MEMOIRS

OF AN

ALTAMAHA RIVER
OUTDOORSMAN

AND
OTHER DRIVEL

William A. Bowers, Jr.

i

ISBN: 979-8-99918539-0-3
Library of Congress Number: 2024920610

Published by

Swampfox Publishing Company

Edited by
Deloris Bowers and Elizabeth B. Hall
Interior Design by William A. Bowers, III
Cover Design by William A. Bowers, Jr.

Cover photos from altamahariverpartnership.org

Printed in USA
for
Swampfox Publishing Company

Table of Contents

Photographs

The following is a collection of hunting, fishing and outdoors experiences that I have enjoyed both living and telling through the years. I dedicate this work to my father William A. Bowers, Sr. who was my favorite hunting and fishing partner and to my son Billy Bowers who has now become my new "favorite." And also, to my grandfather, John Leslie Tuten with whom I wish I could have hunted and my grandfather Jesse Monroe Bowers, who passed away while I was young but left me his fishing genes. Also, it is dedicated to my wife Deloris for putting up with me and hearing all my stories many times over. As it was with my great Uncle Zach, who was chided by my Aunt Kete for telling his stories over and over as he got older. My Aunt would raise her hand if he had already told it as a signal that he had already told it. He was retelling a story once when she raised her hand. He looked at her with her hand raised and said, "I know I have already told it but it is so good I am going to tell it again."

That is how some of these are.

I am going to "Tell Them Again!"

My Two Best Fishing and Hunting Buddies of All Time

Bill Sr.

My son, Billy

v

PROLOGUE

The Mighty Altamaha River flows from the confluence of the Ocmulgee River and the Oconee River at the junction of Wheeler, Montgomery and Jeff Davis Counties in South Central Georgia. The Altamaha travels down and is joined by the Ohoopee River in Tattnall County. It is said that The Altamaha River is the second largest watershed east of the Mississippi River with only the Hudson River being larger. It has also been said that if two drops of rain fall in Georgia that one will come down the Altamaha.

I have spent most of my life hunting, fishing and camping on and around the Altamaha. I have been on every section of the river in a boat. I have also spent quite a bit of time in the tributaries and oxbow lakes that once were part of the main run of the river. The river has always been teeming with fish, abundant with waterfowl and surrounded by the Altamaha Basin which is rich with other game such as whitetail deer, bear, feral hogs and many various small game species.

The Altamaha is also one of the most beautiful places on earth. My ancestors have lived on and along the Altamaha since the late 1700's. It is without a doubt that they knew it as a source for food and in some cases income. Six of the original ferries on the Altamaha were owned and operated by my ancestors and kin. My family members rafted timber down river to Doctortown and Darien to the sawmills. One of my cousins was the last to raft down the Altamaha and could call out the names of all the places along the river.

There was a time when paddle wheelers plied their way up and down the river system. My Great-Great-Great Grand Uncle was the Captain of the "Governor Troupe" that plied the Altamaha during the War Between the States. I have also fished at Doctortown around the wreck of the "Altamaha Princess" which was the last paddle-wheeler to navigate the waters.

Long ago Native Americans lived along the river, and we still find reminders like arrow heads and pottery which are traces of times past.

When I am on the river in a boat, I feel such a familiarity with it as this is the third century that my family has had something to do with "Old Muddy". I have a deep respect and love for that place and all that is involved with it. We still own property on the Altamaha, that has been owned by the family since the 1850's, and when I sit on the bluff watching the sun rise or set, it remains awesome to me. When I sit there and watch the world wake up. When I watch the deer and turkeys and squirrels as they move around, when I see a sturgeon making a humongous splash in the river it moves me greatly. Our family tries to protect and preserve it so my great grandchildren can enjoy it as the family down from my great-great-great-great grandfather, who had a trading post on its bank in the 1790's, have done in the past.

FORWARD

Thanks to my hunting and fishing partners over the years, who were the source of many of the following stories and the inspiration for this collection.

I can't remember exactly the first time that I laid eyes on Cousin Billy, but it had to be at a very early age. My first recollection is when we would go out in the country and visit relatives. In the early 1950's it was common for people to go to the homes of friends and relatives and visit them on Sunday afternoons. This one place that I especially enjoyed visiting was located about four miles north of the small town in which I lived. Billy's older brother, Ronnie, was my age and we played together as children. When we were old enough, we would hunt squirrels together behind his dog, Missey. I can vividly remember tearing through the briars and bushes trying to keep up with Missey as she barked wildly in an attempt to tree a wily gray squirrel, cat squirrels as we called them. In a few minutes we would find Missey at the base of a tree with her head raised barking at the small gray furry critter that was doing his best imitation of a bump on the side of the tree. Most times we were successful although I don't think that we ever placed the population of squirrels in any grave danger. Those days were the beginning of a time in my life that were enhanced by the time spent out of doors enjoying nature and the fish and game that God placed on this earth. We were even conservation minded at that age for none of us would dare kill a fox Squirrel because someone had said that they were getting scarce, and we did not want to further deplete them.

There were also some great times fishing in the little creek that was called "Icebox Creek". When the fish wouldn't bite, we would all shuck off our clothes and jump off the culvert into the water that was so cold as to take your breath. Yes, we would "skinny dip" or in my case "fat dip". Sometimes if the fish were cooperative, we would catch a few bream, warmouth and an occasional red fin pike. I have half ridden and half pushed my Western Flyer bicycle on the sandy dirt road with my tackle in a band aid box and a tomato can with some earth worms that I dug from the edge of the ditch by my house just to fish with my cousins. Unfortunately, times have changed and children that age would never be allowed to ride that far to enjoy something like unsupervised fishing and hunting.

Billy was just a younger kid, kind of nuisance, in those days but when his older brothers moved off a great distance, to go to college and later to work, I was compelled to find a new hunting partner, ergo Billy.

I began to pick Billy up and go hunting and fishing around the community. We would hunt squirrels and doves and would fish when hunting season ended.

Billy's younger brother, Ralph began to tag along with us as soon as he thought he was big enough to hunt and fish. I was blessed to enjoy most of Ralph's firsts. His first deer, duck, largemouth bass and dove were among those firsts.

The stories that follow are 99 and 99/100 percent true and have been the source of many a good healthy laugh through the years as I have recounted them. It is my hope and desire that you will enjoy them to the fullest.

Largest Female and Largest Male In One Day

CHAPTER ONE

FISHING

My father's side of the family is loaded with fishermen and fisherwomen. My grandmother Amorette and her sister Myra were the two fishingest women I have ever seen. They loved it! They had all the patience in the world and they were pretty good at it. My Father's two sisters, Virginia and Myra, were a close second to grandmother and Aunt Myra. They all loved salt-water fishing along with the fresh-water variety.

I can still see my grandmother on the pier at Flagler Beach, Florida holding the line just above the reel between her thumb and first finger, feeling the line to detect a small nibble on her bait. She would fish in Dead Lake and Crescent Lake which were just a few miles from her home. She would not pass up a 'stickup" (a portion of a limb protruding above the water). She fished around every one of them just knowing that a "Speckled Pearch" was there waiting for her minnow to get close. My family fished for fun but they also liked to eat fish. I have heard my grandmother say when she caught a small fish that "If he is big enough to bite my hook – he is big enough to eat."

My grandfather "Pappy" was an excellent fisherman. When he used to run "Veal's Pool" for his brother-in-law in Appling County, Georgia, one of the other men, Freddie, who worked with him would tell me the following.

"Mr. Jesse would catch a Bream, place it on a hook tied to a short piece of line and attach it to a glass gallon jug. He would then place it in the "Pool." Then Mr. Jesse would go up on the porch and sit a while. Directly the jug would begin to move across the pond. Mr. Jesse would get in the boat and paddle over to the jug and pull out one of the biggest "Trouts" you ever seen!"

Pappy also was known as the best sheepshead fisherman in the Flagler County area. He would fish from the bridge at Matanzas Inlet and the Pier at Flagler Beach. He used to say in order to catch the sheepshead that you had to set the hook just before it bites. He operated a Fish Market in Bunnell, Florida. He operated the market with very low overhead because he only sold fish he caught, shrimp he netted and oysters he harvested. My father once told me of a Tarpon he caught and placed in the case at the market. When customers inquired about the huge fish, he would tell them that the Tarpon was the "Silver King", the fish that

2

the President came down to Florida and fished for. Then he would slice some of the Tarpon off and sell it to them. He was good with a cast net and was all-round self-sufficient at his market. When he died my father's brother Gene took over the market and operated it for a while.

Uncle Gene was also an excellent fisherman and was one of the best I have ever seen with a cast net. He tried many times to teach me how to cast one but I was afraid that the lead sinker would pull my teeth out of my head. Uncle Gene loved to "Free line" using mullet as bait for Tarpon, Snook, and Trout. He would use his cast net and get some good "Live" fingerling mullet and place them on a bare hook at the end of his line. He would flip the mullet out and if the fish stayed on the surface wiggling he would fish with him. If it did not, he would reel him in and put another one on. When the Predator fish hit the mullet, it resulted in an explosion on the surface. He caught plenty of snook and tarpon using that method.

My Uncle Buddy loved artificial lures like jigs and popping bugs. He taught me to love that form of fishing. I caught my first big bass fishing with him, actually an eight- and one-half pounder which was my largest for a long time. Once I agreed to go with a few friends from work to Crescent Lake to fish for "Speckled Pearch". At first, my plans were to go stay with Aunt Myra and Uncle Buddy and meet my friends at the lake each morning. My friends would have no part of that. After much discussion, they convinced me to stay in the same motel as them. I knew that Aunt Myra would be disappointed that I was not staying with them so I did not mention it to them. The first morning my friend Ollie and I were in my gold 16-foot bass boat in the narrows, which was at the junction of Dead Lake, Crescent Lake and Haw Creek, trying to find the depth to fish for the perch. I was intent on watching the depth finder to locate the fish and did not pay attention to the boat approaching until I heard Uncle Buddy's voice as he asked what I was doing there. I was caught!

My Uncle Lee was the only person that I have ever known that I truly believe could have lived off the land exclusively. When you ate at his house you did not ask what was in Aunt Nita's pot. You just ate it. He was a tremendous hunter and fisherman in all aspects. He fished for and gigged flounder. He gigged frogs. We ate "gopher stew" (made from gopher tortoise), alligator and who knows what.   He hunted turkeys, calling them with his smoking pipe. He used a .22 rifle loaded with shorts to take the big birds. He also taught me to shuck oysters at the age of 5, because I was eating them as fast as he shucked them. I can still hear the quiet man say, "Here boy! You need to learn how to do this."

I started my illustrious fishing career fishing with my relatives on the East Coast Canal (The Intercostal Waterway). We bait fished mostly for croakers, yellowtail, and drum. I fished with a Shakespeare casting reel (referred to as a "Knuckle Buster") loaded with 20-pound Dacron line and a heavy lead sinker rig with two hooks. I remember one day, in my grandmother's boat, that she, Daddy and I were in the canal fishing between Matanzas Inlet and Flagler Beach. I was catching two Yellow Tails every time I dropped my rig down. I loved fishing that way and when Daddy decided to move, I was upset and pitched a fit to stay. Daddy pulled the boat to the shore and we got out. He proceeded to explain the facts of life and that on this trip he was the boat Captain and the crew would do as he said. He explained it to me in such a way that I never more protested moving in that fashion.

4

There were times when I was with my Aunt Myra and Uncle Norman (grandmother's sister and brother-in-law) and how they would clean the fish in the boat and break out a Coleman stove and fry them there in the boat. Fish doesn't get much fresher than that. I remember how good the fish and hush puppies tasted there in the boat.

I guess that I must have really inherited the fishing genes from my father's side of the family. I can remember when I was young fishing in any hole of water for small bream and stump knockers. Daddy taught me quickly not to waste the fish. No matter how small the fish was if I caught it and brought it home, I cleaned them and presented them for the family table fare. There were some small water holes where Daddy worked and Mother would take me out there with his lunch and I would fish until he got off work that afternoon. My stringer would be a willow limb and I would have it full of little panfish by the time he got off work.

As I got older, I would ride my bicycle out to Caney Creek (or Icebox Creek as we called it) about four miles from town and to some ponds close to town with my "Prince Albert" tobacco can with hooks, corks and sinkers and another can with worms that I had dug. I would catch grasshoppers, crickets, caterpillars, and minnows to fish with. Once I tried to use a cockroach. I placed him on the hook and threw the line out to catch a fish. I was sitting there on the bank of the creek half daydreaming when I discovered that the roach had climbed up the line and was sitting on top of my cork. Fat chance I had of catching anything other than a flying fish.

My cousin Robert would fish with a super small hook (we called them a hair hook) and sewing line on a small flexible stick cut from a willow. It was surprising just how big a fish he could pull from the creek with that ultra-light rig. He was a purist about fishing and wanted to give the fish the best chance possible. He was Billy's older brother and we shared some fine times fishing in that creek.

To this day I like to fish ultra-lite tackle for panfish so as to have much more fun pulling in the smaller fish. Sometimes it takes a small bait to catch a big fish when the conditions are right. I have caught both a 12 pound and a 18 pound catfish on a 1/16-ounce grub using 6 pound line. You have to fight them like a blue marlin in the ocean. It takes time to wear them out. The light equipment can add quite a bit to a panfish experience because you have to even play smaller ones.

Aunt Myra and Uncle Norman had a son N. A., who was a career Navy Chief Petty Officer, that also loved to fish. When he found out that I had begun fishing with popping bugs he bought me a split bamboo fly rod with an automatic reel at the PX and I quickly learned how to fish a fly rod. The popping bugs were deadly for bream and would also attract a bass. When he retired from the Navy, he was either fishing or running the "Fish Camp" at Dead Lake in Flagler County adjacent to Crescent Lake.

There was a pretty girl, that I liked a lot when I was in elementary school, who lived about three miles from town. Her dad said that I could come and fish in his two ponds. I would get on my Western Flyer and hold the dissembled fly rod across the handlebars and peddle the three miles out to fish there. The ponds were full of fish with one producing a 16 pound bass that the other producing a 14 pounder.

Mr. Carter, who lived next door was an influence on my fishing. He and his wife loved to fish and almost always came home with a mess of fish. He liked to fish for "Red Horse Suckers', a carp that lives in the Altamaha River. He would mix up the dough and form dough balls on his hooks and then bake them on. He caught some very large carp, the biggest of which I remember was over 18 pounds. Once when I was bass fishing in the Altamaha, he and Mrs. Carter were on the bank at a county landing fishing. They had their cane poles stuck in the roots along the area that had been excavated at the landing. I trolled up close to them, trying to get a bass when I saw one of Mr. Carter's poles fly from its place in the roots. The fish had taken it from the bank in a fraction of a second. Too fast for Mr. Carter to catch it I looked to my right and the fish was carrying it into the Live River. Only about six inches of the butt of the pole was out of the water and was bobbing up and down like a cork. I pursued it with my trolling motor and had a time catching up with it. I reached down and grasped the butt end of the cane pole and tried to pull the gigantic fish up to the surface. The fish was so powerful that in my effort to bring him up the fish broke the pole in three places and managed to escape. I returned what was left of the pole to Mr. Carter and we both speculated what had taken the cane pole like that. It was either a giant catfish or a striper (that water has produced a 45 pound channel catfish, a 62 pound striper and the world record 22 pound 4 ounce largemouth bass) so the possibilities are many.

Mr. Carter would take things that others would throw away and combine them to produce something better than either. He was a very talented man. He made lamps from cypress knees, pain medicine from willow bark and many a home remedy. Some of them tasted so bad that you would claim a "Cure" so as to not be subjected to any more medicine.

My grandmother (my mother's mother) made sure that I kept the roe from all fish. She would scramble it with eggs and call it "hen eggs and fish eggs." She would cook whatever fish that I brought home. Fried fish with grits and hush puppies with some cole-slaw is a southern feast. She was unique in the fact that she would eat the leftover fish the next day cold. She raised a family during the "Depression" and she did not waste food.

When I was young, my cousin, Gertrude, would take me to the Altamaha River to fish for catfish. That was my first time on the river and my first time deliberately fishing for catfish. We were fishing for channel catfish instead of the salt-water catfish, which I had caught many, but they were considered trash fish. Gertrude would land the boat and head upstream to the base of Lower Sisters Bluff and anchor off. We would bottom fish and catch what the river folks used to call "shine eye cats" (small catfish, which were fried whole). My family could put away several of these little guys at one sitting. Gertrude had introduced me to a body of water in which I would spend many hours and days for the rest of my life. The place we fished was under Lower Sisters Bluff, which my family owns.

I still love salt-water fishing and have done many types of it. I have fished from several Piers up and down the coast, along with surf fishing and fishing in the intercoastal waterway along Georgia and Florida. I have been on several party boats in the Atlantic Ocean and the Gulf of Mexico and have been on many small party charters. Most of my charters have been out of Savannah with some from Brunswick and some in Destin, Florida. My cousin Jeff once hooked into a large king mackerel and just before reaching the boat with him an approximately ten-foot-long barracuda struck the mackerel and the fight was on. We strapped

Jeff in the fighting chair and for the next twenty minutes he fought the behemoth hard. Suddenly, the line went slack and Jeff pulled in half a King Mackerel that weighed over fifteen pounds. The barracuda had bitten off the back half of the mackerel behind the dorsal fin. I don't know how big they grow but it had spots on his side as big as a Dudley Softball.

On another trip, my first wife got sea-sick and was leaning over the side of the boat when we hit a wave and thanks to my father's quick reaction, he grabbed her by the belt and pulled her back in. She was almost immediately cured. Once I had to grab a fellow fisherman, to keep him in the boat when a big grouper pulled at the wrong time and his feet left the deck. He would have swum rather than let go of his Penn International rod and reel, which was rather expensive.

We were at a place off Wilmington Island, Georgia called the Texas Tower and had had some success. The fish had slowed in their biting and the fishing was almost at a halt when a friend Bob took some sliced ham and put it on his hook. We started kidding him but his logic was that anything that tasted as good as ham ought to catch a fish. It didn't. We could see a school of amberjack swimming all around and later I got on a cooler strapped on the bow and took a Cisco Kid lure and started casting it ahead of the jack. They would absolutely not bite. Then we saw a scuba diver with a spear gun surface at a boat that was anchored nearby and realized why the fish would not cooperate.

My cousin Jeff was one of those "Natural Fishermen." When he was only three or four, he would take a stick and tie a string on it and try to fish in the ditch, by our house. He went on vacation with us because we fished on vacation. We would have

9

to stay with him on the pier in shifts because none of us could stay out there as long as he could. Once Daddy brought him a sandwich and drink for lunch. Realizing he could not hold both and his rod, he threw the sandwich overboard and just drank his drink. That Summer, he caught one of the biggest fish on the pier and paraded the fish up and down the pier showing it off.

He ran out of bait and even caught fish without bait using a gold hook and jigging it up and down. I once had him and another little cousin on the pier late one night. We began to catch ribbon fish about three feet long. We did so until we ran out of bait.   The ribbonfish had extremely large teeth and Jeff cut off a section of one of the fish and tied it to a line that was lying on the pier. He began to slap the six-inch piece of fish on the surface and a ribbonfish latched hold of it. Jeff quickly hand-over handed the line in with the fish's teeth still attached to the piece of fish. He repeated this several times to my amazement. We stayed out on the pier until about one o'clock in the morning and when we came into the house, I was in much trouble for keeping the boys out late at their young age.

When we went trolling, we brought back not only King Mackerel, Spanish Mackerel, Dolphin (the fish not Porpoise), Wahoo, Barracuda, Cobia, and Bonita. We would fillet them and sometimes fillet the fillet in order to get them the size that would cook evenly. Daddy would even put Bonita fillets in his electric smoker and smoke them. They were tasty that way. I once ate smoked channel catfish from a 30 pounder that a friend had prepared. He used to run the store at Everett City near the Altamaha River. He sold bait, fished and tied cast nets for a living and always at least had a good story. He asked me to try it but would not tell me what it was until I had tasted the fish. It was excellent and I asked for more.

There was a time when fishing regulations were lax in salt-water. There were very few limits and the size restrictions on Pompano were the only ones that I was aware of. We fished off the pier for smaller fish but also fished for big drum both Reds (Channel bass) and black drum. When the lights were under the pier there were times in the summer when the schools of black drum would be all under the pier after baitfish. When that occurred people would flock to the pier and everyone would catch the big black drum. We were there one night and the pier was wall to wall with people fishing. My sister caught a huge one and while daddy was helping her take hers off, I hooked up on a good one. After fighting the fish a while and keeping it away from the barnacle laden pilings, a circle net was lowered and we hoisted my fish to the pier. I proceeded to get the hook out and rebaited and turned to get my line back in the water. There was a woman standing there in my spot. No rod and reel, just standing at the rail where I had been fishing. I asked her to move so I could get my line back in. She declined, informing me that she was saving MY PLACE for her husband. I asked again but she refused stoically. My friend Neal was fishing beside where I was and looked over to me and winked. Suddenly he screamed "I got a bite" and swept his big Calcutta rod in her direction. She ducked and jumped away from the rail and I reclaimed the spot.

We were on the end of the pier one day fishing for channel bass when one of the guys tied into something. He fought for a little while and then it looked as though he was anchored to the bottom. The fish did not move but Bertha hung on. A while later, Uncle Gene came down to where we were and asked the boy what he was doing. The boy said he was fighting a fish. Uncle Gene

11

said that he didn't look like he was doing much fighting but the boy held on. Uncle Gene then told him that it looked like he had a big ray which had gone to the bottom and formed a suction there. He then asked if the boy wanted the ray to get up and the boy said yes. Uncle Gene went back down the pier and returned with a crab. He wired the crab's pincers around the line and slid him down into the water. He told the boy to hang on because when the crab began walking on the ray's back he would get up. It wasn't long until the drag on the reel began to scream as line stripped out. In just a few moments, a humongous Manta-Ray exploded from the surface and sailed in the air for a short distance then crashing down on the surface breaking the 135-pound test line. One night my cousin Henry and I were on the end of the pier fishing and an extremely large manta ray was flopping around on the surface for a good while. About an hour later the boy came back to fish and we informed him of the big ray and that he flopped around calling "Bertha, Bertha"!

Once when the King Mackerel were running off Flagler Beach, Daddy and Uncle Gene got the brilliant idea to surf fish for them so as to get away from the pier fishermen. In order to get their bait out far enough in the ocean, they were to use grandmother's small wooden boat which had oarlocks and oars. They readied the rigs and started out in the breakers with the bait. There was somewhat of a Nor'easter blowing and the waves were quite large. They made it to the first breakers and then began to be tossed about. They looked like the lifeguards in Australia fighting those waves. I don't think that those two ex-Marines were scared but after a while, they realized that there was a flaw in their plan and returned to the beach.

We took an old Studebaker pickup that my cousin Howard had obtained and cut all the excess material off it. They had some ambulance tires which were bald and some wide split rims welded together and we made a "Skeeter" for running on the Beach. Back then you could drive on every beach if you had a vehicle capable. Uncle Gene installed a spotlight on it and us three children rode in the back with the cast nets and washtubs. We arrived at Flagler Beach and went down the approach onto the beach and began to head South with the spotlight shining into the breakers. Suddenly we saw mullet in the breakers. Uncle Gene slammed on the brakes and grabbed the 9-foot English cast net making a perfect cast into the breakers. It almost took the whole crew to drag the net back to the Skeeter. We filled two washtubs with mullet and headed back. We cleaned the fish while my mother and aunt fried some up. Those were the best mullet I have ever eaten.

We now fish in the pond right behind the house off our deck. There are way too many bream in the little ponds, so I have a rule that if a bream is caught, he does not go back in. My wife, son, daughter in law and I caught 120 one afternoon and cleaned fish until we were worn out. My daughter in law and one cousin have caught 19 and 17 little bream respectively using only one earthworm.

I have spent many an hour on the Altamaha, fishing for both panfish and bass. I have fished and hunted the entire length of the Altamaha River and part of the way up the Ocmulgee and Oconee Rivers which form the Altamaha near Lumber City, Georgia. I have fished up the Ohoopee River which comes into the Altamaha near where Ten Mile Creek joins it. The Ocmulgee is red-stained with the red Georgia clay and the Oconee and Ohoopee are darker clearer waters with way less stain. I would often fish the conflux of the Ocmulgee and Oconee at the "blend line" where the two different colors meet. There is a distinct line where they

13

join and it takes a while for the different water colors to mix. If one of the rivers is high and the other low it can be treacherous there.

On one occasion, I was pulling on willow limbs to try to maneuver my boat under the willow to fish. I was being really careful because I had recently gotten into a Red Wasp nest as big as my hat in another willow tree and had paid the price. As I pulled my boat in, a gigantic sturgeon came from under the willow, blowing, splashing and scaring the heck out of me. I almost gave him the boat from sheer fear. It is hard to describe the blowing sound but suffice to say it instilled fear in my heart. The Altamaha used to be the spawning place for many of this ancient species. Not long ago I watched one from our bluff on the river. They are magnificent when they are not scaring you.

———————————

Stripers also come up the Altamaha and continue up the Oconee to spawn in the rocks there. That is why they are called "rock fish" in that area. Sometimes you will catch them along the Altamaha. I was casting a spinnerbait in the log-roll at the junction of the Altamaha and the Ohoopee trying to entice a bass when a very heavy strike almost took the rod from my hands. I was fishing with a 5000c Ambassador loaded with 20-pound line and a heavy rod. I thought that I had hooked an underwater freight train. The drag was singing, and my line was leaving the reel in a hurry. When it looked as if he would take me to bare spool, I thumbed the spool and reared back on the rod. Suddenly this gigantic striper exploded from the depths and put on more pressure than my 20-pound line could stand. I estimate the fish was 35 to 40 pounds and close to 4 feet long. The Georgia record for stripers that were not landlocked was 63 pounds, caught in the Oconee River near

Dublin, Georgia. I have hooked and caught several stripers since then but never one so large.

There are large catfish in the river. In the old days if you caught a big one it would most likely be a channel catfish. You can tell a channel from a blue catfish by the number of rays in the anal fin. I have never seen a big catfish with enough rays to be a "blue". Several years ago, someone introduced Flathead catfish to the river. They are not indigenous to the Altamaha and as all non-native species do, they have upset the balance in the fishery. They are in competition with the other large predators such as channel catfish, largemouth bass, chain pickerel, and striped bass. One of my friends has caught a 94 pounder on a limb line, so the "Appaloosa" cats, as the locals call them due to their coloration, have a firm foothold in the Altamaha.

I was fishing near the county landing at Eason's Bluff one day. I had run up on one of my oldest friends, Jimmy Lee, who was fishing with a cane pole in a small johnboat. As I was casting to the Appling County bank, I glanced over to the opposite side of the river and saw Jimmy Lee out in the river with his pole bent in a U shape. He had a big fish on, and the fish was pulling him out into the middle of the river. All he could do was hold on. It was a comical sight. Eventually, the fish tired and he pulled in an 18 pound channel cat.

Another friend and I were fishing for bass in the dead Altamaha River Section where the Ohoopee joins the Altamaha. I call the outside of the bend Predator Run. For several years I would catch at least one predator fish when I fished it. It would either be a bass, jack (chain pickerel) or a mudfish (bowfin). That day we filled the boat with mudfish. As we trailered the boat a pretty teenage girl in a bikini came up to the boat. We thought that we had attracted her but as she looked in the boat, she asked what we were going to do with those fish. I told her that I used them to fertilize my tomato plants. She asked if she could have them. Puzzled, I asked what she was going to do with them, since I have once tried to eat mudfish and the more I chewed, the spongy meat the bigger it got. She said that her grandmother made something like salmon balls out of them. The next few times we fished there she came to see if we had any mudfish she could have. Then we did not see her anymore. I wondered if the steady diet of mudfish had done her in.

I used to carry a "Mudfish Tamer" (a weighted billy club) because of the difficulty in retrieving a lure from all of those sharp teeth. I have watched a mudfish literally chew up a lure. A sharp tap on the back where the head joins the body will calm one down to where the hook extraction is painless to the fisherman.

I liked to fish with my fly rod in the Altamaha and make casts so as to drift the popping bug under the willows. I was fishing on the long reach between Eason's Bluff and Iron Mine Bluff one day and was making some pretty long cast with my bug taper line. The boat and bug would drift at about the same speed. When the bug would hit a good shade spot, a big red breast would hit and the fight was on. I made several passes and caught a fish each pass. I had noticed a boat on the other side of the river and he cranked his motor and came toward my boat. As he pulled alongside my boat, he cut his engine.

"How are you making such long casts with that fly rod? What the heck kind of line is that you are using?" He queried.

"Fly Line, what do you use?" I responded.

16

"20-pound monofilament," He answered. I then knew why he could not cast very far.

Once, in Alligator Lake, I was fishing with a lure in my favorite color pattern (chartreuse and fluorescent orange). A large jackfish (Chain Pickerel) intercepted my spinner-bait. He came at almost a 90 degree angle. I poured the steel to him and began to fight the fish. This was the biggest jackfish I had ever seen, somewhere in the neighborhood of 3 feet long. After a few minutes, I thought that the jack (sometimes referred to as a "wolf with scales") was tiring enough. I got him about ten feet from the boat, the line went limp. As I reeled the line in, I found that the jack's teeth had cut the line which is why jack fishermen use a six-inch steel leader for them. The big ones almost always get away.

Mr. Davis operated a landing and little store on Buckhorn Bluff on the Altamaha. I discovered that he liked jackfish so whenever I had landed at Buckhorn and caught any jack, I would give them to him on the way out. He and lots of other folks raved about how good jackfish taste. I would tell them that I did not favor eating a "Bone Sandwich" for the Jack, a cousin of the Pike and Musky, was loaded with bones. I have tried to eat jack but the bones quickly discouraged that effort.

I worked with some guys who would eat a bream sandwich. They would place a whole bream between two slices of light bread and commence eating. In no time the bones would begin to work out the side of their mouth, I am not geared that way. Mr. Davis would tell me that you could make lateral cuts in the fish and fry him hard and eat bones and all like a sardine. I never had courage, to try that. Mr. Davis appreciated the fish and rarely charged me for landing my boat.

17

My wife and I were fishing in Grantham Lake, which is an oxbow lake cut off from the Altamaha downriver from old Doctortown. We had gone to the lake with some friends who had resurrected an old tenant house from his father's farm. We had spent the night before and were in my Fisher Marine, fishing in the lake. We had half-filled a six-foot stringer with large white perch and warmouth. The friend's daughter wanted to go in the boat with us so, we pulled to the shore and picked her up. As we fished along the lake she was playing with the stringer, so we cautioned her to be careful with it. I was intent on fishing and suddenly heard "Oops!" I looked around just in time to see the stringer sink into the black water of the Lake. The little girl's face was red and we were wide eyed in amazement. We took a deep breath and started to fill another stringer. I guess the gators and turtles ate well that evening. We fished the rest of the day and caught the limit of fish as a reward for our tolerance.

We also used to set lines for catfish. Years ago, if you set lines, you mostly caught channel catfish but after some intelligent so and so introduced flathead catfish to the river, that is all you will catch.

My first attempt to fish lines (trotlines and limb lines) almost ended in a disaster. We went down-river from Carter's Bight and set out lines. I was a novice and had not run that section of the river much and never at night. My friend Jackie and I were returning to the landing when we hit a shelf of rock that extended out in the river on the Appling County side and broke the shaft of my 9.5 Evinrude outboard motor. We began to drift down-stream and as soon as we could, we grabbed a willow limb preparing to spend the night on the river. After about an hour of clinging to the limb, we heard an outboard coming up the river. Finally, we saw their lights and signaled them with our flashlight. They came to our rescue although they only had 9.9 Mercury. They managed to get us safely to the landing. We were able to procure another boat to fish our lines (in the daytime). I still remember the location of that rock shelf and steer clear of it to this day.

When I was in high school there were several of my friends who liked to fish and we would go to near where Five Mile Creek empties into the Altamaha River and fish for "jackfish" (chain pickerel). The bait store sold "Baltimore Minnows" which were gold-colored and looked like goldfish to me. We would park and walk down to the "Bonnet Hole" and fish for jackfish. The trick was to cast the baited rig with a plastic cork to the upstream side and let the current take the bait downstream. On the trip downstream the minnow would be intercepted by the quarry and the fight was on. Jackfish are great fighters and those that were in the 20- inch size range fight really well. That was great fun. Larry, a cousin who owned the land and I had talked about going back for old times' sake but never put the trip together. It is a part of my younger days that I really cherish.

I was fishing a line in Collins Lake in the Bullard Creek Wildlife Management Area with a friend. I was pulling the boat along using the trotline as we checked the hooks. We neared the stump the line was tied to, and I was going to untie the line to take up the rig. I had not yet reached to untie the line, but my eyes caught the shape of a coiled Water Moccasin on the stump. My mind raced far ahead of my actions, and in my mind's eye, I had seen the snake striking my hand although I was not yet close. I let out a screech like an old owl and almost jumped into the other end of the boat where my friend was. Afterward, we had a good laugh about my actions, and he never let me forget what I had done.

19

After that I carried a .38 Special loaded with snake shot to dispatch the moccasins that we encountered. I had one friend who knocked a moccasin off a willow into the boat with him. Without thinking he grabbed his shotgun and promptly dispatched the snake and the bottom of his wooden boat at the same time.

I now own a Taurus Judge which is chambered for .410 shotgun. A charge of .410 loaded with #6's or #8's will dispatch a moccasin quickly. It is the quintessential "Moccasin Gun."

Daddy and I fished together all during my adult life. The older we got the more we hunted and fished together, the closer we got. There was a time when he thought that if my Bronco and boat trailer left the yard, he was supposed to be with it. That was one of the most favorite times of my life as we shared the outdoors together.

I used to fish more regularly than I do now. My motto was if there is water I should fish it. Fishing is an accumulation of knowledge, gained through the years. If you can remember what was successful in the past you can catch them in the future.

Eventually, I developed more and more into a Bass Fisherman which became my passion for a while, although I sometimes want to go back to my roots.

Daddy with His 10 Pound 4 Ounce Bass

CHAPTER TWO

BASS FISHING

I also have complete recollection of the first Largemouth Bass that I caught on top water while fishing with my Uncle Buddy in a railroad ditch in Flagler County, Florida. I had caught some bream and a couple of small bass. I spotted an opening next to some lily pads. I was careful to flip the bug onto the lily pad and worked it towards the edge. Then I jumped it into the open water. I can still close my eyes and see the explosion of water when the behemoth engulfed the little yellow and black popping bug. I held on for all I was worth. The big fish circled and moved toward the grass at the edge near my feet. When it was close I pulled with all my might partially moving the fish into the grass but the pole broke in two places. The fish was in the grass at my feet, in shallow water. I know that I looked like Dick Butkus pouncing on a Quarterback as I sprang into the grass and smothered the big bass down under my body. I got hold of its gills and crawled out on the bank. I ran to Uncle Buddy to show him my prize, and we got our stuff together and headed for town. The fish weighed 8 ½ pounds but lost quite a bit of weight as we rode all over Bunnell, Florida showing off my bass. I did not know but my cousin Howard caught an 8 pounder that day in Haw Creek. Not only did I hook the large fish, but he also hooked me for life on "Bass Fishing".

For years after that I was a purist. First, I would only fish with a fly rod and a popping bug on top water. Later when I switched to a spin casting reel, I would only fish with a four-inch Rebel floater/diver. Later while fishing in bass tournaments, I would learn to use all types of lures and even every once in a while, recognize when to use which lure and where. The other important thing is to work at it. Keep casting and keep looking for patterns and fish movement. The more places that you present your lure, "the right lure", the more chance you have of catching a bass. Another thing is to fish the lure all the way to the boat. Many times, I have hooked a bass just as I was about to take the lure out of the water. The bass had obviously followed it all the way there before striking.

In the days when the Rebel was my only bait, I developed a style of top water fishing that I called machine-gunning. It consisted of short rapid casts to the water's edge twitching the lure two or three quick times and reeling the lure in as fast as possible

22

to cast again. It was after I bought my first electric trolling motor that I perfected this, because it was hard to find someone who would paddle you and work as hard as the method requires. When conditions are right, usually early in the morning and late in the evening, this method is awesome. It can present the fisherman with a spectacle that defies description.

One morning Cousin Billy and I went to fish in a farm pond behind an old, abandoned school. As we slipped the old wooden john boat into the water, we decided that I would paddle once around the pond for him to fish and then he would return the favor. He tied his favorite bass lure onto his line, a black rubber worm, and began to fish. When he had completed his round, he had attracted two strikes but was unable to hook a fish. Then as I tied my silver rebel on, Billy remarked to me.

"Black worm...black worm. That's all you need. They won't bite that thing!" he said.

Halfway around the pond and eight bass later he asked if he could use my rig on the next round. From that day on he had an assortment of those minnows in his box.

_____

My first experience fishing a plastic worm was with a neighbor, Mr. Johnny. I had contracted to mow his grass and afterward, we would load up his boat and head to a local pond. He was using a rigged black worm with white spots, and being used to topwater strikes, it was different to feel the slight twitch as the bass took the worm. I got the hang of it eventually. That pond is about a mile from my present house and when I pass it, I think of Mr. Johnny and my introduction to plastic worms.

One fishing trip was in my cousin's pond which had been there several years. I was using my fly rod and placed the Chartreuse Evans Popper just at the water's edge at the dam's corner. I let the ripples move away from the bug and twitched it once. The explosion sounded like someone had thrown a refrigerator into the pond. I flicked my wrist and set the hook. I fought the fish all over that pond. Twice it went under my boat and I had to stick my rod down into the water. Once it jumped while I had the rod in the water, about twenty feet beyond the boat. Finally, I whipped the fish enough to bring it alongside the boat so I could land her. The fat female weighed over 8 ½ pounds and was a beautiful specimen. This was the largest bass I ever landed on a fly rod, equaling the largest on a popping bug with a cane pole. By the way the pole was a Lew's Bream Buster.

There was a time when I was fishing over two-hundred days a year. Often, I would leave after work and fish until about 9:00 PM. We have several pictures, holding bass in my mother's kitchen, with the clock on the wall behind us reading around 10:00 pm. During this time, I was catching quite a few large bass with the largest being 11 pounds 8 ounces. I did not realize it but I was getting a reputation for large bass. I was weighing all the big bass at a local store on the certified meat scales. I caught 35 bass in one year over 9 pounds but I refused to mount a fish under 10 pounds. I am looking at the 11 pound 8 ounce fish mounted on my wall as I write this. She was my first over 10.

Work was slow and we were hanging around the office. I asked to take the afternoon off so I could go fishing. I also asked my boss if he wanted to go with me. He declined. I went home and grabbed some lunch and got my fishing gear loaded in my Bronco. I went to a pond about fifteen miles away that contained some large bass. I had caught several from seven pounds up to one that weighed 9 pounds 8 ounces. The 9 pound 8 ounce came one day after daddy caught a 10 pound 4 ounce monster there (he refused to mount it, which was the minimum weight I had set to mount a bass, so we had baked 10 pound bass that week). The pond had produced one 14 pounder in the past. I decided to fish from the bank instead of taking my boat. As I eased around the dam fishing through the openings in the trees, I got a good hookup and fought the fish to the bank. I weighed the fish on my pocket scales the result was 5 pounds 3 ounces (it turned out it was a male and was the biggest male that I ever caught). I tied him off on a stringer and placed him in the water's edge. I began to move slowly and quietly down the dam. I was preparing to cast when I saw something strange. The more I looked the more it looked like the side fin of a bass flapping above the surface. It was too far away for me to reach with the lure I had on the line. I quickly returned to my truck retrieving a "Little George", which was a chunk of lead with a treble hook and a spinner blade on the rear. These lures are normally used in deep water vertical fishing. I got it because it was small and heavy so I could cast it farther than anything in my box. I moved as close as I could and the fin was still up. I cast the "Little George" several feet beyond the fin and began to crank as fast as my speed geared reel could. I had the rod tip high in the air causing the lure to sputter along the surface. I was "buzzing" a deep-water lure. The fish went under and I thought I may have spooked it but kept buzzing. As the lure neared my position I saw a large dark object under it. I almost set the hook early out of panic. I kept my cool as I watched the fish get in front of the lure and make a vicious strike. I fought the fish for a good time before tiring it enough to bring it to the dam. I waded into the water and "lower lipped" the large fish. I immediately took it to the Bronco forgetting the pocket scale I had. I opened the back of the Bronco and placed the fish in a large styrofoam cooler in the back and started to gather my gear. I was ready to leave. The fish flopped, breaking the side of the cooler out and falling to the ground on the dam. The fish kept flopping toward the water's edge. I hurried to it intercepting the fish just

25

short of the water and it's freedom. I tied a stringer in its mouth and then tied the stringer to my gun rack to secure my prize. When I arrived back to town, I circled by the local store and weighed it on the meat scales.

The monster weighed 11 pounds 8 ounces, more than thirty minutes out of the water. The fish had made the weight to be on my wall. As a side note the taxidermist asked me if I was sure of the weight, I told him the fish was weighed on certified meat scales. He then remarked that he had five in his shop that the owners said weighed more than mine but he believed that mine could have eaten any of them. I had made a request for him to see how much roe was in the fish which he reported that the egg sacs were as flat as cigarette papers. Daddy's 10 pound 4 ounce fish had 1 pound 8 ounces of eggs. This fish was "laid out". With that revelation my fish most likely weighed over 13 pounds full of eggs and fresh out of the water. She most likely had just laid her eggs and was possibly "sunning" herself.

I was weighing all the big bass at the local store on the certified meat scales. I caught 35 bass in one year over 9 pounds but I refused to mount a fish under 10 pounds.

One afternoon, I had a visit from a retired schoolteacher that was famous in our parts for catching large bass and hunting turkeys. He began to inquire as to the methods that I was using, and we talked about the different baits that we had successfully used. Before he left, we had agreed to go fishing in the Altamaha River on Saturday. I was excited because I had heard for years about his fishing prowess and was anxious about fishing with and learning from the old master.

Saturday came and I picked him up with my bass boat hooked behind my Bronco. We launched the boat at the landing on the other side of the river and went to the spot on the river that we called "Predator Run". That stretch of dead river run was the most consistently productive area that I have ever fished. You were almost assured to catch a bass, jack or mudfish every time you went. Any of the three add up to a good fight. As we began to fish the stretch of the bank, I was careful to observe his every action. I began to notice that he carefully scrutinized my actions. We fished all morning together and I learned quite a bit from the old master about lure presentation but neither of us caught a fish in the five hours that we were on the water. Neither of us knew if the other's methods would work, at least by the other's success on that given day. I did, however, burn into my memory just how he fished that Bomber of his. I watched how he would cast to the edge and how he quickly jerked the rod tip down to make the lure dive almost vertically and with his rod tip low, work the Bomber toward the boat. I still use some of the techniques that I learned from him that day and now know for a fact that they will work. The next day he returned to my house. He had a sack full of spinner baits. I had used spinner baits with the Hula skirt flipped backward in order to make it bellow out more. I would side arm cast under the willows and "buzz" the spinner bait to the tip of the willows. Stopping the bait, I would then let it fall under the control of a tight line and "helicopter" into the depths. This action will normally trigger a strike quickly.

When you are fishing for Largemouth Bass, it is very important to pay close attention to the location and conditions that are present when the fish is caught. That is the basis of Pattern Fishing. If you catch a fish in two-foot-deep water by a log near shade that may be the pattern for that day. So, it is extremely important that you pay close attention. Tournament Bass Fishing is hard work because if you are fishing hard enough to win, you will cast a thousand times or more in a day. The other thing is to watch what the other fisherman is doing, if he or she is catching fish. It doesn't take a smart person to observe what makes someone successful. I have learned so many tricks and techniques from fishing partners. Every fisherman should practice that.

One old fishing pro once told me that the secret to winning is to KEEP YOUR LINE WET - the fish will not jump into the boat to get your lure. That considered, the next story will interest any tournament fisherman.

Our local Bass club had a new addition. A "hot" bass fisherman from another town had joined our club. He had waxed all the members of his old club and had lost popularity with the members, as constant winners often will. We had invited him into our club, fearlessly. He was an extremely hard worker and fished a tournament from wire to wire, which most likely accounted for his success in the other club.

The monthly tournament was to be held at Banks Lake near Lakeland, Georgia, a large natural cypress lake about seventy miles west of home. I had seen the lake from the road but had never fished in it. The lake was beautiful with all the cypress trees in it. As a matter of fact, the boat chase scenes for the Burt Reynolds movie "Gator" were filmed there. We didn't know just how tough the lake was to fish until we were on the water.

First thing that morning I was using a Johnson's spoon around the cypress trunks and caught a shorter than keeper bass early that morning. For the next six hours, we did not get a bite. Every boat that we got near had been skunked. Finally, one fisherman said that he caught a bass early that morning but he was too small to keep. I was beginning to think that I possibly could

28

win the tournament with a single fish. I neared the new member's boat with anticipation, absolutely sure that he had fish. He said that he hadn't even had a strike all day.

The partner that I had drawn for the day was one of my best friends, but he and I were both very competitive in whatever we attempted and did not cut any "slack" to each other. This should explain my actions in the next series of events.

The water was running five to seven feet deep all over the lake. It was like a giant bowl, a five-thousand-acre bowl. I had been watching my depth finder all day (I was the first bass fisherman around my home to own such a gadget and had taken much ridicule for purchasing this "worthless new-fangled gadget"). Suddenly my depth finder was registering twelve feet. I looked again to insure it was not an echo reading off six feet because there were light flashes around five to six feet. Sure enough, I had found a hole and there were fish in it! I carefully triangulated some trees so as to mark the spot and without a word changed to a five foot deep running plug that I bought in a closeout sale for twenty-five cents and positioned the boat to cast into the newfound "hole." The first cast with my little blue plug produced a strike and I pulled a keeper sized bass into the boat.

My partner asked, "Where did that come from?"

"Out there!" I pointed in the general direction and cast in the opposite direction.

He cast right behind me, away from the hole. In a couple of minutes, I had worked the boat back into position and fired another cast into the hole which produced a second fish. My partner again became excited but had not discovered the secret. I worked the boat in a circle and for a third time fired the plug into the "Honey Hole" dragging a third keeper out.

My partner then said, "I hope that you have two of them damn ugly plugs so that I don't have to take that one from you."

I pulled a similar plug from my tackle box and flipped it to him without divulging the location of the "Hole".

When we arrived at the weigh-in, I was the only competitor with any fish and was the winner of the tournament. The others wanted to know just how I had been able to catch fish when they couldn't. I proudly related the story of how I had spotted the "Hole" and the fish on my depth finder and proceeded to haul them in.

In the next tournament there were several of the boats equipped with brand new, shiny depth finders. Among them was the new member, who had been the most vocal opponent of the "worthless new-fangled gadgets".

I was the only member of the bass club to weigh in at least a fish in every tournament for three years. That kept me in the top five of the club. I attribute this to the diversity of lures and experience fishing them. One strange thing though was that the most productive lure in my box was a 3/16-ounce green catalpa worm "beetle spin". Virgil Ward used to say on his TV program that it "will catch anything that swims". I rarely fished it in Tournaments. That was crazy!!

————————————————

Another of my fishing buddies was about ten years older than me and was involved in most of the outdoor activities that I was. He shot skeet, hunted birds and deer and loved to fish for bass. For years we chased large "bucketmouths" all around the area where I live. We fished in lakes, ponds and the river together.

This friend used a Zebco 808 and absolutely refused to use a casting reel. He had a unique method of casting a plastic worm that resembled a stagecoach driver popping a whip. He could cast with pinpoint accuracy but unnerved you when the tail of that worm popped behind your ear. I kept kidding him by telling him that the 808 wasn't man enough to handle big fish, but he paid little attention to my remarks.

One day he and I and a third friend were on a bass fishing excursion at Patrick's Paradise, a "Mecca" for bass fishermen, which was near Tifton, Georgia. We had heard about the "Monster Bass" that inhabited the waters there. The three of us were in the largest of the lakes fishing when the drag on the 808 began to sing. My friend finally wrestled a nearly ten pound bass to the boat. He was excited about his trophy. We had only been there about an hour and were in possession of a prize that only one percent of bass fishermen ever attain. We admired the fish and eventually returned to fishing. When he began to reel the 808 in after the next cast, we all heard a noticeable skipping sound. The behemoth had broken three teeth off the gears. I again told him that the 808 was not man enough and the skipping sound was proof.

That place was later purchased by the D N R and now is a public fishing area for Georgia citizens.

The owner of the facility had several geese in the lakes to keep the algae eaten from around the edges. Our other partner was fishing near the edge with a topwater plug when one of the white geese pounced on the lure. The most awful fight ensued and you wouldn't believe how much trouble he had landing the goose. He had even more trouble trying to free the lure from the goose's mouth. It looked for a while that the goose would win, and we were ready to take bets on the outcome when the goose succumbed. He finally had to dispatch the goose to retrieve the lure. Not wanting to waste the goose meat he plucked the rascal. Feathers drifted all down the 100-acre lake, and I was sure we would be apprehended by the owner of the goose.

The only thing that I have seen that was worse to retrieve a plug from was a four foot alligator that almost took possession of a 14 foot aluminum boat of which I was an occupant. He pounced on my friend Charlie's topwater bait and gave Charlie a "Whale" of a fight. Charlie drew the gator up alongside the boat and before I could protest Charlie and Jay, the other fisherman, had hauled the scaly critter into the 14 foot aluminum boat with us. He flopped and struggled until Charley was able to tape his mouth shut and extract the plug. We relocated that "gentleman" to a creek far away from our fishing hole.

———————————

On another trip Jay and I were in another lake known for big fish, Perkins Pond near Odom. I had not fished in a while and when the line came off my Shimano reel it favored a child's slinky toy. This was in the days before "Reel Magic." I was frustrated that I had not checked my tackle before this hastily planned trip. I told Jay that I needed a ten pounder to straighten out my line. Four or five casts later I hooked a very large bass and he gave me a wonderful fight. I lifted him into the boat and weighed him at 8 pounds 8 ounces. I looked around at Jay and said that even though she was not ten pounds that my line was straight and ready for action. Jay just shook his head amazed at my blind luck.

———————————

Most Bass fishermen are tackle collectors and I am no different. Every new lure and fad are consumed by anxious fishermen attempting to gain an advantage over their scaly adversary. I have amassed a collection of tackle and fishing paraphernalia that is unreal. I have foot long plastic worms, lures with five pounds of hooks, and gadgets that emit all kinds of smell, taste, and sounds. One of which is the little twenty-five cent lure that I mentioned earlier. I have for a long time been partial to blue lures. I have caught many fish on blue worms and it stood to reason that blue crank baits, spinner baits, and topwater lures would work well. Bill Dance once stated on his television show that any color was good as long as it was "Blue". One day I was in a variety store in a neighboring town and saw a closeout display. Being naturally curious and cheap (not thrifty but cheap) I ventured over to check it out. There on the table was a pile of small- lipped crank baits, several of which were "BLUE"! The price was an amazing twenty-five cents. I scooped all of them up and bought the whole lot of them. On the next fishing trip, I tried one of them and caught fish right away. The most amazing thing about the lure was that it contained a sound chamber and you could hear it from under the water. The lure ran two to five feet deep and made quite a lot of racket. Throughout the next several years, when I would be in a bind to catch fish, I would pull out the Twenty-five cent special, and most of the time it would catch fish. I have often stated that I must have been crazy, for the two most productive lures that I have ever used, were the ones that I used least in tournaments. Although I enjoyed quite a bit of success, I know for sure if I had used them, I might have been on TV like John Foxx, Bill Dance or Rowland Martin. Bass Fishermen are funny creatures!

On one occasion we were holding a tournament in the Altamaha River and I had caught a good stringer of fish. I had located five places that were holding fish and spent the morning fishing the first four and had been pretty successful. I knew that my partner for the day fished a lot in the fifth place, so I was in no hurry to get there assured that he would choose that place during his half day. We were only about a half mile up river when my half day expired. (For those that do not know, in some tournaments the partners alternate the choice of fishing location - one chooses the locations for the first half day and then the other chooses the locations for the second half day). When I mentioned the place, he said that he hadn't caught a fish there in two or three trips. My heart dropped! I felt like I was in the running for first place, but was depending on the last "hole". I had not missed catching at least "ONE" bass there every trip in over a year. It was my most consistent "Honey Hole" in that area. Matter of fact, I had caught several large bass there including one 9 pound 8 ounce. I was obliged to go where he chose for the rest of the day and did not catch another fish. I did manage to hook a 2 pounder about fifteen minutes before the tournament was over but did not set the hook very well in the swift water and lost the fish. When the weigh-in was over I had come in second by one ounce and had missed the big fish prize by one ounce.

The next day at the tackle shop the tournament winner and I were discussing the tournament and I related my misfortune with the one of my fishing partners that had won the tournament. He laughed and said that it would not have made any difference in the outcome. I disagreed and made him a proposition. Since we could leave right away and arrive at the "Honey Hole" at about the same time that I would have on the day before, I challenged him to a friendly match. He agreed immediately and we took my boat to the river.

This fisherman was one of the best "live river" fishermen in those parts. By "live river" I mean fishing in the main run of the river. The Altamaha runs three to four miles per hour on average and is very difficult to fish with any success because of the current.

34

This friend was a "plastic worm only" fisherman at the time and was as good at it as anyone with whom I fished.

As we pulled into the backwater of the slough (pronounced slew), I tied my twenty-five-cent special on. We began to cast around the cypress trees and on the third or fourth cast, I caught a keeper bass. Within the next half hour and one hundred yards of water, I had boated five keepers one of which was nearly four pounds. The plastic worm had produced not even a strike! My friend stuck with his favorite weapon for one full circuit of the oxbow lake, finally catching one keeper bass. I asked him why he didn't try a "crank bait" and he answered that he would like to but didn't own one. I loaned him another Twenty-five cent special that I had and we tore up the bass all afternoon.

Being a smart fisherman, he recognized the need for diversity, and until the day he passed he still loved his plastic worms, but his box also contains a few crank-baits just in case.

———————————

One spring I had taken off work to go fishing at Lake Seminole in Southwest Georgia with some friends. We booked lodging at Jack Wingate's Fish Camp. When we tried fishing there the first day, the fishing was very slow. I went to the "Spring Creek" Section of the lake and could see "Monstrous Bass' in the clear water but could not entice any to bite. I fished hard around duck blinds and trees and in holes in the moss to no avail. When we went back to Jack Wingate's lodge for lunch, I met with one of the guides who shared with me some smoke-colored worms (clear grayish worms) and the advice to use light line. I went back and fished hard catching only two small ones. The next day I went up the Flint River arm and got into some muddy water, like the Altamaha River, where I felt at home. I caught some small bass including one Flint River Shoal Bass (a red-eyed bass with a smaller mouth than a largemouth and a larger one that a smallmouth bass.). "Old Sem" had not held up her reputation and we were disappointed. We cut our trip short and headed home.

I still had the rest of the week off so I went the next morning to Davis' landing and proceeded to fish Half Moon Lake, one of my all-time favorite fishing places. I caught a limit the first day on a purple worm and a limit on the second day on a blue worm. My friend, Weyman, and I went on the third day. As we began to fish, I told him of the experience of the last two days. I suggested that one of us fish purple and the other fish blue to see what they wanted today. He informed me that he was planning to fish a black fire-tailed worm so I tied on a purple. I caught a couple of small bass and as we approached a log jutting down into the lake, I cast the purple worm along the left side of the log. About ten feet from the bank my line twitched and I drove the 40 size hook home. I fought the nice bass for a few minutes and then placed him in the boat. Unhooking the fish and straightening my worm I cast on the opposite side of the lake to another log and tied into another big fish. After I got him into the boat, I heard Weyman rifling through his worm box. He quickly removed the black firetail and replaced it with a purple and began to tear the bass up. When we got time to weigh them one of my fish was seven pounds and the other was seven pounds and two ounces. These were pretty nice bass for back-to-back catches.

On the Saturday afterward my father and I were back at the "Honey Hole" and we were working into a little slough where I had missed a fish for the last three days. I made a perfect cast and was ready when the fish picked the worm (a blue one) up. I was using the same rod and reel that had tamed the two seven pounders like puppies two days before and set the hook with all force possible. The fish streaked out to the middle of the lake passing my boat on the right like a runaway freight train. My reel was a 5000D (direct drive) with no drag unless the handle was released. I held the handle and applied pressure on the fish. "Crack!!" The reel handle broke in my hand and the reel dropped into the lake. I caught the line and managed to retrieve the reel and recover my crippled rod. When I could get the slack out of the line the fish was gone. The rod was a number 6 action Lew's Speed Stick which was so stiff that it could double as a pool cue in a tight. I had another rod just like it and switched the 5000D over to it still shaking my head at what had happened.

My father asked, "What kind of a fish was that?"

"I don't know but if it was a largemouth, George Perry would have to move over." (George caught the World Record Largemouth Bass on June 2, 1942 about 25 miles upriver from where we were). My father and I sat there for a while trying to take in what had just happened. Just around the bend was the log where the first of the two seven pounders had been caught before. I was demonstrating to daddy just how I had worked the worm earlier when my line twitched and I drove the hook home again. The fish streaked toward the mouth of the lake and towards the Altamaha. I lifted the rod and attempted to turn the fish. "Crack!' There was that sickening sound again. A second rod handle had snapped in my hand and I was again trying to avoid losing my tackle. Again, the fish was gone. I do not know if it was the same fish although it felt the same. I am not sure of the species, but when you consider that a 22 pound 4 ounce bass, a 45 pound channel catfish and a 62 pound striped bass had come from the same waters, anything was possible. This does not consider sturgeon of over eight feet in length and flathead catfish of over 90 pounds have also come from there. My balloon had been deflated, and the rest of the day all I could think of was what could have been.

Weyman and I fished and hunted together regularly. We met on a trip in 1964 to the Boy Scout National Jamboree at Valley Forge, Pennsylvania and have been good friends ever since. At one time he was the drummer in the "Rock Band" that I was front man and lead singer for.

One cold January day we were bass fishing on the Ohoopee River not far from where it joins the Altamaha River. It is a beautiful little river with tannic acid water and white sand. There are lots of fish in it and we were fishing ultralight tackle for the bass. I was attempting to make a cast in a seemingly perfect lair for a hungry bass when a puff of wind caught my small Rapala lure and took it into a limb 10 or 12 feet above the water. I maneuvered my Bass Boat under the limb and stood on the bow trying to save my lure. I was reaching up with my rod tip to free the lure when suddenly the boat was no longer under me. I plunged straight into the icy water. I shot up out of the water and hit my head on the swivel seat knocking me back into the icy water again. Weyman was so busy laughing at me that I could have drowned for all the help he was. On the second attempt, I catapulted into the bow of the boat. The first thing I thought about was my wallet. I pulled it from my pocket and discovered that even though I had been the water twice my wallet was hardly wet. It must have all happened so fast that the water could not have gotten to my wallet. I must have looked like a wet possum for Weyman could not stop laughing at me. He must have been my "bad luck charm" for that was not the only time he was with me when I got wet. Once we were setting out decoys in my little aluminum bass boat when I leaned over to correct a neck wrapped decoy and the bolts holding the swivel seat broke loose causing me to go headfirst into the Altamaha River Sound. But I will discuss that in another chapter.

Weyman and I were fishing in the mouth of a lake on the Altamaha early on New Year's Day. I saw a swirl and flipped a Rebel Pop Top out in front and when the ripples settled, I gave it a slight twitch. It sounded as if a large bream had "Kissed" the plug like a popping bug. I flicked my wrist and immediately knew that I had a "Hawg" on. I quickly told Weyman to get the net. He did not sense any urgency so he did not move fast, getting the net. I always sat my large tackle box on the net when trailering the boat so as to keep it from blowing out of the boat while transporting it. It was still on the net when the Bass (all 29 inches of him) cruised by the port side of the boat. When Weyman saw the fish, in the clear water, swimming just under the surface he grabbed the net and almost threw my tackle box out in the lake. The next pass he professionally netted the monster and threw him into the boat. The fish was skinny due to the fact that it was mid-winter and she must not have fed well. She weighed only 9 ½ pounds despite the fact she was 2 ½ inches longer than my largest bass of 11.5 pounds.

I still love topwater fishing and the excitement that it brings. I love to see the strike, hear the splash and feel the tug. I have learned through the years to fish almost every way that a bass can be caught. I fished enough tournaments to discover that a tournament fisherman must be resourceful and use different techniques but Topwater still is my greatest thrill. There is a bank on the Altamaha that the best lure is topwater even in the swift water. I fish that cut bank (deep water on the outside side of the river bend) with Devils Horses, Zara Spooks, Scrambled Eggs, and dish faced poppers like the Lucky 13 and Rebel Pop Top. The fish there will readily hit the topwater plug and the trick is to quickly get them out into open water and away from the trees and logs underwater there. I always use heavy line on that bank and a stiff rod for that purpose. The last thing you need to have is a large bass on the line that decides to tangle up on the limbs of a big tree which had fallen into the river. If a fisherman gets into this predicament, it is either swim or lose the fish. The excitement on that bank is beyond parallel. Not only the anticipation of the strike but the plan to get the fish out in open water is in effect. The current of the Altamaha is another factor on that bank as it is all up and down the main river.

There is a place near Doctortown known as "Dick Swift". It is the only place in the river that I ever found that my 24-volt Rebel trolling motor would not pull upstream. All it would do there was to hold you still against the strong current. A friend that lived in Jesup, Ollie, was an avid bass fisherman. He liked the area around "Dick Swift" and fished it regularly. His method was to drift with the current and fish the cut bank. When he was in my boat was the only time he could sit still and hit the same spot several times. Plenty of fishermen in the Altamaha, Ocmulgee, and Oconee utilized small boats with a small outboard motor with "Foot Steering" to be able to overcome the current and fish upstream. My large trolling motor would accomplish that feat to an extent. Ollie used a rig which I adapted to quickly. He would place an 8 inch black worm on a black Johnson's spoon and cast it against the bank retrieving it just under the water to the boat. I do not know if the rig resembled the eels that are plentiful in the Altamaha or the water snakes and moccasins that are also abundant in the river. No matter, the strikes are vicious and the fish that will hit that rig are usually good sized. I changed to purple spoons and purple paddle tailed worms and have had much success fishing them. I have seen bass hit snakes swimming in the water before and the Georgia Record Striper was caught on an eel in the Oconee.

On a patriotic note, Ollie and I were fishing in Crescent Lake in Central Florida one morning. We were in the "narrows", the bottleneck where Dead Lake, Haw Creek, and Crescent Lake join. We call it the "Deep Hole". The water there is up to 36 feet deep when the lakes around run 11 to 12 feet so it is always a good starting point to fish the transitional water to find the depth the fish are in. It was foggy that day and you could hardly navigate the lake. We picked our way to the "narrows." We had just begun to fish when a shape descended out of the fog hitting the water. Suddenly we could see the spread white tail and the white head of a Bald Eagle started to ascend up into the fog with a "keeping size" bass in its talons. We both put our fishing gear down and just stared up into the fog as the eagle disappeared upward. It does not get more beautiful and stirring as to witness that in the "Wild."

I liked fishing a Rebel or Rapala floater-diver, "Machine-gunning". I could set the trolling motor on slow and begin to circle a pond. I could cover much water using this method which was a combination of topwater and crank bait fishing. I have circled a pond and caught up to twenty bass when the "bank runners" were active. Lots of time I could pattern the fish with that method and then use either topwater or "cranking" to catch fish. I have caught loads of bass using it and a trolling motor doesn't get tired like a fishing partner that is paddling can. It also doesn't get jealous if you are catching many fish.

Another important thing is to remember the color of the lure and the conditions where you are successful. I have "red banks", "blue banks" and even one is a "chartreuse bank."

A good memory of locations and also remembering the type of lures is important. I have topwater, spinner bait and worm banks where I remember the locations and what bait I used.

I lived in Jesup for a while and had a pass to Morgan's Lake on the Long County side of the river. There were a great number of fish there in that old oxbow and I was a regular visitor. I would catch mostly large bass but it held a goodly number of Crappie (White Perch as we call them in South Georgia) there too. The lake is notorious because General Sherman (The Union General that all true Georgians have a great dislike for) sent two regiments to cut the trestle at Doctortown so the Confederates could not reinforce behind him as he went into Savannah. It seems that the confederates who were defending the trestle consisted of young boys and old men of the militia with Two 32 pounder cannons, one on each side of the track and a Campbell Siege Gun mounted on a flat car. They had surveyed the track and had the cannon trained on the Morgan Lake Grade (the long fill across the flooded lowlands of Morgan Lake). They had posted skirmishers to fire when the "Yankees" were on the grade as a signal to fire the cannons. All went as planned and when the exploding shells hit, the Yankees jumped from the grade into the lake. It is said that they feared the alligators and moccasins as they plunged in. All South Georgia Boys knew that December was not a month in which the cold-blooded reptiles or biting bugs were active on the Altamaha. The Yankees did not know it. The trestle is still there!

42

The mouth of Goose Creek (the old Appling County Wayne County boundary) is an excellent place to fish for bass. The sandbar there has always been a good producer with plastic worms. There have been several local tournaments held at both Jaycee Landing and Riverside Park Landing which are both downriver from Goose Creek. I have some banks and spots which are color-specific but the Goose Creek mouth seemed to not be selective. All colors worked there, as long as a fisherman used plastic worms. I have caught many bass and shot many ducks there but the close proximity to the two landings means it gets fished regularly. That section from Oglethorpe Bluff to U. S. 301 has always produced lots of fish.

As a side note, Oglethorpe Bluff is one of the 6 or 7 tallest bluffs on the Altamaha River. Its name comes from the legend that when General Oglethorpe and Chief Tomo Chi Chi were exploring the area on the West side of the Altamaha the indigenous Indians (Muscogee Creeks) on that side of the river jumped them and were in chase. It is said that Oglethorpe rode his horse down the tall bluff and swam the Altamaha River to escape them. I do not know if it is true but it is an interesting story. The Altamaha River was the White Man Red Man divide until the 1813 Creek Cession. The 1818 Georgia Lottery was when Appling County was created out of that land and it was divided and opened for settlement.

I had another friend, Gary, whose father was an excellent outdoorsman and the son inherited the genes for it. We have fished and hunted together many times. We have been through quite a lot together. We were in a 25 acre 47 year old mill pond one day trying to catch some bass. I had rigged a 3/16 ounce Beatle spin with an oversized hammered Colorado blade. When the lure was retrieved it would stay on the top of the water with little effort. It would also run horizontally instead of the normal vertical position. It made lots of sputtering and was an excellent buzz bait. Gary looked at it as I was tying it on and remarked that it looked like a "Bat-winged Vibrator" and inquired if I was really going to fish with it. I shrugged his remarks off and began to cast. The old pond was loaded with stumps, all of which I imagined that a lunker bass was just lying in wait for my bait. After a few casts, the water exploded by the stump and an extremely large "Bucket Mouth" was giving me a great fight. I landed him and proceeded to put more in the boat. Gary never said anything else derogatory about the little lure. He just marveled at how it would toll the fish up. We had fished for an hour or so and we were digging in the cooler for cans of Gatorade to help us in the hot environment. We were near the end of the pond when we spotted a small wooden boat. We recognized the fellow. He was part of the family that owned the land around the shallow end of the pond. We pulled my boat alongside his boat and we began to talk. Gary noticed a stone crock in the bottom of his boat and inquired as to what he had there. (His family was known to make a little "Shine" from time to time.) He answered that it was "Tea". Gary asked if we could have some and he handed the crock to Gary. He took a snort as did I and we both dove into the cooler for something to chase it with. All there was to drink was Gatorade so we chugged some down. We might as well have taken an IV and mainlined it, for it went into our system like it was riding a "Fast Freight". In no time at all, we were all giggly and could not cast without putting our lure in the tree or on the bank. We may have converted from Bass Fishing to Squirrel Fishing. It really did not matter anymore. I have always been careful when offered something to drink after that. It was several hours in the sun before we were fit to drive to town.

Gary and I were fishing one day in the river and decided to change locations. We were making our way carefully upriver from Carter's Bight toward Hell's Shoals Lake but the river was very low and treacherous. We picked our way up each sandbar trying to find the way across the bar. We approached on the Tattnall County side and saw an opening to an oxbow lake. Once we were in the mouth the water was plenty deep so we began to fish. The first part was narrow and we caught a couple of nice bass. As the oxbow began to widen, I was looking at a likely spot to cast when we got close enough. A coot was walking off the log which was leading down into the water. Just as the coot stepped off the log into the water, to make his escape from us, the water exploded around him and he disappeared below the surface never to return. This made Gary and I fish even harder trying to catch the fish that could swallow a full-grown Coot. It was all to no avail. We fished all around the ever-widening oxbow and came upon some cabins along the lake. Presently a man in a small boat entered the lake. I was not paying much attention to him until he drew close to us. He spoke and I turned to see a double-barrel shotgun in the bow of the boat.

"You got anything?" he inquired.

"A few," I replied. Although I wanted to say, "a .308 and a .38 special, how about you?" But I bit my tongue.

He began to inform Gary and me that we were trespassing. I knew we had driven in from the river and the Altamaha was a "Navigable Stream" and questioned his statement. He said that we needed to come to the hill so he could call the sheriff. I knew the sheriff. He had been a Georgia State Trooper and gave me my examination for my driers license. Finally, I told him to call the sheriff and we would wait for him in the boat. I knew that on land I might be trespassing, but I was not sure about being on the water.

I told him that if the sheriff told me I was trespassing, I would believe it and would go with him. This ended our conversation and as soon as the man was out of earshot, Gary convinced me to take the boat back to the river. I found out later that Jimmy Carter, when he was Governor, was salt-water fishing in what some people considered private property that he got the Attorney General involved and cleared that question up but the fresh-water question had not been cleared up. I did not have the backing like the Governor, so I let it alone. I still think about the fish that ate the coot!

I was fishing in another pond one day using a 3/16 ounce green Beetle Spin. We were in the deep end and I was working the lure low and slow in the deep water. All of a sudden it felt as if I had hooked a stump. Frustrated, I thought that if I pulled a little, I could pull it loose. Suddenly, I realized I had a fish on the line, "A Big Fish". As I fought the fish it first ran directly away from the boat. Then it turned and streaked to the left. I brought to fish around and it went hard right. After another turning of the fish, it began going away again. I finally began to gain some line of the fish. I had it coming to the boat with its head and shoulders out of the water. As it came to the boat my partner had the net that daddy and I had already landed a 9 pound 8 ounce and a 10 pound 4 ounce bass in. My partner tried to sweep the fish instead of getting his head in and suddenly there was my prize pinned alongside the boat with the head outside the net on one side and the tail on the other. I hollered "Grab Him in the Mouth" but instead, my partner tried to jiggle the net trying to fold the big bass into the net. Having enough of our game the fish flopped. With the head out of the water and the line tight. The hook straightened and the fish slid from between the boat and the net, sinking into the deep. I had my Lew's Speed Stick in my hand and had visions of Zorro and his rapier but my partner was too good a friend. I asked him why he did not grab the fish in the mouth and told me that the week before he had "Lower Jawed" a mudfish in the Altamaha and his fingers had yet to heal. That was the second biggest bass I ever had on my line. Judging by his lack of fitting into the net my estimate was that he was over 14 pounds.

I love to night-fish. The darker it is the better. My favorite lure at night is the Devil's Horse with propellers on both ends. The trick I learned early in fishing at night is to be consistent. Don't mix it up. The fish will be feeding by sound and if you get cute, he might miss the bait. Daddy and were fishing in a good friend's pond one night. It was so dark that we would turn on a flashlight pointing up and circle it around to determine where the cypress trees were. Nothing is worse than to cast and never hear the lure hit the water. That usually means that you will have to go and retrieve it from a limb if you can. I got a bearing on the tree limbs and cast the lure. I heard the lure splash down. The method I like is to twitch the rod and count two, three, four and twitch again. I was working the lure this way and suddenly, it sounded as though someone had driven a Volkswagen into the pond. I fought the fish, controlling him the best that I could.

We did not have a net with us and when I got the fish alongside the boat and told Daddy, "Grab him in the Mouth!"

To which he replied. "There are nine hook points on that darn lure. I am going to check with the flashlight before sticking my hand in all those hooks!" He did and lifted a beautiful 7 pounder into the boat. I also liked to use a Fred Arbogast lure called the Jitterbug. A steady pull is all that is necessary to be successful with that lure.

There was a form of bass fishing popular on the Altamaha River many years ago. It was called "Jigger Fishing." Men would rig thick Calcutta cane poles with 135-pound test Dacron line and wrap it from the handle to the end leaving a short piece of line off the end. They would cut a lizard shaped piece of rubber from a tire inner tube and place treble hooks in it. They would go along the outer edge of the river and beat the water with the tip of the pole. They would do this all among the tree tops and logs and trash on the edge. When a Bass would hit, they would walk the pole backwards and throw the fish in the boat so fast the fish could not react. They used to catch many large bass using the "Jigger Poles". I never tried this type of fishing. I believe it would wear a person out.

Billy's first bass

I now have several small ponds on my property and can fish anytime I want. I have bass in four of the ponds and will just "catch and release" them. I began "Catch and Release' quite a long time ago. There is no telling how many thousands of bass I have released. The largest was over nine pounds. My father was not inclined to release bass. His family members were all avid fishermen. Not for sport but for food. He was not keen on releasing bass and the biggest one of his, we ate weighed, ten pounds four ounces. He liked to bake big bass with dressing.

My friend Jerry and I planned a trip to the Suwannee River to catch Suwannee Bass. The world record fish was just a little over 3 pounds and we were sure that us "Super Fishermen" could easily top that and get our names in the record book. We landed the boat at Stephen Foster Park which only permitted a motor less than 10 horsepower. We began working our way down the river. I quickly discovered that a Mann's 4 inch blueberry jelly worm was the bait of the day. We had "Texas rigged" them with small bullet sinkers and small worm hooks. We patterned the fish to be in the roots of Tupelo trees and either caught bass or very large warmouth. The largest bass we caught was just over 2 pounds and the warmouth was a little larger, but no world record. I did find out that Jerry made the best homemade Ham Salad I ever tasted.

My grandmother did not like "flip filleting" bass. When I started that method of fish cleaning she protested aggressively. She did not want me to waste fish although you could pick up the fish and see through the meat left on the backbone which I saved

49

that piece for her. She liked cold fish as good as anyone I have
ever known. She was the one who would have me save the roe of
my catches and when she had enough, she would cook up some
"HEN EGGS AND FISH EGGS" by combining them and
scrambling them up in a cast-iron skillet. Later she was not fond
of my new catch and release habits. I guess when you raise a
family in the Great Depression you want all the food you can
acquire and throwing fish back struck her the wrong way.

    I was fishing a tournament one weekend in the lower
Altamaha River. The tournament was based out of Two-Way Fish
Camp near Darien. There were far too many fishermen with boats
so I decided to enter "No Boat." By doing this I would be drawn
and paired with a partner with a boat. I drew a fisherman from
Welaka, Florida. He had a 17 foot Stryker Bass Boat with a
blueprinted 175 Mercury Black Max outboard motor. As I settled
down in the seat, I noticed he had a "Hot Foot' which was an
accelerator pedal like in racing boats. I secured my equipment and
asked if he had ever fished this area before. His reply was that he
had never been in the Altamaha before. This retort caused me
some anxiety, because unfamiliarity with this river can be deadly.
He asked if I was familiar and I said I was. He then told me to let
him know by hand signals where to run in the river.

    The rules called for a four-boat ooze-off start and we were
in the front row with several fast-looking boats. On an ooze-off
start when the signal is given, the boats would slowly accelerate
until they reached a buoy in the river at which they could give it
full throttle. Some quarter-mile distance away loomed the U. S. 17
bridge. Before the signal to start I asked what he wanted me to do
to which he said. "Sit on your hat and hold on!"

As the signal was given, he held back and let the others get about halfway to the bridge then he shot the gas to it. The darn thing lifted out of the water like a top fuel dragster and passed the other three at the end of the straightaway. While we were speeding up the river, I was hitting him on the shoulder to direct him away from the sand bars although no more water than we were drawing, we most likely could have skimmed over the submerged bars. When we got about three miles up the river and the other boats were no longer in sight, he backed off to a reasonable speed. He later told me he had been clocked at 75 miles per hour.

We began a long day of fishing, and I quickly noticed he was using Zebco Number One reels (push button spin casters) but I made no remark for most bass fishermen at the time fished casting reels like the Ambassador 5000. I was using Lew's Speed Spools which were made by Shimano and would cast farther than a 5000. That day I had to use many different casting techniques in order to get to the fish, from overhand and side arm to under-hand both left and right-handed.

Throughout the day I showed him many good spots in the Altamaha delta. And we caught some bass but not enough to place in the tournament. We enjoyed each other's company and as we began to secure the equipment to make the ten mile trip back to the weigh-in site he remarked, "I've seen a lot of fishermen who use those darn reels, but you are the first I have ever seen that fished all day without a backlash."

I had not given it any thought until then, but that was one of those lucky days that I went without a backlash. My reputation is good in Welaka, if nowhere else, for I have gotten some backlashes that you could "write home about". Most of those were when the lure hit something on the back-cast. I guess starting with the old "Knuckle Busters" gave me an advantage with a casting reel. I kept spare line in the tackle box for those occasions when the only answer is the cut the line off and start over. I have created "bird nests", before, that a mockingbird would be proud of.

In another tournament in the lower Altamaha, Jerry and I were partnered up and were at the top of Swan Lake fishing. There were bass there but you had to fish through the mudfish. We were using my "Mudfish Tamer" and dispatching the toothy critters. We left with a sizeable catch of largemouth but there were at least 20 "Grinnels" floating. I glanced back and could not help thinking about the girl at the landing on the Ohoopee River.

Bass Anglers Sportsman Society was having a big tournament in Welaka, while I was visiting relatives in Bunnell. I had not brought my boat and was not intending to enter the tournament, but I had brought some tackle in the back of the car. The Boy Scout motto "Be Prepared", is something to remember, so I had both salt-water and fresh-water tackle with me. I borrowed Uncle Buddy's boat and went to Dead Lake to try my hand there. I had been fishing for about an hour, when I approached a dead fall tree in the water. Although I was not used to Uncle Buddy's rig and the trolling motor controls, I positioned myself for a cast and intended to walk the six inch Strawberry Jelly Worm down the branches toward me. As I worked the worm along the branches, I saw the 25 pound test Golden Stren line twitch. I caught up the slack and put all my strength into the hook set. I drove the hook home and set it hard again. It was like pulling dead weight toward the boat, which made me wonder what was on the other end of the line. All I knew was it was heavy. Possibly a small alligator or snapping turtle. As it neared the boat, I saw it was a huge bass, the largest I had ever had on my line. I must have stunned it with the hook set for it was not fighting. When the fish was within ten feet of the boat and possibly saw the boat, she came to life and dove deep pulling the bow of the boat around. She was headed back to the treetop! I tried to locate the trolling motor control to pull her into deep water to no avail. I almost stomped a hole in the floor of the boat looking for the unfamiliar foot control. The fish went back into the treetop despite all my efforts. I held the line tight wondering if I should go in after her or if I could get her loose from the limbs. After a few moments of the line sawing back and forth on the tree limbs, the line broke and my prize was lost.

I got a good look at her and knew by her length and girth that she would dwarf my 11 pound 8 ounce trophy. She looked to be over 30 inches long and was at least 24 inches around. I would have estimated her in excess of 16 pounds. The big ones have a habit of getting away. To this date, I have never had a bass on and seen it that was larger than that one. I can close my eyes and still see the whole scene rerun it in my mind.

There is an old saying. "If your heavy rod is bent double and your line is a hummin' high "C" and the boat moveth toward the bass – THAT'S A HAWG".

Offshore Fishing Rig

CHAPTER THREE

OFFSHORE FISHING

As I have fished salt water all of my life, I have enjoyed all of it from intercoastal waterway fishing, pier fishing, surf fishing and most of all the deep-sea fishing. I have fished this method up and down the Atlantic from Savannah, Georgia to Ponce Inlet, Florida. I also fished the Gulf of Mexico in the Destin, Florida and Apalachicola, Florida area. I have taken many large fish using this method on both party boats and individual charter boats. The following are some of the interesting stories about those fishing trips.

The bulk of my deep-sea fishing trips have been out of Savannah, Georgia area off Wilmington Island, Georgia. The charter that we used there was on the Miss Judy with Captain Judy Helmey. We took many charter trips with her as the captain.

Most of the time when we went out, we were either trolling for fish such as Barracuda, King Mackerel or Dolphin (now called Maui Maui), or we were bottom fishing are Snapper, Vermillion, Grouper or Black Sea Bass. Both types of deep-sea fishing can be very productive if you hit the conditions right. The most successful trip that we took from Wilmington Island was to a place called the 135-foot ditch. This location is about three hours out of port. It is also where the Gulfstream runs. On one of these trips my cousin, Jeff, hooked a big King Mackerel. This was giving him all he could ask for. The drag was squealing and Jeff's heavy-duty deep-sea rod was almost bent double. He was in the fighting chair hanging on for all he was worth. As he worked the fish close to the boat suddenly the drag on that saltwater reel began to scream. Jeffrey hung on with all he had. After a few minutes the line looked as though it had dead weight. As he retrieved his line there was half of a King Mackerel (cut off at the dorsal fin) on his hook. Trailing behind was a Barracuda that appeared to be close to 10 feet in length. The spot on the back end of the fish looked as large as a Dudley softball. What was left of the King Mackerel weighed better than 20 pounds. At that time the Georgia record for Barracuda were in the neighborhood of 8 feet long.

On another occasion when my first wife and my father were with me. We were bottom fishing, when suddenly a big Grouper was on her line. The pull caused her feet to lift from the deck. Only my father's reaction, of grabbing her by the belt, kept her from being pulled overboard. On another occasion my friend Bill that was with us often, was nearly taken overboard by another grouper that was sizable. Divers have reported that some of the Spotted Jewfish that they had encountered were as large as a Volkswagen so you can imagine what an 800 to 900 pound fish can pull like.

There were times when certain species were running the excitement can be nonstop. I have seen it with Black Sea Bass, and before you could get your bait to the bottom you would have two on your double hook rig. The same has occurred with the Snappers, speaking both Red Snapper and the Charleston Snapper. When trolling with Captain Judy, we have encountered King Mackerel that would be in such large schools that the action would be nonstop and many times they would be up to three on lines at a time which can cause an interesting dilemma in successfully landing them. Another interesting fish to get a large school of is a Bonita. When you get one on, it is like hooking a freight train and will give you a superb fight. They are a red meated fish and most people only want to use them for cut bait. My daddy took several home from one trip and smoked them on our smoker at home. They were excellent when prepared that way. One of my friends would bring Barracuda home and make what he called 'Cuda Critters". There was another occasion when Captain Judy's Striker did not show up. I became her Striker for that trip.

On some occasions instead of going all the way out to the 135-foot ditch we would go to the Texas Tower which was closer to the coast. It was a communications tower in the ocean and being a structure, really attracted a lot of fish. The Amberjack would school in tremendous schools of 40 to 50 fish. You mostly would catch them trolling on the occasion when the schools would sound as the boat crossed over them. I sat on a cooler on the bow and casts a Cisco Kid plug in order to entice one of those 30 pounders to pounce on it. One time my friend, Bob, who was frustrated with not getting a bite placed a piece of ham on his hook trying to entice one of those big devils to hook up.

I would fish off Saint Simons' Island with my good friend, Neil. He had a 24-foot North American boat, that was really good to fish from. We would go out and troll for Spanish Mackerel in the sound between Jekyll Island and St. Simons Island. On one occasion we were trolling in an area where the schools of fish would be 5 to 7 acres large. We were encountering problems with the fish sounding as the boat passed over therefore minimizing our hook ups. I took a small open faced spinning outfit and hooked on a silver spoon. I would cast out into the school and sometimes have eight or ten hookups before I got back to the boat, but I most always had a fish on when I did reel in. The action was so furious that in no time we had filled all the coolers up with fish and had no more room to place any more fish in. I really believe that I probably caught half of the fish we had using that method and the other three fishermen caught the remaining half.

On one occasion fishing with the same group, I hooked a big Cobia off the St. Simons sea buoy. Christmas Creek on Cumberland Island is reputed to be one of the largest breeding grounds of sharks on the Atlantic coast. On one occasion, fishing at the deep hole which is located between the south end of Jekyll Island and the north end of Cumberland Island, according to our depth finder the deep hole was 80 feet deep near the mouth of the big Satilla River. We were fishing there one day for bottom fish when we spotted the shape of a shark under our boat. The boat was 16 feet long and the shark was longer than the boat. We made the decision that we needed to find another place to fish that was safer than that. Two of my friends who lived in Brunswick and fished for sharks regularly caught a 980 pound Tiger Shark from the beach on the south end of Jekyll Island just inshore from that deep hole.

On one occasion my friend had agreed to take a television fisherman with him. I was asked to go along, which I readily accepted the offer. We went to the mouth of Christmas Creek and cast out in the breakers to cast. I hooked up with a Barracuda on a Garcia 5000 casting reel. I saw that the tv fisherman's wife (the camera person) was filming me. I loosened the drag and lifted the rod tip so as to make the fish jump, which it did several times. I was sure I would be on television after that. We fished the rest of the day with much success. The only bad spot was when I was about to put a wippin' on that tv fisherman for how he treated his

57

wife, which was nasty. I watched the show for several weeks, to see me fighting the Barracuda. I finally saw the fight but he had edited the film to look as if he caught the fish. I then wished that I had put a wippin' on his lying behind.

When we vacationed in Destin, Florida we were fortunate to fish in the Gulf of Mexico on a few occasions. On one of the charters, I hooked a large Cobia and turned it over to my nephew to fight and land. He did a great job and got the experience of a lifetime. The fish weighed over 25 pounds and we had it cleaned by the boat hand. The restaurant would prepare your catch and add trimmings for your supper. We asked the other family on the charter to join us for supper. That fish fed 14 that night and was scrumptious.

There was a time when the Engineering company I worked for took the employees on a trip to Apalachicola, Florida to observe our dredging operation in the Gulf of Mexico near there. While there I ate oysters every way possible. My coworkers kidded me about eating oysters every meal. I told them that if I were in Vidalia I would eat Vidalia onions and if in Texas I would eat beef every meal. What was wrong with eating oysters in the oyster capital of the South. On that trip we went on a party boat to fish. The wind kicked up and the seas were very rough. All but three of us got seasick. I fished hard although I almost had to lash myself to the rail.

Bill's Eight Pointer

CHAPTER FOUR

DEER HUNTING

Although dove hunting and bass fishing are two of my favorite outdoor pastimes, I enjoy a host of other outdoor activities including deer hunting. I must admit that the bulk of the humorous things that have occurred to me have either been during or around deer hunting.

My first experience at deer hunting was taking a "stand" beside a two-path road, listening to a pack of July, Blue Tick or Black and Tan hounds as they chased a deer through the dense flat woods near my home. In that form of hunting if you are either lucky or placed on a known "runway" you can get a shot at the fleeing whitetail as the dogs drive it by. In the protocol and tradition of South Georgia dog hunting everyone on the hunt shared the meat with the owner of the dogs and the shooter taking the larger portion of the meat. Dog hunting was not only an organized hunt but a social event in the old South. I was never successful in taking a buck on a dog hunt but I did get to chase the dogs that would not respond to the "cow" horn that was blown for them to come back. I guess that this may be the reason that I decided that other forms of deer hunting might be more attractive to me.

My next recollection of deer hunting was crossing the Altamaha River in a leaky old boat with a tired old outboard motor, to still hunt in the river swamp in the bordering counties with my cousin, Billy. The season in my home county was closed because the deer population had dwindled. The Georgia Game and Fish Commission had restocked the county with Texas and Wisconsin whitetail deer and kept the season closed for seven years in order to allow them to repopulate the depleted stock. They must have known what they were doing because they now are forced to issue permits for farmers to control hunt them to avoid crop damage and the limit had been expanded from two bucks to five deer (two bucks and three does). Although my first buck was taken in Tattnall County my trips across the river were almost as unproductive as my dog hunts so I was compelled to search for a type of deer hunting that I enjoyed or give it up.

In about 1970 the season reopened in the county and my cousin, Billy said that he knew where we could kill a deer on opening day. Although I had accompanied Billy on the excursions across the river without success, I still agreed to go along on the opening day expedition. We were so excited about the season reopening, although it was a relatively short season of only a couple of weeks and could hardly wait until morning. I slept on the floor of his grandparents' house in front of the fireplace because he convinced me that it was closer to the hunting area. It was four miles closer.

Far in advance of first light, we were up and ready. We scooped up our gear, which at the time was modest, and we proceeded on our way. Ignoring the overhanging bushes, I drove my 1969 Ford LTD down to a ford over Tenmile Creek. We grabbed our shotguns and coats and I followed him into the unknown wilderness of the Tenmile creek swamp. Even though I did own a pair of military rifles, a .303 Enfield and a 7.7 Arisaka, I had never hunted deer with anything but a shotgun. I was armed with my trusty Remington 1100 and Billy had a 2 9/16" chambered Browning that would jam with 2 3/4" shells unless the shells were ringed with a knife so that part of the hull would be fired with the load thus shortening the overall length of the shell.

As we proceeded through the woods, I noticed something about Billy that was to later become his trademark. He could not walk in a straight line. His zig-zag style of walking translated a short walk into a cardiovascular workout. I fully believe that we walked for thirty to forty minutes before he declared that we were "THERE". A later check of the aerial photographs revealed two things: First, we only traveled about three hundred yards from where we were parked. Second, we could have driven to the spot from a road on the other side of the creek. The latter will become important later in this story. He had read somewhere that if you could take a stand off the ground, the deer would have more difficulty in smelling you and he said that I must climb a tree. We were in a plantation of young pine trees and the largest tree there was only about six inches in diameter. Now you must realize that even though I was not a large baby, I quickly overtook the larger babies and never was considered small. I could not envision my 220-pound body up a six-inch pine tree. Nevertheless, Billy insisted that I must hunt "right there". I found a large stump in a clump of palmettos and set up my stand there. The stump was located at the junction of two plowed fire breaks and I sat there facing the wind, which in hindsight was probably the only correct thing that I did that morning. Billy proceeded on forward and I later learned he found an oak tree big enough to climb.

The events that occurred next are forever burned in my memory. It was a cool, foggy morning when daylight finally decided to break. The birds were just starting to sing and the black of night was slowly turning to the gray of first light. There is nothing more exciting than watching the world come to life in the morning and I am still in awe of the Creator every morning that I get to relive this happening. I had, in my infinite wisdom, deduced that my best shot would be out in front of the stump where the fire break veered off down the ridge and was prepared to take my first buck. I fidgeted a little and then settled down pulling the hood of my lined navy-blue jacket (we did not have camouflage at the time) snug around my head. I peered nervously down the grade waiting for my buck to emerge. Suddenly as I glanced over to my extreme right, I saw a frightening sight. A buck that looked like the Hartford Insurance logo was standing broadside looking straight at me in the firebreak. What happened in the next few seconds seemed like hours to me. As soon as I could get my heart out of my throat, I began making a feeble attempt to think. Now you have to realize that this was the first "live" buck that I had ever seen while hunting and I was fighting off "Buck Fever".....and loosing. My shotgun was loaded as per Billy's instruction, with a slug first followed by two 00 buckshot shells and I was wishing that slug was not in the way. It was laying in my lap pointing in the opposite direction of the buck. I did have enough sense to know from my old squirrel hunting days that I must not allow the alert animal to see any motion, or else he would spring into the gall berry bushes directly in front of him. I devised a plan. I would slowly, ever so slowly try to turn the shotgun around toward the direction of the buck. My plan was to keep the gun low until the last minute or until the buck looked away and raise it deliberately and squeeze the trigger. My back up plan was that if he saw the motion and bolted, I would bring the gun up fast-firing the slug out, on the way to getting on target. Then I would fire the buckshot into him broadside. Some plan. I had only gotten about one-fourth of the way around when the buck snorted at me. Plan B was in effect. I swung the gun as fast as possible and fired three shots so fast that they sounded like one shot to me. I thought I saw the rear end of the buck slump but I was in the process of being overwhelmed by all the adrenaline that my body could dump into my system. I jumped up and ran to the spot where he was standing expecting to find him just into the gall berry bushes like the birds and squirrels always were. I cannot describe the empty feeling in the pit of my stomach when I saw that he was not there.

I heard something behind me and saw Billy coming up the side of the ridge toward my position. I could hardly talk when he approached me. It was like I had forgotten how.

"What did you shoot?" he asked.

Finally, I managed to say, "A big buck and he went that way." I pointed down the other side of the ridge, and we began to try to trail him.

We followed the trail he was on for about 200 yards to the creek and lost the trail. Thinking back, I am not sure that we were even on the right trail for we were both inexperienced at trailing wounded deer. I suspect that many a deer is lost by hunters that do not know how to trail a hit deer. Three days later, a man that lived near there found a twelve-point buck dead and decomposing within 200 to 300 yards of that spot. I will always believe that was my buck and that I should have kept on searching for the buck instead of giving up so soon. He had the antlers mounted on another cape later, and it made me sick to see the beautiful rack on a mount hanging in his office. I have always believed that if I had been using a rifle that I would not have taken such a low percentage shot and would have either killed him outright or never shot him. That day I exchanged the shotgun for the 7.7 Arisaka and never used a shotgun again.

But the story does not end here. I went back to my stump and Billy started back to the oak tree. In just a few minutes I heard a shot from his direction. At first, I thought that he had accidentally shot himself while climbing the tree so I rushed off in his direction. When I got to him, he was under the tree looking up into the branches of the tree.

"I got him!" he exclaimed.

"Got what?" I asked.

"A big buck!" he blurted out

"Is he up the tree?" I inquired.

"No!" he stated flatly.

"Then which direction did he go?" I pressed him.

He pointed off further down the ridge, and I began to look in that direction. Not fifteen yards from the base of the tree was a sandy fire break. I began to walk down it, looking for tracks crossing the break and there they were. And there he was! A heavy-bodied eight-point buck. His size was enhanced by the small rack just the size of your fingers if you put your hands together in the shape of deer antlers.

Billy pounced on him "like a chicken on a June bug", grabbed his head-turning it up toward his face. I thought that he was going to kiss the damn thing!

"I'm going to cut out his tongue and eat it!" he blurted out. I knew then that he had been reading too much about the Old West and the Indians.

"Don't you think we had better cook it first?" I joked.

He looked at me funny and said that we needed to cut a pole to carry him out. That accomplished we lifted the pole with the 175-pound deer and started back toward my car. After about fifteen minutes I was absolutely sure that he was lost. You only have to pass the same tree two or three times before it becomes obvious.

We had been on our way about ten minutes when we heard doors slamming on the road and deerhounds being placed on a trail. Within a few minutes the pack of hounds trailed up to us and we had to almost fight them for the deer. We finally discouraged the dogs and made our way to the car. It must have taken an hour to get back to my car and we promptly tied the deer on the hood (with no regard for the car's finish) and headed to Billy's uncle's house to show him off and dress him.

That night we camped where we had parked that morning and we had exchanged the shotguns for rifles. I had the 7.7 mm Japanese and Billy was using my 303 British Enfield with a ten-shot clip loaded with 215 grain cartridges in it.

We hunted the next morning without success and were sitting around the campsite during lunch preparing to return to the woods. I had even found a Blackjack oak tree on an isolated ridge that I could climb and had found plenty of deer tracks on the little ridge. Some friends had come down to the ford and found us camping there. They visited for a while, listening to us recount the events of the morning before. Billy was the star because he had killed the only deer close around.

After they departed, we heard the rattle of another vehicle coming down the two path road and watched as the Volkswagen beetle approached. I had seen the fellow before but did not know him very well. We greeted him as he exited the vehicle. He asked Billy about his deer and Billy relived the event once again for the new audience.

Then to my surprise, the visitor stated "You killed that deer in front of my dogs and rightfully half of him is mine! If you kill another in front of my dogs, I'm going to take the whole deer!" he threatened.

Suddenly "fire" jumped from Billy's eyes.

"If this gun kills a deer....." He shuffled the bolt of the Enfield, throwing a 215-grain cartridge in the chamber and glared at the now unwelcome visitor. "He'll be mine HOOF, HAIR, HIDE AND ALL and I'll kill the first S....O....B... that tries to take him from me!!!!!"

The visitor, sensing the urgency of the moment wisely retreated to his vehicle and left. I was certain that if he had made any further threatening gestures, he would have been a causality, and I would have been a witness to it all.

The remainder of the season was uneventful and I was forever hooked on hunting from a tree stand. For the next several years there were several of us that spent so much time perched in the trees that we thought we were becoming like hoot owls.

Cousin Billy was a true meat hunter. He would take to the woods in search of what he called a "Small Game - Mixed Bag". Loosely translated, it means to take to the woods in search of any edible game, bag it, cook it and eat it. Just because he was deer hunting didn't change that mentality as is evident in this occurrence.

We were in our climbing stands on the edge of an old fallow field. The field was shaped so that we could not see each other but could cover the entire field. Billy was using a single barrel 12-gauge shotgun, at this time with a buckshot. About an hour before dark a shot rang out from his side of the field. Knowing that he had killed the big buck whose tracks had caused us to hunt the small field in the first place, I climbed down from my position in the oak tree to go help trail the deer before dark. When I rounded the bend in the field, I saw him stooped over in the grass in front of his tree. As I drew near, I noticed that he was picking up several things from the ground. What I did not know was that a covey of quail had bunched up under his stand. Seeing this he had quietly slid the buckshot out and inserted a high brass Number 9 shot it in its place. When the covey bunched up just right, he cut loose. He had limited out on quail with one shot. Looking up at me while picking up his last quail, he grinned and said,

"Small Game...Mixed Bag!!"

On a separate occasion when Billy was camping at the creek, I visited him to plan the weekend hunt. When I pulled up to our campsite, he had a fire roaring. He was cooking a squirrel on a spit and was cleaning a wood duck. He had again been hunting the "Small Game...Mixed Bag". Hunting season was his signal to move into the woods and commune with nature. He said that he had taken the duck as it was "Glidden' into the creek." I later discovered that was code for swimming in the creek.

I remember a very cold Thanksgiving, we were all planning to hunt in the "creek" on Saturday, and Billy, who would become a vagrant during deer season, was planning to bivouac for the next week. When we started to the stands the temperature was 18 degrees. Now for those that are used to the winters in Canada or Alaska 18 degrees does not seem cold, but in South Georgia, that's cold to us. I took a friend, Dwight, who was home from college and put him into one of my stands. The stand that he was using was on the way to my stand and was a board jammed in the fork of an oak tree limb. He had never hunted deer before, so we gave him a crash course in deerology. The stand that he was using was on the way to my stand about halfway between my stand and where we parked the vehicles. The others had to cross a swollen branch on a foot log due to the extremely wet winter. Billy and his

68

brother Ralph were in charge of placing the other two hunters in their stands. One of the other hunters, Lewis, was another cousin of mine. He had played tackle on the high school football team and was a good-sized man. Add to that the fact that he often carried along quite a bit of gear. We were to later learn that in the dark instead of finding the loblolly pine with the easy to climb limbs, Billy mistakenly tried to put Lewis up a dead pine. When Lewis protested, Billy informed him that he had climbed that tree before and there was nothing to it. Then Billy tried to physically lift Lewis up the limbs which were rotten and broke off causing them to end up in a pile at the bottom of the dead tree. Billy finally gave up and Lewis decided to fend for himself.

The other hunter was Dwight's roommate at Valdosta State College and Ralph took him to his tree. As the sun came up the temperature dropped to 12 degrees. My hands got so cold that I could not tell whether I could feel the trigger or not. The thin gloves and clothing that I was wearing were grossly inefficient to keep me warm. At some point, I realized that I could not shoot a deer if it climbed up the tree with me. As I made my way back toward Dwight, I began to whistle using the recognition whistle that I told Dwight that I would use, as I approached his position. I whistled but heard no answer. I drew closer to the stand and since Dwight had not answered my whistle, I made sure that I kept trees between Dwight and myself so as to not get shot for a deer by the inexperienced hunter. Dwight's father-in-law had loaned him an Arisaka Japanese 7.7 military rifle to use, and I saw that it was hanging on a limb above Dwight and the wool military blanket that Dwight had taken with him was completely covering his upper body. I realized that I was in no danger from him and neither was the deer. As I reached the bottom of the oak tree I called out to Dwight and asked if he was ready to go. "Catch my s__t." He said and began to toss me everything that he had with him in the tree.

69

He gingerly scurried down the tree and we made our way to where the cars were parked. I asked him why he did not answer my whistle, to which he informed me that he could not whistle.

When we arrived at the cars, we found that we were the first to come out. We began to gather some wood to make a fire and warm up somewhat. All the wood had ice on it and was going to be hard to start until Dwight produced one of his college textbooks and began to tear pages out to start the fire. Just as he finished tearing up his textbook, I found a tar cup (a cup attached to a pine tree to catch the gum that flowed from the face of the tree which had been scraped to cause the gum to flow). This material is highly flammable and an excellent fire starter.

We had the fire burning pretty well when we heard the crash, as Dwight's roommate had slipped from the log as he was trying to traverse the log back over the frozen branch, when he slipped off the log and broke through the ice, getting him wet to about mid-thigh. His pants looked starched as they were frozen, when the wet cloth met the 12 degree air. He hustled over and almost stood in the middle of the fire to thaw out. In a little while, we heard Lewis coming across the log and through the gall berry bushes to our location. He joined us at the fire as we waited for the other two. The fire was so hot and the air was so cold that we had to continue turning, like we were on a rotisserie, because we were freezing on one side and burning on the other.

We waited quite a while and as we were getting somewhat hungry, we took Billy's "Bivouac" pack out and investigated his stash. He had some blueberry newtons which tasted good to all of us. He also had some potatoes and tin foil which we placed in the area of the fire which had begun to coal up and was right for cooking. We knew we could replenish his supply, and surely, he would not bivouac with it that cold. After a while, Ralph quietly emerged from the bushes saying that he thought he smelled oak smoke. Still no Billy. Just as we were about to organize a search party (because he surely had frozen to death), Billy came into sight. When he discovered that we had eaten his supplies he was "Mad as a Wet Hen" and would not listen to our apologies and excuses and offers to resupply his expedition. I thought we would have to knock him in the head to get him calmed down. We took him to town and re-outfitted him and took him back to the "Creek" and left him there.

I well remember Ralph's first deer. He and I had been to Statesboro and had acquired some Interarms Mausers. I had bought a 7 x 57 mm and he had bought an 8 x 57 mm. On opening day of the next season, we were in our places along Tenmile Creek. Just after the crack of dawn, I heard five rifle shots in succession coming from the direction of Ralph's stand. By stand, I use that word loosely, because the stands back then were climbing up a black pine or an oak tree and sitting on a limb. After hearing the shots, I climbed down from my oak tree and headed in Ralph's direction. I went through the branch and up on to the oak ridge where he was supposed to be hunting and spotted that cotton top white head of his through the scrub oaks. I got to him and calmed him down and he began to tell me what had happened. He had been up a real small scrub oak, and the deer came straight under his stand. He shot and the deer bolted off. He kept shooting until the deer disappeared. I looked under the tree and it looked as though you had opened up a commercial-sized ketchup can and poured it out on the ground. I knew he had hit the deer well. We began the trail in the direction of the deer had gone, and quickly found him with three bullet holes in him. As far as I know Ralph had never practiced shucking the bolt fast in order to get shots off quickly, but he had fired them just a fast as you possibly could. The first shot was all he needed but being a young hunter, he did not know that. I'll never forget we hung that buck up and I was going to field dress him for Ralph but he said he wanted to do it. I asked him if he knew how, to which he replied he did. I handed him my Case XX sheath knife, since he did not possess a knife of his own. Immediately, he plunged the knife deep into the stomach cavity which caused a foul smell to emit. I knew he had punctured a gut and it was not going to be pretty.

I asked him if I could finish it, to which he relented. We quickly field dressed the deer and went to the creek where we flushed the body cavity several times to rid it of the undesirable material that might be in there. Although I have retired that little Case XX knife, I sometimes take it out and as I look at it, I can't help but remember Ralph's first deer.

I remember a few years later when I got a call from Ralph to come and help him with the deer he had killed. I got there and helped him get the 200 pound, 10-point deer out of the woods. A 200 pound 10-point deer is a large one for this area. Eight-point buck is the largest I have ever taken and 185 pounds is the heaviest. My son, Billy, has taken a 200 pound 10-point, but they are rare. Anyway, we got the deer out of the woods and took it to his grandmother's house where we dressed the deer, wrapped it in plastic and took it into town to hang it in the butcher's freezer for a week. After we got through, Ralph told the story of how he took that buck. He had borrowed Billy's model 762 Remington BDL pump (a beautiful rifle with basketweave checkering on the wood). Billy had cautioned him not to mess his rifle up so Ralph had it in the zippered gun case as he entered the woods. His plan was to climb the tree and then take it out of the case so he wouldn't skin it up. He got to the base of his tree, but before climbing it he heard a noise off to his left. He quickly unzipped the case removing the rifle and chambering a round. Two does were slipping across in front of him in the firebreak. He froze, watching the two does, as they moved off away from his position. Suddenly, from behind the does, he caught a glimpse of movement. The big buck was trailing the does and never saw Ralph as he raised his gun to his shoulder, shooting the buck in the neck and dropping him in his tracks. I often told Ralph that although he was a good hunter, he was also a lucky one to have taken that deer. The tree Ralph was going to climb was a scrub oak. As long as he hunted, he always climbed the skinniest, ricketiest little trees you have ever seen in your life. For a long time, all he would do is either jam a board or a boat cushion in the fork of one of those little skinny trees and that was his stand.

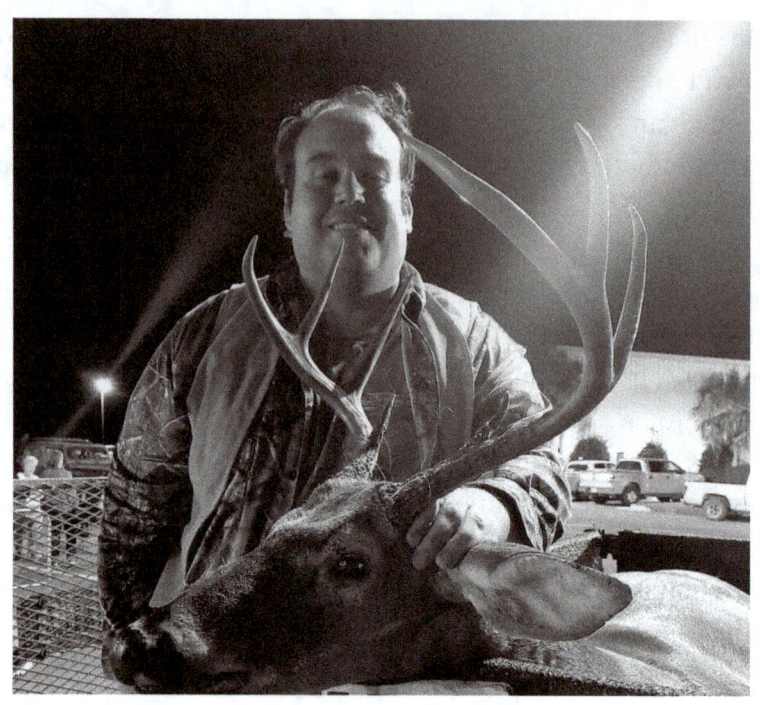

Billy's Nine Point

CHAPTER FIVE

MORE DEER HUNTING

My first buck came from Tattnall County. Jackie, my
cousin, and I had gone over there to hunt in an area that had been
clear-cut and replanted with small pines. He told me, he knew
there were deer in there, but he had never hunted them from trees,
just dog hunted them. We went in with my Bronco and I drove
blindly through the fire breaks until Jackie said, "This is the place."
We got out and all I could see was little planted pines, which
brought me into remembrance of my first hunt in Appling County.

74

I knew that I could not climb any of those little pines but as I shined my flashlight around, I spotted a tall tree in the midst of the short-planted pines. I decided I might be able to climb the tree with my "Hug and Hump" climber and Jackie said he knew where a clump of oak trees was and he would go there. The tree was growing at an angle and was not straight up so I had to be particular how I placed my stand and how I climbed with it. I was limited in the direction which I could face due to the angle of the tree. As a matter of fact, when I climbed and got into position I was facing back toward the Bronco and could see it over the short trees. This was because I was 20 feet up that crooked tree. I could see all the way down the firebreak in both directions and the nose of my Bronco was parked in the intersecting firebreak, so I had a clear shot. It wasn't very long before I looked down beyond where the Bronco was parked and there was a little buck quickly making his way up the firebreak. He hopped up to my Bronco and stopped looking directly at it. T couldn't believe that all I would have had to do was sit on the bumper and I could've taken the deer. He stayed there a moment, and then resumed his movement toward me. When he was about 20 yards from me, he stopped broadside and my .308 Remington model 600 barked, knocking him immediately to the ground. I went back to the Bronco and drove it up to him where I could lift him onto the tailgate and slide him in the back. We got back home and Jackie kept telling me how pretty that deer was and that I ought to mount him. I finally conceded that I would do just that. He is still on my wall although he was not a big one, he was a perfect six point and is still a beautiful deer. When I look up at the mount, I relived the experience over again.

We all had seen this larger doe which we called "Big Momma" as we hunted in the Ten Mile Creek area. At that time the limit in Georgia was two bucks. The shooting of does was prohibited. Very few folks took their two bucks back in those days. Later as we began to hunt with bows and muzzleloaders the taking of does was permitted. Daddy told me that once she was in the gall berries by his stand. She was so large that he was sure it was a buck. Every time she raised her head he would tighten up on the trigger. He told me that if she had come up with a twig on her head, he would have surely shot her. He said he was sure that she was over 150 pounds and might be as much is 200.

The deer population got its size from the Wisconsin Whitetail genes and the antlers from the Texas Whitetail gene pool which was stocked in the county. As far as I know "Big Momma" died of old age. We had no knowledge of anyone taking her although every one of us had had her in our sights at one time or another. It is still difficult for me to take a doe because I was overtrained to take only bucks. Now the limit in Georgia includes several does, not including those taken on Wildlife Management Areas.

I have enjoyed many a good hunt on Georgia's Wildlife Management Areas. I used to hunt Bullard Creek WMA every Archery, Primitive Weapon and Firearm hunt. My house was only about 20 miles away, so I could easily get there for the daily check-in. Now, in Georgia, there is an Annual Sportsmen's Hunting License. There is a Wildlife Management Area named Big Hammock that is directly across the Altamaha River from our property on the river. I have hunted there several times. Both WMA's have rifle and pistol ranges on them so I utilize those facilities fairly regularly.

We had a group of friends who would come from Columbus, Georgia, Virginia and Maine to hunt the primitive weapon hunt with us. They were all retired military competition shooters and were excellent hunters. We would set up camp in the camping area of Bullard Creek and hunt for the week. The only setback with the WMA hunts was, if you killed your one deer you were relegated to camp cook duty because you could not hunt anymore. Due to that fact I would hunt in the swamp of the Altamaha, hunting for wild hogs until about Thursday of the week before looking for deer. We had a great time of fellowship and visiting with those friends. My retired Colonel friend, Gene, taught us much of the German Hunting tradition and how to build a "Hokesits." This was a ladder stand of sorts, which was made from natural material and made it much better camouflaged that one made from boards. It had armrests and a shooting bar that you placed across the armrests in front of you. We met them every year at the Bullard Creek Wildlife Management Area. We camped in a little cluster in the camping area and oft times shared meals.

After hunting in those stands, my cousin Henry and I would buy rough Cypress 2" x 4" lumber and build something very similar to what Gene taught us to build. The main difference is that the Cypress would last much longer than cutting little hardwood saplings to supply the components.

One season when we were camping there, daddy had crushed his hand in an accident at work. He had this funny looking brace on his hand with little pins sticking out his knuckles and corks on them. He was unable to climb because of that hand. We had hunted hogs the first part of the week to not take a deer and had not become the camp cook. Daddy was using a folding dove stool and I would drop him off at the location where he wanted to

77

hunt and drive my Bronco on over closer to my hunting area and pick him back up in the afternoon. My "hokesits" was located in a great place. There were deer trails everywhere. It was up against a small oak tree where I could see five or six trails.

On Friday afternoon when I came to pick daddy up, he told me go and drag his deer out. I was not even aware that he had shot. I have heard several shots in that direction but could not distinguish his 45-caliber muzzleloader from any of the others. He had a small button buck that he had tied all the feet together so you could carry it like a suitcase. But it was tender meat, as we would later discover. When we got back to the camp, he told how he was sitting on the dove stool and the deer came out and he just put his elbow on his left knee, laid the gun in the fork of his splint and used it as a bench rest. He had drilled the deer at 90 yards dropping him in his tracks, which is unusual for a 45 caliber round ball to do. My sister had just recently given birth to my new nephew and daddy was anxious to get to Atlanta to see him so he pulled out that night went on home preparing for his trip the next day.

The next morning, I went to my stand shortly after the crack of the day I saw a deer moving from left to right in my direction. The deer was in some planted pines which made it difficult to place the sights on the deer and hold it long enough to make a shot. Eventually, the deer worked so far around to my right that I had to shift the gun left-handed. The reason was that the little oak tree my stand was leaned against had lots of dried leaves and if you wiggled any, they would all rattle like a large rattlesnake. As I was settling down preparing to make a left-handed shot the deer turned around and started retracing her steps. Still holding the gun left-handed, I found a gap in the planted pines just in front of where she was walking and held the gun in that opening, waiting for her to step in. This would be like the old days at the shooting galleries

78

of the Carnival when I would use what you called "ambush lead" in front of the little duck targets. Shooting just before they got there and thus knocking them down. I set up in the opening, and waited for the deer to step in. When the deer was in the opening I adjusted and shot the deer. We had decided that when shooting those round balls that had no expansion properties, we needed to try to break a leg so they would not run so far. I aimed to go through the left leg into the lung heart area. As I touched the black powder rifle's trigger off, the smoke of the black powder obscured my view. To my right, I suddenly heard a large sound that was likened to an expulsion of air from lungs. I reloaded the rifle, climbed down out of the stand and began to head for the last place I saw the deer. A good rule of thumb is to go to the point where you shot the deer or to go to the point which was the last place you saw the deer to begin trailing. With a muzzleloader and a round

ball, if you don't get a low exit hole, you won't have a blood trail to start with. The body cavity has to fill up and then begin to drip before you see blood in order to trail. I went to the last place I saw the deer and started down the trail only seeing tracks no blood. I came to a fork in the trail with both forks full of fresh tracks. I decided to take the right fork since that was in the direction of the sound that I had heard. About 20 yards down the trail, a deer was lying with its head pointed back toward me. My first thought was that could not be the deer I shot as it was going the other way. As I approached the deer, I took the muzzle of my gun and poked the deer. I then knew the deer was fresh. As I stood there, I realized that the deer had run until it had died in full run and that the sound I heard, was the deer hitting the ground as it flipped over, expelling all the air from its lungs. I drug her back to the Bronco, loaded her up headed up to the check station. Daddy had checked in the last deer the day before and I had just checked in the first deer that morning. That was a little unusual and remarkable. We went over to the tree with it and hung the deer to start to dress and clean it, when I looked around to see daddy's LTD pulling up. He and my mother had decided to stop by and see how it had gone that morning before heading on to Atlanta. They only had to go about 3 miles out of the way in order to do that. He was tickled to see that I had taken the next deer even though it had been about 10 hours later.

A few years before a 12-year-old boy, hunting with a 20-gauge shotgun, had shot an eight-point albino. Although he knocked him to the ground with the first shot, every time the deer would wiggle, he shot again. He even reloaded. When the deer finally quit wiggling, he quit shooting. The deer was messed up some due to the five 20-gauge slug holes in him but the boy was as tickled as could be. There have been quite a few Piebald deer and several albinos taken on that particular management area.

I can reassure you, without a doubt, if you deer hunt, you will make some mistakes. You will miss and you will lose deer. The big ones will always manage to get away. Not counting the big 12 point in 1969, that I shot and lost. The first big one that I lost on our property snuck up behind me. When I turned around on my ladder stand to try and get a shot, I almost got over balanced and fell to the ground. The buck was possibly a 10 point but was at least an 8 point and a pretty good size.

Billy's Ten Pointer

On another occasion, we were hunting one of my favorite areas on the management area during bow season. A humongous buck jumped out in front of me the last evening of the archery hunt. He had a tremendous and tall rack so when the muzzleloading season came around I was back in the same place hoping to get a shot at him. Lewis, Gene and I were staked out in that area hoping that one of us would get a chance at the big deer that I had seen. In the middle of the week, the weather had gotten rainy. Anyone who hunts with black powder knows the first rule is you have to keep your powder dry. Gene was hunting about 400 yards from where I had seen the big buck while I was hunting about 100 yards west of where I had seen him. That evening when we came back to the Bronco, Gene was extremely excited. Gene was a career Army officer and had hunted all over the world. His den was a trophy room lined with mounted heads on all four walls. Under the heads along three of the walls was his immense gun collection. He had built vertical racks and the room was filled with all types of long guns under the trophies. We needed to fire our muzzleloaders so that we could clean them and not risk moisture in

81

our powder. Gene had said that the big buck had come out on him. He said he raised his rifle, sighted carefully and squeezed the trigger. The cap had snapped. The powder did not go off. The buck was not affected by the popping sound so he placed another cap on the nipple. He repeated the sequence with the deer only looking up. He tried one more time with a third percussion cap without any luck. He told me that was the only deer he had ever mounted and had on his wall before he pulled the trigger. Then the deer had just walked away disappearing into the pine woods. He said that was about as great a disappointment as he'd ever had since his powder was wet enough to inhibit ignition. He placed a new cap on there at the Bronco in another attempt to clear his rifle. When he pulled the trigger, the charge went off and the rifle cracked and he had the funniest look on his face. He was one cap away from taking the gigantic deer. As a side note during rifle season Lewis had a chance at that big boy. Again, it was raining and he was up a short tree in a climbing stand with the trail in front of him forking about 5 yards in front of the stand and going to each side of his stand. The gigantic buck was coming straight toward him. His scope, without his knowledge, had fogged up. He lifted the rifle to take the easy shot and could not see through the scope. In an attempt to get the scope cleaned off the deer moved too fast toward him. He planned for the deer to either go on the trail to the left or right of his stand but instead the deer walked right straight forward under his stand and when he looked through the scope all he could see was hair because he had left it on the high-power. Needless to say, he missed him. All three of us had seen that buck that year and he was still walking in the woods.

As the rifle season in the county ended, I received a report that a friend of mine, who owned property adjoining the wildlife management area and pretty close to where we were hunting, had killed a super large buck. I went to the taxidermy where he had taken the buck to take a look at him. He was a 12-point typical with his G2 point forking on both sides making him a 14 pointer. I believe this was the buck that I saw and it made me sick to know that I couldn't take him although I was happy for my friend.

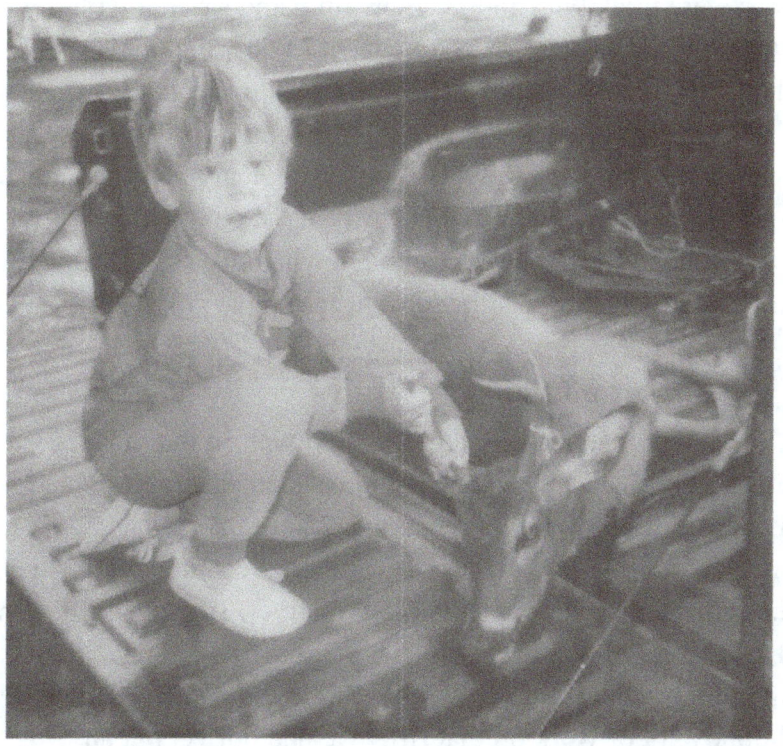

My son, Billy, and Deer

I had seen an albino eight point (not a piebald but a pure albino) at a place we called the triple break one year before hunting season on Bullard Creek WMA. Needless to say, I spent all three hunts in that bay where I had seen him. I never spotted him with a weapon in my hand but not because I didn't sit on him.

The first big one that I lost on our property snuck up behind me and when I turned around in my ladder stand to try to get a shot, I almost got overbalanced and fell out. The buck was at least an 8 and possibly was a 10 point was going away from me. The bushes were thick but I found an opening and sat in it with my rifle waiting for him to appear. In retrospect I know that was not a good high percentage shot I took on him and when I went over there to look. I was sure I had absolutely missed him. I was hunting from a rough cypress ladder stand that my cousin Henry and I had made. It was 16 feet tall and sturdy but I was just facing in the wrong direction that day. That was opening day and I was in the big buck contest and I am sure that that deer would have placed.

The second big one that I missed was on our place. I was hunting from that same stand. My father had passed away and I had decided to try to kill one with his 7.7 mm Arisaka that we had sporterized. He had two types of Norma bullets in the box where he kept his ammunition. He had four or five 130 grain bullets and had 2 ½ boxes of 180 grain bullets. I assumed that he would have been hunting with the 180's, so I took them with me. Although we had done a lot of work on that rifle, we had not yet put an adjustable trigger in it with a good safety, so we were relegated to the full military trigger and safety. It is difficult to noiselessly to take the safety off that rifle, so you have to be very careful with it. I had made up my mind to stay in the stand until 9 o'clock that morning. That would've resulted in me staying there for over three hours after daylight. About 15 minutes before 9:00 o'clock my behind had just about gone to sleep sitting on that plywood seat. Placing the rifle on safety and slinging it over my shoulder, I began to come down the 16 feet of steps. About halfway down the ladder, a fine eight point came out. There I was like a cat squirrel on the side of the tree with the trophy out there just waiting for me to take him at about 60 yards. I hung on as best I could to the ladder rungs and quietly took the safety off the rifle. Clinging to the ladder with all of my might, I drew a bead on the only target I had, which was the neck. I squeezed that old hard military trigger and the rifle cracked. The deer looked in my direction and before I could chamber another round bounded off into some dense brush to his right. I investigated and found no sign that I had hit the deer and trailed the direction the deer went, for a good way, just in case. This was another opening day. This was another big buck contest placing deer, that I had lost. When I got back, I decided I might better check the sighting of the rifle which I had not done before going hunting. The rifle was sighted in for the 130 grain bullets because it shot very high at the yardage with the 180 grain bullet. I made two mistakes that day. The first mistake was not checking to see how the gun was sighted (I have never made that mistake again). The second mistake was not staying in the stand until 9 o'clock. Had I stayed until nine I would've had a perfect shot with a rest, at the body in the lung heart area. That target is an eight-inch circle and although it would have shot high, it would still have hit the vital area and I would've taken the deer.

On another opening day, I was hunting pretty close to the river, in a place that I call my "smokehouse". Through the years I have taken more than 20 deer in that spot, and other family members have taken some there to. The spot is not good until after Thanksgiving, when all of the hardwood leaves have fallen. Sometimes it's a good place to hunt early in the season, if you are careful about shooting lanes. Now we trim shooting lanes there to see the quarry. I was about 30 feet up a longleaf pine with a good vantage point to watch the main trails, where I had taken deer before. I could also see both the two path farm roads in my front to my left. I spotted movement to my right in the dense bottom that drained to the river by the big bluff. The buck moved in my direction and toward the two-path road. I was hunting from the two-piece climber that I had made and it faced the tree giving the hunter a perfect rest for a precise shot. The deer moved but stayed behind a leafy, brushy bush. I quickly noticed that he was wet and had most likely just swum the river. The field test for a trophy is if the antlers are wider than the ears when he faces you and when he profiles if the tips reach beyond his nose. This buck qualified in both categories. I held my rifle on the point just beyond the bush so that when he stepped into the clear I would be instantly on target and take him. You could tell by his attitude that he sensed something he didn't like. He stood there for over five minutes and never took that one more step that would've placed him in my zone. I was getting nervous, as he refused to move forward. I was not going to take another bad shot and chance my bullet striking a limb and deflecting. After about five minutes he retraced his steps and disappeared into the thick bushes of the hardwood drain. He never offered me a shot. The rest of this story is that I stayed in that stand until almost noon. I climbed down and scurried to my Bronco taking care of all those things that I needed to and grabbing my sandwich quickly making my way back to the stand and climbing back up the tree. I stayed in that tree except for that one short period of time, which was maybe 10 minutes at the most, the whole day until it was black dark when I came down. I hoped to get an opportunity at what was the largest buck I have ever seen in all my years of deer hunting.

The only one with a bigger body that I've ever seen come out of this county, field dressed 212 pounds and took five of us to hang him up on the nails to skin him. We estimated him at 268 pounds on the hoof but his antlers were nowhere near the size of this river monster that I had seen. His antlers were bigger than the 14 point the friend of mine got near Bullard Creek around that time. Another big one got away.

On another trip I was hunting pretty near to that "smokehouse" tree, Henry was hunting on one side of the drain and I was hunting on the other. This rather nice buck came between us. Due to the dense vegetation, I only saw his antlers for a while and then his legs for a little while. Henry also saw the buck as he passed him but was unable to get off a shot.

Henry had a ladder stand on a tree that we called the Henry Tower. We placed a 16-foot cypress ladder stand there, and it was up on the top of the hill which overlooked the bottom. He took several deer from that stand and once I had climbed it with my two-piece climber after the ladder had finally succumbed to the weather. I was facing the bottom when a large yellow antlered eight point came quickly from my left. Instead of turning left and going down to the bottom in my front, he took the right and went behind my stand. You do not have to hunt in the two-piece climber very much to know that the shot directly behind you is the most difficult to take. I tried to turn around in the stand almost falling 30 feet to the ground, as the buck quickly moved to my rear. I did not like the shot I had at the deer going directly away from me but I thought that I might be able to make it and take that trophy. He didn't and I didn't.

I am about to subscribe to the theory that once you climb the tree with a climbing stand and you think you know the direction you want to hunt. Then, turn the stand around 180° because they are going to come from behind you invariably. I lost another large 8 to 10 point buck in that same circumstance in the bottom on the stand that we call the little saddle. He came out behind me and there again I was in the situation of trying to turn around and shoot 180° from where my stand was set up. I have come to the conclusion that I need a stand like a bought for Billy. He has a tripod with a swivel seat and they can't slip up behind him.

I was hunting one opening day in my "black gum stand", which was where I had nailed boards for ladder rungs on the side of a big black gum tree. I built a small platform in the fork of the tree, with a perfect limb on which to sit directly above the platform. Off to my left I could see a pretty good distance, although some brushy shrubs obscured part of my vision. It had not long cracked day when, I saw a large pair of white antlers coming through the woods. All that I could see was the antlers. I could not see the deer but I brought my little .308 carbine up swinging the scope to full seven power magnification. When the deer emerged from the thick brush, he was looking straight toward me. I placed the crosshair on the knot of his chest, where his breastbone was and touched off the trigger. Instead of falling like three more bucks that I had shot in that same place, he just turned his head and looked. It rattled me, so I tried to slip the empty cartridge case out and another cartridge in the chamber, slowly and quietly, which was a mistake. Had I shucked it as fast as I could, I could've gotten the second shot. Before I could chamber the second round, he bolted off to his left and was quickly in some dense brush. My mind was completely blown for I knew without a doubt that I had held the sight picture right and I squeezed the trigger and also that deer should have hit the ground like a sack of potatoes. He didn't. He had run off to the swamp. I had taken a nice 6 point from that stand that was almost in the very place as that deer and dropped him in his tracks. I was baffled.

When I came out of the tree and went to the truck, I test sighted the rifle. It was dead on at 100 yards. I shot through the mouth of a plastic Coke bottle that I had jammed in the fork of the little tree and the bullet went out the casting sprue in the rear of the bottle. There was nothing wrong with my sights. The scope was dead on in 100 yards. I had shot at 60 yards. There is no way I could've missed. I went back that afternoon climbed back up in the black gum and had not even settled down when I saw a deer moving in my rear. I turned around and saw that the antlers were fairly high above the head and dropped the rifle down, squeezed the trigger. The deer collapsed. I went over to where the deer lay, I had hit perfectly where I had aimed. The only problem was that this was a cow-horned spike. The tines were over 12 inches tall. I had not taken enough time to look because I saw they were way above his head. As a side note, the next Saturday I was in the stand and like most hunters, was still fretting about missing that big deer, which would've also placed in the big buck contest. I sat there reliving the instance from the Saturday before and with my scope on 2 ½ power, I lifted the rifle, reliving my shot at the deer. I discovered that one of the black gum limbs, which were about the size of my finger and was about eight or 9 feet in front of my muzzle had a semicircular cut off right where my crosshair was looking. I had hit that limb, which had been focused out by the high-powered the scope and there's no telling where my bullet went, it just didn't go where I wanted it to.

I finally placed one opening day in the Big Buck Contest. I was sitting in the black gum stand and heard something behind me and to my right. It was splashing through the water that I knew was in the firebreak. I turned and positioned myself for the shot. When the buck stepped out my little .308 dropped him in his tracks. I gathered my equipment from the stand and climbed down to retrieve my prize. I grabbed him by his antlers and started to drag him up the hill. The hill was fairly steep and about every 30 or 40 feet, I would have to stop and hassle like an old hound dog, trying to catch my breath. My lungs would burn and I was just dumbfounded as to how I could've gotten in such bad shape over the summer. When I finally got him up to the two-path road I threw him under some bushes and said, "you wait here buddy while I get some help" and I went searching for Henry.

I got back to the truck and he came scrambling out of the brush from the tower. "I heard the shot; did you get anything?" He inquired.

"Yeah, I got a pretty nice six-point but I'm bad out of shape, I had to leave him by the road up there and you're gonna have to help me load him." We pulled the truck up to where the deer lay under the bushes, waiting for me as I had instructed it and when we tried to lift it the doggone thing was a struggle to get in the back of the truck.

When we arrived at the Big Buck Contest check-in site, we were behind a pickup truck with a humongous buck in the back. That buck later won the Big Buck Contest and scored close to 150 inches, Boone and Crockett. We had learned that the buck had been eating horse feed all summer long, and he was large. My buck looked small beside him.

90

As the official was taking the photographs and checking my deer in and inspecting the tag, a friend who was the local taxidermist came up to me and said, "Bill, are you gonna mount that thing."

"Ronald, I have one 6 point on the wall and I do not need another" I replied.

"If you'll cape him out and give it to me, I might use the cape and in turn I will mount the antlers on a buckhorn kit for you." He replied.

That got me to thinking why he would want the cape of a little deer. So, before I cleaned the deer, I weighed him and found that he was over 185 pounds which had made his antlers look a little smaller. I then caped it out and dressed the deer and put up the meat. I came back that night to the measure of the antlers, for the contest. I placed with that six-point buck since he was big enough to beat several smallish eight-point bucks. I gave Ronald the cape and the antlers and he was true to his word, he presented me with the antlers mounted on a Buckhorn kit.

My wife Deloris tried very hard to enjoy the things that I did. When she planned to hunt deer with me, I acquired a Winchester 30-30 for her to use from my cousin Billy. The only problem was that Billy had been injured in an accident at work and could not squeeze the lever safety on the Winchester, so he had it removed. He told me that he had it put up and would get it for me to put back into the rifle. To this day I have not seen the part, so I had a gunsmith friend to get another one and install it, so that she would be as safe as possible in the woods.

On the first day, she hunted I dressed her in blaze orange a-plenty to protect her and had instructed her on shooting her rifle, identifying the deer and knowing where to shoot. When I put her in the "Number One" ladder stand that morning, I told her that it was doe days so if it had hair, shoot first and ask questions later. I also told her that if she shot, I would wait fifteen minutes and come to her. I instructed her to stay in the stand until I came and got her out. I went on to my stand which was about 300 yards away on the other side of the branch. About thirty minutes after sunrise, I heard the little Winchester bark once. I looked at my watch and waited the agreed-upon fifteen minutes and headed for her stand.

I was careful and anxious as I rounded the head of the branch. I looked in the stand and she was not there. Suddenly to my right I spotted a pumpkin looking thing moving around in the brush. As I approached her, I scolded her for not staying put where I had instructed her to stay. I asked her what she had shot and she replied that two does had come out near her stand and she had shot one of the does. The other had run off and then had come right back to where she had shot the first one. I asked why she did not shoot the second deer and she told me that she thought that one was all she could shoot. She then showed me where the deer was when she shot it and told me that the deer had gone in the direction that she was looking. We went to where she stopped looking, and she said that that was the last place she saw the deer. There was a split in the trails there. I looked down the one to the right and saw nothing nearby so I stepped through the gall berry bush on the left trail and right behind the bush was the deer.

"Here it is, and it is a buck!" I told her.

"What!" She almost tore the whole bush down coming to me and was so excited to see the smallest six point rack that I have ever seen. His ears were longer than his antlers and the antlers

92

were dark brown. "I thought it was a doe," she said, "I can't believe that I could have taken the other deer too!"

I had the antlers placed on a Buck Horn Kit and every time I look on the wall at it, I have fond memories of her first deer hunt. She still claimed that stand until we cut the timber including that tree and hunted there every year.

The next year she was in that stand and a short-legged eight-point came out close to her but, she said that her heart was pumping so hard that she could not hold the rifle steady, while he was close. After he moved away and was at least a hundred yards away she calmed down enough to take a shot. My cousin Henry and I looked for two hours for that deer finding only a drop of blood every twenty yards or so, until it played out and we could trail the deer no longer. My boss had seen that same deer while hunting there earlier in the season and could not get a shot at him, but he also described him as a short-legged eight-point.

We replaced the cypress ladder when it deteriorated with a steel tubing ladder. She used that ladder stand for a few years until we had the timber cut. We cut the tree the ladder stand was on. We were not sure how she was going hunt in the "Honey Hole." That problem was solved the next opening day when she won a Wal-Mart gift card at the Big Buck Contest and used it to procure a tripod. That stand was the best, most productive stand on our property. Ten of us have taken over 40 deer from it through the years and the game camera there has taken more photos of big bucks than anywhere else on the property.

Before she acquired the tripod, Deloris was hunting in the "Henry Tower" and I was hunting in my black gum stand. On one occasion, when I decided to come out. I was to pass directly behind the tower, so I stealthily made my way into the rear of the tower. As I approached the stand, she made motions to me to get down and to be quiet. Keeping low, I quietly eased up behind the tree the stand was against and kneeled there. There were five or six does down in the bottom playing around. Deloris later told me that she had been watching them for a good long time hoping that a buck would come out since it was not a doe day. She has a knack for seeing deer and attracts them much better than I do. I sometimes call her a deer magnet because that ability to attract deer.

On another occasion, Deloris had sent Billy home with his grandparents so she could hunt and informed me that she would walk out to the highway about 9: 30 and go to her mother's house to see Billy and help with Thanksgiving dinner. She was hunting in the "Double -Tree" stand which I had built in two maple trees that were side by side. Our woods had been clear-cut and I could see her from my perch 40 feet up a pine tree in my climber. I watched her as she walked and the five does, that I had been watching at about a hundred yards from my tree. As she neared the does on the two-path road that ran through our property, the does instead of bolting froze about twenty feet from the road. She walked right past them and never saw them. After she was out of sight the does began feeding again as if nothing had happened.

She never liked going to the stand before daylight by herself nor did she relish leaving the stand after dark and coming out of the woods. Once she swore that something was following her. When she stepped so did it and when she stopped it did also. I reminded her that she was carrying a loaded gun so she should

94

not be afraid. She never bought that at all.   Now she rides her four-wheeler to the base of her stand and will step off the four-wheeler onto the ladder and did the reverse coming down. I guess she figured she could outrun anything in the woods on her Arctic Cat. Now Billy takes her in our Kubota side by side to the stand and picks her up.

We placed a trail camera near her stand and poured some corn out in front of the camera. The corn was visited by two eight pointers and two boar hogs. She asked what she was to do if the hogs came while she was in the stand and I told her that we needed some sausage and she was to shoot. A few years ago, we had four 8 pointers by her stand the night before opening day. We discovered this after we had come out of the stands and she hadn't seen anything. The next time she hunted her luck had changed. She was shooting a brand-new Remington 700 youth in 7mm-08 that I had purchased for her and had it sighted in perfectly. An eight point that we later identified as one of them on the trail camera came out on her a mere 25 yards away. She related that she raised the rifle, had the deer in her crosshairs but could not pull the trigger. I guess she had buck fever like she'd had on that eight-point years ago. She then said that two other bucks came out on her, but they were smaller so she didn't even want to shoot them, since she could not shoot the big boy.

After that, I bought a .243 Remington youth rifle to replace her 7mm-08 because I had decided that fear of being kicked may have contributed to her not pulling the trigger. I tested that .243 the year before and "smoked" a doe at 80 yards with it out of my "Condo."

Later in the season, my son, Billy decided to hunt in her stand one day. I heard his .270 bark and a moment later I heard it bark a second time. The cell phone reception is so good out there now because there's a tower close our property, so I sent him a text. "Was that you?"

I knew that the sound did not come from his stand which was 300 yards further beyond his mother 's stand so I was confused. Again, I texted, "Did you get one?" To which he answered. "No. I got two. I got the eight point and then I got the doe he was following." The eight point he got was similar to one of them that was on the camera but not the one his mother had let walk.

I took her 7mm-08 and smoked a little buck at 140 yards with it recently. There's nothing wrong with that rifle and I look forward to hunting with it some more. That same week I used my Uncle Zack's .35 Remington, which is a model 141 Remington pump to take a six point that apparently had been in an automobile accident. His left rump had a large patch of hair missing and the skin had a cut in it. His antlers were all broken up and I told Billy that he probably was still addled from his automobile accident which aided in my being able to take him so easily.

My son has been hunting his whole life in some fashion. I started taking him to the deer woods when he was three. He would go with this little pair of binoculars and his canteen. He would be dressed in his camo and have a little bag filled with candy. The first time he hunted with me we sat on the little rock cliff in the middle of our property, after it had been clear-cut. You could see for a good long distance. As we sat up there, he would look through the binoculars a little while. Then he would take a swig of water. Then he would dig around in his pack for some hard candy to eat. He always loved to go in the out of doors and I always enjoyed taking him along.

He started shooting at three when I purchased a little short-stocked Daisy BB gun with a safety. I would get a box that a washing machine or dryer came in from the appliance store and take it out into the backyard to set up his range. I would thumbtack the target on to the side of the box and we would sit there while he shot BBs at the target. The great thing was that the BBs wouldn't penetrate but one side of the box so you could recycle them by getting them out of the box and shoot them again. I used that little BB rifle to put him through safety training. We later switched to a little Ducks Unlimited pellet gun that I had won. I had some small steel silhouette targets and we would set them up on the board in front of the big cardboard box and he would shoot at them practicing silhouette shooting. I used those two air rifles to put him through safety training and to install gun safety in his mind, at a very young age.

He later graduated to a Chipmunk .22 rifle and further honed his skills. Although his hunting indoctrination was squirrel hunting and dove hunting, I would carry him deer hunting at least once every year.

When he was four, we were in the "black gum stand" where he sat on the platform between my feet and I sat on the limb. I well remember that he was there with his binoculars, canteen and candy and I spotted two does that were making their way toward the stand. Billy had not noticed them as they were approaching. He began to dig around in his bag to get another piece of candy and the noise spooked the two does which were within 20 yards of the stand. They blew and with their white tails raised, they scampered off.

Hearing the noise Billy looked up and saw the deer running and said, "Shoot them, daddy! Shoot them, daddy!"

But it was way too late. We hunted in that stand when he was five and saw deer on that occasion also. After we got out of the tree on that occasion, we went to get my daddy's climbing stand off the tree where Henry had left it thinking he was going back that afternoon to hunt. I was not wild about leaving stands in the woods. That's why I had backpack straps on every one that I made. As we approached the location on the "Hickory Point", out jumped a spike buck. I pushed Billy to the side and tried to get a rifle sight on him. Just as I shot, he ran behind a little tree and tree bark flew everywhere. When we got back to town to the feed store, he had to tell everyone there about me missing that little buck. I had to have another good talk with him about telling everything he knew, when it would embarrass daddy.

———————————————

By the time he was six, he was equipped with a .410 single shot shotgun loaded with slugs. We had relocated to a stand I named "the DoubleTree" stand. I had nailed boards for ladder rungs and had fixed a platform with a seat above it. He was sitting again between my feet as I watched a doe approach us. She was on the trail that would've carried her within 10 yards of the base of the tree where our stand was. Billy had been looking off to the left, which was a much clearer area and I reached down and tapped him on the right shoulder and pointed in the direction of the deer. The deer was in the gall berries and you couldn't see a whole deer, just the head and an ear and a nose or a tail. When he looked to the right, he didn't see anything so he turned back to the left. I reached down and tapped him again, pointing my rifle in the direction of the deer. He obviously still didn't see anything and let out a fairly loud, "WHAT". At which the doe turned tail and bounded across the ridge. He turned around and looked up at me and said, "I guess I messed up, didn't I daddy?" I took the time to explain to him that sometimes you wouldn't see a whole deer you have to look for movement, maybe an ear, maybe just a big round eye or just some slight movement in the brush because they were camouflaged really well.

We finally got to the point where he had switched to a 20-gauge Remington 870 youth pump and would climb, with the two-piece climber, a tree 20 or 30 feet away from me and hunt. Later we got farther and farther apart, with me always keeping him in sight. On one such occasion, I spotted a large eight-point buck to my left. Lifting my dear call, I grunted twice and begin to clash my rattling antlers together. I saw the buck as he moved towards us. Looking at Billy expecting him to shoot the deer at any time. The deer was within plenty close range to take a shot but Billy did not fire. Eventually, the deer moved on away from us. When we came down, I asked him why he had not shot the deer. He told me that all he could see was the head and neck because the rest of the body was obscured behind the brush. He reminded me that I had taught him to shoot in the lung heart area, which was the high percentage shot and he didn't have a shot at it. I guess I had over trained him.

Finally, I traded for a Marlin Model 336 in 30-30 Winchester and mounted a scope atop it. I loaded some 125-grain jacketed hollow point 30-30's, like those that I loaded for Henry, Cousin Billy, and his mother. I had placed him on a ladder stand atop the "White Oak Acorn ridge" where there was plenty of deer activity, and I positioned myself about 200 yards away in my quadpod stand. He shot his first deer at about 45 yards, and after a little trailing we found the deer. He had hit a little forward of where he wanted to but it still made a deadly shot.

I actually had traded earlier to get him a model 600 Remington in .222 but he never had taken a deer with it, before switching off to the 30-30. When we were trying to sight it in at a friend, Roy's house. We were on the bench at 100 yards and I allowed Billy to fire the first shots. When Roy and I went down to look, we saw that the three shots were high and to the left, so we adjusted the scope accordingly we had Billy to shoot again and this time they shot low and to the right, much further than we had adjusted for. We clicked back upward and left and he shot again. He shot high and to the left. We were mystified because we knew that was a good scope and we knew we were adjusting correctly. Billy told us that he didn't know why it had not hit the middle because when he saw where they hit, he adjusted his aim to correct for it. The boy was using "Kentucky Windage" and was canceling out our corrections. Once I explained to him to keep aiming at the same place, he zeroed it in nicely and you could place a dime over three shots at 100 yards with him shooting.

I later traded the Remington 600 .223 for him a Winchester Model 70 Featherweight in .270 Winchester caliber. At first, he didn't like it because it kicked a little bit too much and as a 14-year-old he had not experienced any recoil with his rifles. I had loaded his .270 cartridges hot enough so that they would shoot relatively flat and they kicked a little. So, the first season he would not shoot the .270. He took my .22-250, which was another Winchester Model 70 and hunted on the "Quad-Pod" stand. I took his .270 and went around to the "Property Line" stand and killed a nice buck at 240 yards with it that morning. That afternoon he was back in the quadpod. I hadn't been up the ladder stand but just a few minutes when I heard the .22-250 crack. A moment later it cracked again. Another moment later a third shot. I thought I might better go check and see what he was up to. I climbed down the ladder and started to traverse the 600 or 700 yards I was going to get to the truck, when I heard "Old Blackie", my four-wheel-drive F 150, crank up. I walked past where the truck was parked and headed toward the "Quad-Pod". I heard the engine revving and I heard the truck as it came back up out of the food plot. I'd been teaching Billy how to drive out there in the woods and had left the key in the pickup. He had gone to get it to retrieve a deer and already had him in the back of the truck, when I finally made it to the "Quad Pod". I inquired as to what had been going on and he said that seven deer had come out into the food plot. He had shot the biggest one. He said the deer then scattered and he saw one trying to slip across the two path road toward the "Henry Tower". He shot that one, which disappeared, but didn't know if he had hit it or not. A third deer had crossed the little road that led to his mother's stand, so he tried to shoot it also. We walked down toward the "Henry Tower' and there the second deer was just a few yards off the road. We went back dragging that deer to the pickup threw her in the back and went to see about the third deer. I found where just off the road to his mother's stand a chunk of bark was blown off a pine tree, about mid deer high off the ground. Obviously, while he was swinging on that deer and touched his trigger off, that tree jumped out in the way and saved the third deer. He had done something that I had never done before which was take two deer together out of one stand. In the days and years to follow he's done it numerous times. I don't know if it is patience, luck, skill or what but I no longer consider it a fluke when he does it. I finally accomplished that feat.

On another trip, he was again in the "Quad Pod", watching a doe and two yearlings on the food plot, when he spotted a coyote approaching from his right. He sensed that the varmint was stalking the deer, since he was heading in that direction. Lifting the .270 in position he placed the crosshairs on the coyote, dispatched him before he could mess with any of his quarry, the deer who were out in front.

Billy moves through the woods without making much noise and taking his time. This has resulted in him taking many deer using that method, including his biggest, a 200-pound 10 pointer he took with that .270. Although he will shoot a Ruger Number One in .257 Roberts, a Ruger RS I in .30-06. He will also take a deer with his granddaddy's old sporterized 7.7 mm Arisaka (now with an adjustable trigger) but most of the time you will find that .270 in his hands when he is hunting deer.

Billy's wife also loves to hunt and is an excellent shot to boot. I remember when she took her first deer with a Remington Model Seven in 6 mm Remington that I bought her for Christmas. She and Billy were sitting in the "Black Box" stand and I was down in my "Bills Condo" hunting. I heard a shot and was preparing to wait to see if I was to be called upon to help. Then I heard the second shot that sounded different but coming from the same direction. It confused me for a moment because even though a layperson may not notice it, I know the sounds of every rifle my family hunts with and my ears are still good enough to pinpoint the direction from which the shot came. Both of those shot sounded as though they came from the same place but they had a different sound to them. The first seemed to be a sharper crack than the second. Finally, I could stand it no longer I came down out of the "Condo", straddled my trusty old Polaris four-wheeler and headed back toward the "Black Box." As I neared the last turn before coming to the stand, there was Billy and Toni. I pulled up and got off the machine just about the time Billy found her deer. We placed her deer in the basket on the back of my four-wheeler. Billy told me to pull out on the food plot where we could pick his deer up. Upon arriving at that deer, I found that he had taken a fine 7 point. He then explained to me that after she had shot her deer and was anxious to go look for it, he exhorted her to wait just a few minutes and give her deer a chance to expire, since it didn't drop in its tracks. He had an ulterior motive. In short time the buck that was following her doe stepped out and he shot it with the .257 Roberts, dropping it in its tracks. I said he was a good deer hunter, didn't I?

I took a fall, when the "Quad Pod's" anchors pulled loose and could not walk for several days. Eventually, I believe, that fall turned into an injury that resulted in me having to have my right hip replaced. I don't walk as much anymore. During that same time, I tore loose the ligaments in my shoulder and had to have surgical repairs made to it and to my right hand. Then when I recovered after my hip was replaced, the doctor would not allow me to climb even my ladder stands so I designed "Bills Condo." I engineered, measured and sawed the boards and my wife and mother-in-law put the components together. We painted them and then with the help of Cousin Billy, my son Billy, my cousins Cherry, Angela and Ricky and my wife and mother-in-law we went to the woods, with me mostly supervising, and erected the condo. This was a 6 x 6 shooting hut atop an 8 foot high platform. That way I was able to avoid missing even one of my deer seasons after the surgeries. I am like Deloris and drive my Polaris to the beginning of the stairs leading into the condo, shut it off and climb up in there. Then opening the windows, I can hunt. I have taken several deer from there including an eight-point buck with the largest rack I have ever taken. I shot him with my .257 Roberts which is a Ruger Model 77. I shot him on opening day and he measured around 100 inches Boone and Crockett. The problem is that I shot him late in the afternoon and although I made as good a hit as you could make on him, he ran so far that we did not find him that afternoon after he quit leaving a blood trail. The next day we went out there and I took the four-wheeler and I rode the firebreak he was headed toward and found him lying about 20 yards from where we had last found blood. He had crashed through the middle of the thickest bunch of gall berry bushes you've ever seen. He did not take the trail to the right or the trail to the left. He went straight ahead through the bushes. He would've placed in the big buck contest in one of the last two places, but in the money.

I acquired a Savage 6.5 Creedmore with a special scope that had incremental marks to 600 yards. I took a deer at over 155 yards with it and dropped it in its tracks. My most recent deer rifle is a Savage Weather Warrior in .308 Winchester my son gave me as a Christmas present. It shoots less than 1-inch groups with factory ammunition. Although when we change the stock to a youth stock, in order to fit me, there was one more thing that you had to do to the new model Savage 110's that we didn't do. That error cost me a very large buck because it snapped twice with me at 80 yards. To date, I have taken deer with 25 different rifles in various calibers and have settled on the Creedmore and the Weather Warrior as my choices now. My longest shot is a little over 200 yards from my condo. They will serve me well at that range. At age 69, I took four deer including the eight points. At age 70 and 71 was fortunate enough to take four deer each year. At 72 I took one at over two hundred and 60 yards and dropped it in his tracks. I chased a 10 point that was on my camera all season but never got an opportunity to take him. I passed up several of those waiting for him to show up.

Uruguay Dove Shoot in Sunflower Field

CHAPTER SIX

DOVE HUNTING

I come from a long line of outdoorsmen that have learned to both enjoy nature and to reap the bounty that the Lord has provided for us to use. I cannot remember the first time that I went fishing, for as far back as I can recollect, I have been fishing beginning with saltwater fishing with my father for croakers, yellowtail, drum and whiting from a little boat in the Intercoastal Waterway in east-central Florida.

I remember squirrel hunting with him at a very young age.

I vividly remember my first dove hunt, so vividly, that even now when I drive by that farm and see the old barn, I still get a warm feeling inside and can feel the cool, crisp autumn air. I can still remember the smell of the burning gun powder from the little single-shot .410 that my father had borrowed for me to use. I didn't kill a single dove, but I was hooked for life. Dove hunting has been one of my favorite activities since some 75 years.

I can remember many a dove hunt where I would shoot two boxes of shells and only have three or four doves for the fifty shots that I had taken. Two factors contribute greatly to such a low success ratio. One was that I was not shooting a gun that fit me. The second was that I could not shoot very well. Fortunately for me, I was able to remedy both problems on a skeet field. This is a good piece of advice to anyone that has these problems. Seek professional help!

I can remember a couple of funny happenings that stand out in my years of dove hunting. Early after graduating from a .410 single shot, I shot my Uncle's Remington Model 11 autoloader in 16 gauge. Bear in mind that this is a Browning A-5 that Remington produced before the Belgium-made Browning's were available on the American market. I then graduated to another Uncle's Model 11. This was a 12-gauge, military surplus, with a parkerized finish with a Cutts Compensator on the barrel. Neither of these guns ever fit me because of the drop that model is famous for not being compatible with my short neck and tendency to lean into the stock. Anyway, the sear on the 12 gauge was worn and would not hold. This caused the shotgun to double fire or triple fire according to how many shells were in the magazine. I borrowed a Remington 1100 with a 28-inch modified barrel from my cousin Ralph and retired the old Model 11 temporarily, until it could be repaired. This friend of mine, Billy, was to join us on a dove hunt but his shotgun was in the shop, and he asked if he could borrow my old gun. I told him of the problem it had, he said that he could shoot a single shot safely. He agreed and we went to the dove field. Now you must understand that the old gun would not multi-fire every time but you never knew when it would.

The place where we were invited to shoot was in a field adjacent to a farm where the owner had planted millet to attract the doves and was having a large shoot comprised of the more affluent hunters in the area. I took up a position between a small water hole and a round bay which proved to be an excellent place because the doves would come from the big shoot and fly between the two. I won't tell how many doves that I killed because I am not sure about the statuette of limitations but suffice to say that I was more successful than I had ever been before. My cousin Billy was on the other side of the round bay shooting the model 11 Remington. I could tell where he was because several times I heard the gun multi-fire. After the hunt was over, Billy returned to meet up with me and knowing the answer, I asked if the Model 11 kicked hard when it multi-fired.

He answered, "Yes, but it sure will kill a bird when it does!!!"

On Monday morning I was at Ace Hardware and selected a new Remington model 1100. I did not have much extra money so I went to the bank and borrowed the $135.00 to purchase it. I had found a gun that did fit me and I liked it. It has brought down many a dove, particularly due to the fact that the standard pull of the new Remingtons fits me well.

107

Another thing that comes to remembrance is my father's approach to dove hunting. Even though this rugged ex-Marine was an expert marksman with a rifle and a pistol, he had never quite mastered the art of shotgunning at the speedy little gray doves. He was not a bad shot but his shotgunning was not on the same plane as his rifle and pistol shooting. To compensate for this, he would always position himself near a large tree or a power line. In order to save shells, he would patiently wait for the doves to attempt to light. When the dove had slowed to a stop and almost landed, Daddy would nail him. He always said that there were other advantages such as not having to look too hard for the dove. We had a close family friend, Billy that subscribed to the same philosophy. The two of them would invariably seek out those places conducive to that kind of hunting.

A good friend, Calvin, invited the three of us to hunt doves with him. When we arrived at the fifty-acre field, Calvin and I headed on into the middle of the field. We beckoned to daddy and Billy to follow but they had already reconnoitered the power line on the west side of the field and the tree line on the north side. They set up near the corner, where the two joined. When the hunt was over, we all had a limit of doves. When we counted our shells, we discovered that the two of them had only shot one more shell than they had doves and that daddy had not missed a shot.

You can't argue with success!!

Once we were hunting in a large field with just a few friends and shooting was fast and furious for a while, but then it cooled so the group, Daddy, Lamar, Bart, Bobby, Calvin and I gathered in a group to discuss the shoot. As we were standing around talking, a dove flew broadside a good distance away. Daddy, who was on that side of the group, lifted his Winchester 101 over under with skeet barrels (Choked for a 21-yard shot optimum) and fired. The bird began to helicopter and circled round and round in a tight spiral to the ground. Calvin ran over and retrieved the bird. He stepped the distance back to us. He stated that the bird had landed 93 yards away. Now I know my father would have liked for us to have believed that it was skill, but we examined the bird declaring that it must have died of a heart attack. Upon close examination, we finally discovered that one pellet had hit the bird in the head. Daddy was proud of his prowess that day.

For years I hunted doves without the benefit of a retrieving dog and had to learn to mark my downed birds well so as not to lose them. The first lesson is to not take your eyes off the downed bird until you have walked to it. This excludes you from looking at other incoming birds and taking other shots because you will lose track of where the original bird fell. A hunter that is serious about retrieving downed birds must adhere to these rules.

It never failed that when a single bird came over and I knocked it down. Even locking my gaze on the location where it fell and starting toward it. That is when large droves of doves take that opportunity to enter the field like unto a Kamikaze attack. It is extremely difficult to not look when it sounds like World War III has just broken out. Invariably you sneak a peek at the incoming birds and lose track of the location of your downed bird. The old saying that "a bird in the hand is better than two in the bush" also translates to better than twenty flying over the field! Altogether too many times, I have lost downed birds by not observing this simple rule.

Some of my friends have dove hunted in South and Central America, saying that one of the most enjoyable aspects of these hunts is the "bird boys". Saying that they are excellent at retrieving your birds while you shoot other birds. This takes the pressure off the shooter since you don't have to mark your birds.

On my South America hunts, we had excellent "bird boys". Some folks say that one of the most enjoyable aspics of those hunts is the "bird boys" that are excellent at retrieving and take that pressure off the shooter. They also would load your second gun, take your equipment to the field, bring shells, beverage and other necessities for you in the field.

I once took my two stepdaughters dove hunting with me. They were both "Cotton Top" blondes and we spent quite a bit of time dressing them in the appropriate attire so that they would not stick out like the proverbial "sore thumb" in the cornfield. They were only six and seven years old but they actually did a pretty good job of "fetching" the downed doves. As long as I dish-ragged the birds so that they wouldn't move the girls would run over and scoop them up for me, but if one was only winged and was flopping, they would stand and point at it until I could come and pick it up. My little "Golden-Haired Retrievers" did a jam up job of pointing and retrieving that day even though they were also "Golden Haired Pointers".

Doves are interesting 'critters" to hunt. They are almost as "funny" as the "Critters" that hunt them. Although there are many dedicated dove hunters in our area, there are equally as many "funny critters" that participate in dove hunting. I have seen quite a few of them in my many years of hunting. I have seen many odd and interesting occurrences while hunting them.

I have seen a single dove fly by almost every hunter in a large dove field and attract as high as one hundred shots and escape, apparently unscathed, only to turn around and make yet one more pass through the field. I once read that, all things considered, the average cost of dove meat, based on the number of shots fired at them, is around twelve dollars per pound. I am sure that this dove's cost would be much higher.

Quite a few dove hunters will shoot at any dove that was in sight, regardless of the range. I have also seen them shoot at anything that flies across the field. They must have had great difficulty in identifying the feathered game. My cousin Henry and I once had to hit the ground and take cover when a whitetail doe "flew" between us and some other hunters that couldn't tell fur from feathers.

I remember once a long time ago, when I was very young, hunting in a cornfield with several adults from my town. My father placed me safely on the far end of the field. This limited my chances of getting a shot at the doves and limited my exposure to the other hunters. I remember a low flying dove coming into the field. One of the men cried out to the hunter down the line from him.

"Too low! Don't shoot! Turtle dove anyway!"

The next hunter, who was a local doctor retorted. "D---! He'll eat!" and fired twice at the bird.

Every hunter in the direction of the bird hit the ground. I could hear the pellets striking the corn stalks around me. That "critter" should have stuck to medicine!

I cannot describe just how bad a wing shot I was to start with. With a grandfather who was renowned as the best wing shot in the county and possibly South Georgia, I was not holding up the family tradition. My friend, Bobby, introduced me to skeet shooting and I liked to go to the range with him. The first time I ever shot was in Claxton at Kicklighter's Skeet Range. I was shooting a Savage Fox BSE double-barrel, choked improved cylinder and modified. I broke six out of 25 which was pitiful. I could have easily quit right then and there, but I stuck with it and became quite good after a while. The most that I broke without missing was 235 straight with my twenty gauge in competition. Skeet shooting improved my wing shooting, exponentially. Trap, Skrap (combination of Skeet and Trap), Five Stand and Sporting Clays can sharpen your skills at wing shooting.

I have made three trips to Uruguay, in South America to hunt Golden-eared Doves. I went with some longtime friends including Bobby, the one who taught me to love skeet shooting. He later became World Skeet Champion in 1973. He broke 762 straight birds in that win and ended up with a 935 run before he missed. Also along was another bird hunter, Mr. Dave, that I had been around and known for years. He was the very best birdshot that I have ever seen in action. At home when I saw those two in a dove field, I would make my way to the other side of the field, to avoid them killing everything that might have come to me. We went with several other friends, which is the key to a successful and enjoyable hunt.

I purchased two Beretta 390 20-gauge shotguns for my first trip (I had been told that my Remington Model 1100's would not hold up to the strain of 1000 shots or more a day) and that I did not want to shoot a 12 gauge. It took some adjustment and altercations to the stocks, but they finally fit well and I could shoot them very well.

As we went through the TSA inspections at the Jacksonville Airport, we must have looked strange. Although some of our group were old veterans at this international hunting, some of us were novices and knew absolutely nothing about what was in store for us. We were wide-eyed and in awe of everything around us. We flew to Miami and had a five-hour layover there. Near midnight we embarked on the 777 headed for Buenos Aires, Argentina. Nine and a half hours later we arrived and I had not slept a wink. About daybreak, I looked out the window to my left and at 33, 000 feet saw this gigantic river snaking to the East as far as the eye could see. "My God!' I exclaimed. "That's the Amazon."

We spent about two hours in Buenos Aires and caught a flight to Montevideo, Uruguay. I thought that we would never get through customs, and if the guide had not been there, we might not have. We were loaded into a small bus and spent the next two hours driving back South towards Argentina. We arrived at the field where our bird boys and a wagon of shotgun shells were waiting. We got out of the bus, changed clothes and grabbed out shotgun. Then we were led to our assigned shooting stations. I remember hearing my grandfather Tuten telling of when the birds would "black the sky" but had never seen doves in the quantities that I saw there. My plan was to shoot a flat (10 boxes of shells) each morning and each afternoon, so as not to spend too much on the $10.00 a box shells. Birds were everywhere. I shot every shot and angle conceivable and killed many birds. There was a small river at my back, and I would hear the birds splash down, as I shot them. Being a South Georgia Bird Hunter, I did not want to waste any birds so I modified my shooting to avoid them hitting in the water. You must understand that the doves have very few natural predators in South America and are considered a pest by the farmers. They do as much as 50 percent crop damage to a sunflower field. They sometimes poison them and kill 25 to 30 thousand birds there in the field. When some young women in the Montevideo airport asked what our business was there, we answered to dove hunt. They then referred to the doves as being like rats to the Uruguayans.

After the first morning, my friend and longtime shooting and hunting buddy, Jeff sidled up to me. I could tell that he had something important to tell me. He said that he had been placed by Mr. Dave, that morning. He said, "I am not going to hunt by that old man anymore because he kills everything that comes by him. He even killed three with one shot! On purpose!" Jeff had learned on that day what I had known for a long time.

We went on to have a great time there and I went back two more times, the last time to take my son, Billy, after he had graduated from college.

Billy hunted beside me all but the first day and I could not shoot for watching him have a great time. I can still remember when he killed his first dove, flying. He was seven years old and killed it with a single shot .410. By the time he had shown it to all the hunters in the field, it had almost ruined. He has always loved dove hunting from the time when I would take him with his youth BB rifle and he would send that single pellet skyward toward the streaking gray feathered object.

114

That first day they let me out about halfway down the hill as we were moving through dropping the hunters off. We had the most pigeons I had ever seen coming in from our left. I was knocking them down pretty good but I noticed that the one that was station just beyond me was wearing them out. My bird boy who normally didn't pick up doves filled two croaker sacks with those great big pigeons. As they picked us up for lunch, I found that Mr. Dave was the one that was let out just past me which explained why so many pigeons were falling over there around him.

Billy told me after shooting beside Mr. Dave that the only way for a dove to get by him for someone else to shoot was if there were more doves than Mr. Dave had shells. He also said that at one time he thought that Mr. Dave was throwing dead doves over the bushes at him. Billy even got to the point that he was trying to drop doves on my head. With the practice available a shooter can become pretty proficient.

On the first trip, I had the best day shooting that I will ever have. I had vowed to only shoot one case in the morning and one in the afternoon (1000 shells total). I was being selective in my shots and only shot one out of every drove. The droves were 30 to 50 birds each and were coming one right after the other. When the day had come to an end the doves (908 of them) were so thick that you could hardly walk in clearing without stepping on one. My coverall clothed cousin, Buster came out of the trees to my right and began to traverse the clearing, stepping gingerly to avoid the doves.

He came over to me and said, "Boy! You really wore their asses out today!"

Our guides were also funny. The lead guide/bird boy, Jorje was extremely funny. I once told him that I could take him back to Georgia and give him a four-wheel drive pickup and he would be a "Redneck' in less than a month. We were on our way to the field one morning and went through this small village that had a statue in the center of it.

I asked, "George, who is that statue of?"

He replied, "National hero."

I asked, "What did he do?"

George replied, "I do not know. He is just National hero."

On one occasion Ray, another of my shooting buddies, and Jeff stood back-to-back in the field, like Butch Cassidy and the Sundance Kid, trying to ensure that doves would not sneak up on their rear.

I have always shot the rear or the fringe birds, so as to not disturb the other birds. That way you would get a shot at multiples in the flight. Bobby taught me how to kill multiples in Uruguay. He said to shoot a bird in the middle of the flat, and ofttimes they will be flying so tight that you will get another bird with the same shot. I put that into practice one afternoon, getting over 20 sets of multiples including three with one shot (like Mr. Dave). I was calling the double before shooting. I would say "dos!" And when I knocked down two birds with that one shot my bird boy would repeat "dos!" When I knocked down three with one shot, I had called "dos" as they approached, but three folded and my bird boy said "no tres!"

The secret to having a great time on a trip like this is the group that you go with. For the most part the folks that I hunted with were a pleasure to hunt with. But one evening on the way back, it was hot and the air conditioner was not working well so I let my window down. The guy in the back of the bus began to fuss constantly until I put the window up. When we got off the bus my cousin Buster said, "Bill, I could tell you had about had it with that fellow because you had begun to swell up a mite!"

On the second trip, we had a fellow I had known all my life along with us. His daddy and mine had worked together for years. When I started high school and joined the baseball team, he was the third baseman. Now I have been playing third base all my life. He was a senior and I was a freshman so they placed me in left field. I was down in the mouth to start with until I realized that my bat had me in the game and not on the bench. I was glad to see him graduate so I could have third base. His whole family worked with my daddy and they all loved to hunt. He was no exception he was invited to go along on the hunt, which he gladly accepted.

We were at the Jacksonville airport going through the TSA inspections. And I was sitting on the bench putting my shoes back on, when he went through the metal detector. You were supposed to empty your pockets before going through the metal detector and then pick them up after you made it through. He went through and the detector squealed. The TSA officer who looked like Arnold Schwarzenegger, looked at me and then sent him back to check his pockets and go through again. A second time caused another squeal. The TSA officer looked my way and sent him back again. Finding some more metal he placed in the basket, when he went through the third time another squeal emitted. The officer made him stand on the footprints and had him to remove his belt. They then use the metal detector and told him he could go through.

As he started to go through, the officer smiled at me and snapped a latex glove on his hand loudly and said, "hold on I want to check one more thing".

Jack's eyes got big and fear spread over his face. The officer then told him never mind. You should've seen the look of relief on his face.

On one trip, at the Miami airport a stick of chewing gum in my shirt pocket almost got me strip-searched, so I know the feeling.

On another trip, James, the game warden who rode with me to the field in an earlier story, had retired, and was on the hunt with us. I asked him one of the afternoons as we were eating how it felt to kill that many birds. He just grinned.

One hunt in my county, DNR Game Wardens "wolf packed" the field. Wink had not had a good shot when the warden took his gun to check the magazine's capacity. About that time a dove flew right over him. He stared at the bird and then at the Warden. If looks could have killed, that would have been one dead Game Warden. After the shoot, the Colonel told Wink that the warden did not check his gun's capacity. Wink began to get red all over again until he noticed he was shooting an over under.

On one big shoot where there were plenty of birds, I tried to shoot birds that would fall close so I would not have to chase long range birds down. I liked shooting a skeet barrel to not try and stretch my shots, In Uruguay I shot Fiocchi No. 7 shot and could kill a bird at over 70 yards. Only one No. 7 pellet will bring down a dove.

I am now getting to where I cannot hunt like I once could but I still enjoyed a good dove hunt and recently my son, Billy, had limited out before me once and limited one time when I did not get the limit. I guess it is now the changing of the guard. I am no longer the most proficient dove hunter in the family. All good things must come to an end one day.

I was invited to come and participate in a shoot, two counties north of where I live, on the late season opening day. My friend, who had issued the invitation, asked that I find a few additional hunters so that we could cover the peanut field well. I made several calls and could only come up with one, a neighbor and a good bird hunting partner, G. B. We rolled out in my Bronco that morning about 4:00 am in order to make it there on time. It was eighteen degrees outside which was a little cold for dove hunting but the stalwart pair trudged onward. We took positions about sixty yards apart due to the small number of hunters in the field. The ground was frozen and hard. When the day began to crack the gray rockets began to come into the field to feed. The shooting was hot and heavy as the orange-breasted "tourist birds" (migrated from the North). Within thirty minutes I had my limit on the ground and G. B was close behind. We quickly made our way to the Bronco, and turned the heater on so we could thaw out. All the way home we talked about all our hunting buddies were not tough enough or man enough to come with us and had missed an excellent but very cold shoot. We also discussed how we were so sparse that birds were able to land between us out of range for either of us to shoot. A cup of steaming hot coffee never tasted or felt better than it did that day.

119

I have used many shotguns throughout the years but my two favorites are the Remington 1100 (12 gauge) and the Beretta 390 (20 gauge). The Beretta is what I used in South America. I shot a Beretta 392 on my last hunt. The reason that I liked them better was that they fit me better. If a shotgun does not fit, it is difficult to shoot well. I have tried some ill-fitting shotguns that made me look like a duffer. I tried to avoid using them for that reason, I recently, at a Ducks Unlimited Banquet, won the third of a certain make and style. I tried to shoot the first one and it would not fit so I traded it. I sold the second one I won and when I won the third one, I said that I would trade it to someone. It was a nice camo model and Billy, who was sitting with me, looked it over. He then informed me that it would fit him so I gave it to him. I do not know why I keep winning that type of gun. I have won two more since. But I have seen folks in a dove field with an ill-fitting shotgun look like a monkey trying to hit those seventy-five miles per hour feathery objects.

Recently, Billy and I were at some dove shoots out at the Southern edge of the County (which has always been a great area to hunt doves). The Big Satilla Creek area has something that attracts doves and has as long as I can remember. We hunted the Saturday before Labor Day and both of us limited pretty quick. Then on Labor Day, we went again and when the smoke had cleared, he had his fifteen but I only had seven. We had hunted together since he was four and hunted with his BB gun and this marked the first time that he had bested me in the United States. While we were in Uruguay, he killed more than me but I credited that to the fact that I was too busy watching him have fun and did not shoot as much as I could have. It is a great feeling when you see your son, student and protégée reach maturity in hunting as he had then. He is actually a better natural shotgunner and has better hand-eye coordination than I have.

I know I am no longer able to hunt like I once did but I still enjoy a good development and, on these hunts, when my son, Billy, has limited out before me once and limited one time when I didn't get the limit.

I bought a mojo dove decoy and put it to use not long ago on the edge of a big dove shoot. The birds were not coming well to me and I was separated a good distance from the other shooters, but when the dove saw the wings flashing on old mojo, they would come to take a look. I killed the limit fairly quickly but because all of my birds were ending up more than 50 yards away after being shot, I told the owner of the field that I got a limit, heatstroke and the cardiac workout that day. I later found out he didn't like the mojo dove so I most likely will never take it back to a field that he owns.

Dove Hunting in Uruguay

A Brace of Mallards

CHAPTER SEVEN

DUCK HUNTING

Duck hunting is a disease that is contagious and there is no known cure. I had my first experience at it while still a teenager. We went to a "roost" to "shoot" wood ducks. Now before you brand me as a poacher and a "slob" hunter, you must understand that we were ignorant of good conservation practices and federal waterfowl regulations, if there were any at that time, against hunting later than thirty minutes before sundown. Also, you must consider that we never hit anything anyway. Those dark objects approaching us through the trees at what seemed to be near the speed of sound were awfully hard to hit. Nevertheless, "Roost Shooting" was a social event in South Georgia at that time. We lacked the large lakes and were eighty miles from the coastal marshes and had no concept of decoying ducks.

Later, we learned to slip along Ten Mile Creek and jump shoot the feeding ducks. We also learned to go to the creek before daylight and shoot the ducks that flew in to feed on the acorns. My first story involves a morning hunt on the creek. A friend of mine, Bobby, who was an excellent shot and had some experience in duck hunting, was part of the hunt. Bobby had been in a motorcycle accident that left him with a severely broken leg that required extensive surgery, pins in his leg and the use of a bulky leg brace. This only slowed his shotgunning and duck hunting a bit. He later would become a World Champion skeet shooter, obviously overcoming all the setbacks of the accident.

The three of us plodded along the path, crossing the ford of the branch that led into the creek. Approaching the beaver dam, we began to spread out in anticipation of the daylight flight of ducks. Bobby suddenly felt the "Call of Nature" and began to peel out of the camo coveralls. Visualize him as he laid his shotgun and crutches on the ground beside him, coveralls around his ankles, one leg stiffened with the brace and the other bent supporting his weight. This was an awkward position at best. Suddenly we heard the Ker-eee, Ker-eee of approaching wood ducks. Instinctively, he scooped up the autoloader and fired. Two ducks were coming in, one from the left and the other from the right. "Blam---Blam" "Sploosh---Sploosh" He dispatched the two Woodies from his precarious position. He had a tracer shell as the second shot and in the near darkness of the early morning, it appeared to me that the tracer ball hit the second duck square. This was the very best "Squat-Shot" that I have ever witnessed. A feat that will most likely never be duplicated, a distinction that I am sure he does not relish.

On one cold and icy morning, I was trying to cross the beaver dam in Ten Mile Creek when I slipped on the ice and fell feet first into the creek. It did not take me long to examine that cold water, and quickly scrambled out of the cold water and walked to the hunting place I wanted to occupy. I looked down and noticed that my camo pant legs were frozen and looked as though they were starched. I shot a "woody" and spotted another duck headed my way. The Remington 1100 jumped to my shoulder and the bird rolled tumbling into the grass. I went to retrieve the duck and looked at the reddish topknot on the bird and thought I had shot a woodpecker. Upon showing it to Bobby, he told me it was a hen Hooded Merganser and when cooked it would taste similar to sardines.

Another morning, two of my cousins, Lewis and Ralph, and I went to jump shoot some ducks that I had spotted roosting in a small pond near my deer stand. It was cold for South Georgia and the ground was frozen. We arrived at the pond about one-half hour before daylight and planned our assault on the feathered critters. Our approach to the pond was across the corner of a field, without any cover.

We split up and crawled on the frozen ground to the edge of the pond. As we raised up, the ducks spotted us and sprang from the water frantically. As they tried to make their escape, we began firing at the fleeing birds. In the few moments that followed, we managed to down six birds, only one of which was on dry land. This was before any of us had retrieving dogs. We pondered our options to retrieve the downed ducks. Finally, two of us convinced my younger cousin, Ralph, to shuck off all his clothes and swim out and retrieve the ducks. We built a fire and assured him that he would be in no danger of freezing. He retrieved the ducks and was almost blue with cold when he reached the fire. That is when we discovered we had "Fish Ducks" Hooded Mergansers.

Ralph was thin and blond in appearance, and when we told my dad about the event, he began to call him a "Fair-Haired Retriever."

There was a pond called "Horseshoe Pond" near the airport in Appling County. There was a dove roost nearby that had quite a lot of doves but this lake had hundreds if not thousands of ducks coming into it at dusk. I have heard many stories of people shooting ducks there and killing and losing lots of ducks. I did not want to shoot the roost so I began reconnoitering the place in the evening and coming back the next morning and trying to get a couple when they left. I had heard of people killing several ducks there but were not retrieving many. The limit on Wood ducks was two per day so you didn't need many opportunities if you were a fair shot. I would park a good distance from the pond and slip in there while it was still dark. There was a place near the middle of the pond where there was enough cover for one to quietly slip up to the water's edge at the widest part of the pond. At first light, the ducks will begin leaving slowly which is followed by the mass exodus a little later. The exodus is hastened when the first gunshot rings out. A couple of us could get in the right position and get our two ducks pretty easily. That was a good place until the timber company that owned the land and pond drained it to promote pine tree growth.

As my enjoyment of duck hunting increased, I began to branch out and try other forms. My hunting evolved from "roost shooting to jump shooting". From there I progressed to drifting down the river and past shooting those ducks that flew over or jump shooting those that were resting at the edge of the river. I even bought a dozen decoys but I didn't have a clue as to how to use them. This next story recounts one of the times that I tried to learn to hunt with decoys.

We were working in the next town between Thanksgiving and Christmas. The weather had turned nasty. The rain and cold had halted our work that morning, so I asked the boss if I could take the rest of the day off to hunt ducks. Since we could not perform anything productive, he allowed it. I hurried home, changing into my camo clothes and scooped up my gun and decoys. I drove out to a small pond that a cousin owned and began to set up my decoys. This was a classic "duck pond", with flooded trees covering over half the pond. I knew that wood ducks roosted in the pond and hoped that the weather would cause them to stir around. I cut some brush and built a blind, on a small washout, on the edge of the dam and placed my decoys about twenty-five yards out from the blind. This pond was only close to two houses, one of which was that of my boss.

It was about 2 o'clock in the afternoon when I finally settled down in the blind. My intention was to hunt until dark or until I had bagged a limit of ducks. I had not seen any ducks and was thoroughly wet from the constant drizzle of rain. I had been in the blind for over an hour and was getting restless when I spotted some movement on the other side of the dam. Under my breath, I scolded myself for not bringing along some buckshot. I would be really upset if a ten-point buck walked out to take a drink of water with me unable to take him. Number five shot is not effective on big game.

127

I stared in that direction and again saw movement. This time I could make out the shape of a young "Homo-Sapien" in the edge of the trees. I then recognized my boss's son, Jeff, armed with his shotgun. He had obviously just returned home from school and had slipped down to the pond to try to jump shoot a duck. I could tell when his eyes focused on my decoys. He began to sneak down the dam with his eyes locked on my decoys. When he was close to my blind, he slowly raised his shotgun most likely wondering why the ducks had not yet flown.

I startled him when I said, "They won't float if you shoot holes in them!"

He jumped around with the funniest look on his face. I then realized that it was not smart to startle someone with a loaded shotgun. I also understood why there weren't any ducks in the pond.

Bart, a friend of mine, had just completed Dental school in North Carolina, and returned home to establish a Dental practice. I began to visit him and his wife. He told stories of duck hunting on Currituck Sound, while he was in school. I was captivated by the stories of thousands and thousands of ducks in the air at one time.

Our friendship began when I was a Boy Scout and he was a Junior Assistant Scoutmaster of the troop. I remember vividly the coffee that he used to make on campouts. He would begin on Friday night by boiling coffee in a pot over the fire. The coffee on Friday night would be so strong that you would pour a cup and use your knife to cut it before the cup was full. He would continue to use the same grounds all weekend, adding water when the coffee would get low in the pot. By Saturday night the coffee was just about the right strength and by Sunday at lunch, it would be weak as dishwater.

We talked duck hunting all spring and during the summer he began to prepare for the fall waterfowling on the Georgia coast.

He and my other friend, Bobby, that I earlier mentioned as being such a proficient hunter, hunted together that season and had quite a bit of success on the marshes of the Altamaha River Delta. I heard their stories all the winter and into the spring. Deep in my heart, I desired an invitation to hunt with them so that I also could tell stories of the coastal hunts. Finally, it came and I looked forward to the upcoming season with an excitement that cannot be described.

Summer approached and he began preparation for the fall. He had purchased a mold and began making Styrofoam decoys. He had hand-painted them and they were beautiful. They looked as good as any other decoys that I had ever seen. When he finally retired them, I requested and was given a hen to use as a decoration in my home. Every time I look at the decoy, I remember all those hunts and all the stories, too numerous to relate. It was a time of learning and a new adventure in my life. Most of the rest of my good duck stories came from the next five or six seasons of hunting on the Georgia Coast.

Bart took a stout aluminum john boat and converted it into a duck-hunting machine. He built a wooden frame and constructed flip up sides of plywood. We made a trip to the marsh and harvested marsh grass to lace in the elastic cord that he had attached to the sides and flip-up portions. We spent several days getting the boat ready. The day of completion arrived, and we were admiring it as it sat ready on the trailer. With the flip-up sides laid down for transport, the marsh grass protruded off the sides and resembled wings. Someone said it looked like a big turkey and he christened it the "S S Turkey."

I had never seen a "boat blind" and was greatly impressed with the Turkey's possibilities. It was built with fore and aft compartments for hunters and a center section with over fifty magnum, styrofoam decoys. He had equipped the decoys with a large diameter line and special weights to avoid tangles. The thirty-five horsepower Evinrude motor on the stern seemed a bit much for an aluminum boat, although I later learned that it was just right. My friend had even wired running lights, a large spotlight, and even small interior lights. There was a shelf running the length of the boat on both sides that was perfect for shotguns, shells, coffee and other goodies necessary for the successful duck hunt. The "S S Turkey" was the Winnebago of motorized blinds.

We left home at 3 o'clock in the morning and headed for Two Way Fish Camp near the town of Darien. Darien is one of the oldest towns in Georgia and is located on the north side of the Altamaha River Delta. During the early 1800's it was a seaport and a sawmill hub and was important to the economy of Georgia. Now it is home for a large shrimping fleet and is a sport fishing Mecca. It is also a haven for waterfowlers due to the location of Federal and State Wildlife refuges located in the delta. Two Way Fish Camp is located across the South Altamaha River from Champney Island which is part of the Altamaha Wildlife Refuge. Buttermilk Sound, our destination, was a good nine miles downriver from the fish camp.

There was still over an hour of darkness as we cast off from the floating docks and headed east. Everything looks the same in the marsh at night, and it was a strange feeling to be plowing through the water for the first time, headed to an unknown destination. I must have felt like the men on Christopher

130

Columbus's ships did as they left the Canary Islands and sailed west to the unknown world. We arrived and set up the decoys, pulling the "Turkey" up near the edge of the marsh grass on the shore. There were several small grass-covered islets nearby, and I supposed that we looked like just another islet. As day broke, we were able to down a few Teal that were the victims of taking too close a look at our decoys. Neither my friend nor I could call ducks so we depended on the decoys as the only attractant. It was an excellent hunt but nothing laughable or extraordinary happened. Nothing except I had found the type of duck hunting that I could really fall in love with.

We returned to that area many times after that and enjoyed many an hour of feathers and fellowship.

Opening day one year we launched the "Turkey" into a diked in area on Champney Island to hunt the first two days. The season opened at noon so we spent the better part of the morning trying to position the boat just right in the shallow water of the old rice field. The water was only about a foot deep, the mud was about two feet deep which made the going tough. By eleven o'clock that morning we were inside the boat eating our lunch. We gave one last look over the decoy spread and were satisfied with the look of it. The weather was almost perfect, clouded, rainy and the wind was lightly blowing. You couldn't ask for it to be any better. We looked over toward where we had launched the boat and spotted the Department of Natural Resources Game Manager peeking at us from the saw grass at the edge. He later told us that he could not believe that anyone would have gone to as much trouble as we did to launch that big a boat into the shallow pond.

All our work paid off because right at noon two Ringneck ducks came into the decoys and I knocked one down. I crawled out of the "Turkey" and proceeded to bog my way over to the downed duck. It was about seventy yards away from the boat and the going was rough. While we had worked with the boat, we always could hold onto the boat for support and could rest while leaning on the boat. This retrieving of the Ringneck did not offer that luxury. Instead, I was on my own. My lungs were burning, and I was muddy from stumbling in the soft bottom, I finally made it back to the boat. The last stumble that occurred, I had rammed the butt of my Remington 1100 autoloader into the mud to keep from falling face-first into the gray mud. I rested for a good ten minutes hanging onto the boat before climbing in. Man was I worn out! I had to disassemble the 1100 and swish it in the water to remove the mud from the action. A little later some more ducks came in, and I downed one about forty yards off to the other side of Bart.

When I didn't make any motions to get out of the boat again, Bart asked, "Aren't you going after that one?"

"Naw!" I could see the duck in the open water. "He's not going anywhere. I'll get him in a little while."

I wasn't about to go wading again so quickly. Hopefully, I would knock another one down near it and get two with one trip.

In just a few minutes Bart shot one down about ten yards from mine. He scrambled out the stern of the boat to retrieve his prize.

"Get mine while you're over there."

"Alright!" He said as he headed for the duck.

Unknown to us, there were deep ditches that divided the sections of the old rice field. And unknown to Bart there was one between the two ducks. As he grabbed the first duck, he took two or three steps toward the second and plunged into the deep ditch. For a moment the only evidence of him was a giant ripple and his floating hat. Just as suddenly as he disappeared, he surfaced with water spewing from his mouth. He reminded me of "Moby Dick", the great white whale. He floundered over to the other duck and made his way back to the boat. It was all that I could do to keep from exploding into laughter.

He looked at me and said, "The next one you kill, you go get."

Later that day, as we retired for the night, we discussed the day's events. We decided that all those paintings that you see with a duck hunter, his back to the rising sun, wearing waders and holding a brace of ducks were not what they appeared. The hunter was just standing there wet and muddy, with his lungs burning, trying to rest and catch his breath.

The next morning, we were back in the "Turkey", which we had left in position, waiting for the first beams of daylight. We thought we saw something in our decoys, so we counted them. Sure enough, there was an extra decoy. That meant that there was a duck already in the decoys, feeding.

Legal hours were just beginning when my old friend, Bart said "There he is!" Then he raised his gun.

Blam!! Bart fired. Styrofoam blew everywhere and a coot half flew and half ran from a spot near there. Suddenly the sky was black with ducks. We did not get a good shot at them and were amazed at the sight. We did not see many ducks after that.

Later that morning, at a local store, another hunter said that there were about five thousand Blue Winged Teal in the back pond on Champney Island.

"Some fool!' He snarled, "Shot about daylight and scared them all off!"

We agreed with him and suggested that the hunter that would do that should be drug for five miles behind a pickup truck.

Not too many trips in the "SS Turkey" convinced me to build my own blind boat so I would always have one at my disposal. I looked the "SS Turkey" over good and had some ideas of my own. I converted my aluminum bass boat, which was slightly smaller than the "SS Turkey", into a blind boat. I painted my 20 horsepower Johnson outboard Marsh Grass Tan and took a WD 40 straw placed in the nozzle of a can of black spray paint and painted little black streaks down the sides of my boat (which was also tan) and my motor to camouflage it. Instead of using ¼ inch plywood I built a spruce frame and utilized plastic woven feed sacks stapled to the frame to save weight. I spent the afternoon with the chemist at Tom Sawyer paints in Brunswick mixing the best color to use. I painted the sacks to match my boat and bought the bungee cord to affix the marsh grass. One trip to the marsh and I had enough marsh grass to finish the job. The "SS Pond Squaggin" was born.

(Bart later dubbed it "The Altamaha Dredge" due to my habit of running in shallow water and kicking up mud. In some cases, while motoring in the sound, kicking up clams and mud.)

134

Daddy and the "Squaggin"

You learn hard lessons hunting in the marsh. Things like having replacement parts, to your guns and spare props and shear pins for your outboard motor. One friend, David Earl, carries a small toolbox with him that contains not only his shells and calls but these other essential things. He calls it his "Pick Ass Box." We all learned the value of this type of preparedness at one time or another. I remember one night when the "Turkey" threw a propeller while Bart was reversing the direction of the engine to clean the marsh grass off the propeller. Instead, he cleaned the propeller off the shaft. He was lucky enough to flag a passing boat down and get towed into the docks. From that time own, he always had a spare with him. I had a military ammunition can with spare props, pins, spark plugs, boat plugs, and other miscellaneous hardware.

The time came when I decided that decoys were just not enough. I felt that I needed to learn to call ducks in order to enhance my duck hunting. I went to the local sporting goods store and bought a simple call and proceeded to attempt to learn the art of duck calling. The main trouble was that no one around knew much more about duck calling than I did. I tried reading the instructions and being an old trumpet player, I developed a feeding chuckle. I had also read that you should be careful when quacking because a wrong note would send the ducks in the other direction quickly.

I remember the first time that I tried the call in the blind. We were in the "Turkey" on the edge of the sound. I saw a duck about three hundred yards away and began to chuckle on the call. For whatever the reason, the duck turned and came our way. We dispatched him with one shot and I took credit for calling him in. Bart always insisted that the duck just saw the decoys and turned to them. I cannot say for sure, but my confidence in my duck calling was awfully high.

I really didn't learn the art until one of my cousins married this guy named Bobby that had spent quite a bit of time hunting ducks. He especially had years of practice on Reelfoot Lake. Now we were hunting from the two boats and this new friend became my hunting partner. We made a deadly combination. Due to competition skeet shooting, I had become quite proficient at shotgunning, and he could call a duck away from an ear of corn.

During that season my ear became tuned to his calling style. I called along with him and by the close of the season, I had become quite proficient. The fourth member of our regular party was another close friend, Weyman. Like I said before we had met at the National Boy Scout Jamboree at Valley Forge Pennsylvania in 1964 and later played in a "Rock Band" together. He had assumed my position in the "Turkey" after I had built my boat. He had also become pretty good at calling and was an excellent shot. We had gotten to the point where we would let one duck hit the water in the decoys, shoot another duck and take the first duck when he sprang up from the water. We thought that we were becoming pretty good duck hunters.

The four of us planned a trip to South Carolina to hunt in the great Santee-Cooper reservoir. We even flew up in a small airplane to "SCOUT" or "Reconnoiter" the area where we would hunt. The fearless Captain of the "Turkey", Bart, had an aversion to flying, so he sent a small Instamatic camera and a pocket full of film for me to take photos for him to look over after the trip. We used a six-passenger single-engine aircraft. We had no Navigator, save myself (a feat I performed using a road map), and with the crop duster for a pilot.

For those that do not know about crop dusters, let me explain. They are either fearless or crazy; the jury is still out on them. Their job is to fly slow-moving aircraft over crop fields and spray them with pesticides. Those that fly in the Midwest have pretty large fields without many trees. In South Georgia, the fields are small and are usually lined with tall Georgia pines. It is obvious just where on the spectrum they fall.

The other three and our crop duster pilot embarked on our reconnoitering mission. The flight to the lake, Lake Marion, was uneventful, with the possible exception of me looking at highways and towns so that we could determine our position. In no time at all we arrived at our target, the confluence of the Congaree and the Wateree Rivers. Due to my excellent navigating, we flew right over Stump Hole Landing Number 9, the landing that we would use.

I could not believe the ducks that were on that lake. I thought that I had died and gone to Duck Hunters Heaven. We made passes over the area from every direction and I captured it all on film for the missing hunter. When we were satisfied that we could find our way in the dark we headed back south. Instead of retracing our path, we decided to fly back down the coast and look at our coastal hunting area and then up the Altamaha River back home. We, for the most part, enjoyed the coastal flight until I discovered on the "real" navigation maps that I had found in the plane, that we were in United States Air Force restricted air space. We took a hard right and quickly vacated the "no fly zone".

We arrived at the point where the Altamaha River empties into the Atlantic Ocean and began to photograph and scout the area. We were flying low, just over treetop high when Weyman spotted a huge Fallow Deer Buck in the marsh of Little St. Simons Island.

"Turn around." He cried, "Look at that buck."

Suddenly the crop duster pointed the wing on my side of the plane toward the ground and began a sharp 180 degree turn only a couple of hundred feet above the marsh. My heart jumped into my throat and I realized that the "Turkey's Captain", Bart, was extremely smart. I never liked the really scary rides at the county fair and this turn was very much like them.

When we finally leveled out, so that I could speak again. I grabbed Weyman by the shirt and said, "Don't you ever do that AGAIN!"

We returned home and I delivered the film and camera to Bart. We had a good time relating to him the events of the trip and had a many a laugh, as we relived the happenings.

The day finally arrived and three of us packed the "Turkey" and headed north. Something had come up that had caused the fourth hunter, Weyman, to cancel his participation in the hunt. We decided to leave the "Squaggin" on the roost and take only the "Turkey".

The first morning on the lake we saw more ducks even than we had seen on our scouting trip. There were layers of them flying in different directions. We were braced for the most exciting duck hunt of our lives. The first three ducks in our decoys were two widgeons and a pintail which we collected beautifully. Then we spotted our quarry, Greenheads, five or six of them. We began to call and turned the birds. They swung around to the south and began losing altitude. They were only a couple of hundred yards away, heading in our direction when it happened. The mallards were still dropping into the flooded timber and passed over a small green clump in the lake.

Blam! Blam! Blam! One duck fell and the rest turned straight up to the sky in escape mode.

"What do they think they are doing? Those were our ducks! Don't they have any etiquette?" My duck calling partner, Bobby, was beside himself.

Some hunters were set up downwind from us and had shot at the mallards as they turned into the wind to approach our decoys.

"You don't shoot ducks that another hunter is calling in. Crank up the boat and I'll give him a lesson in duck hunting etiquette."

It took both of us to restrain him. I have never seen someone so offended by the inconsiderate actions of other hunters. Finally, he calmed down and our hunt was resumed.

We had been doing quite well in spite of the hunters downwind shooting at every bird that approached from that direction, whether they were in range or not.

The wind finally changed direction and our problems with the "Dyke Shooters" as my friend called them, were minimal. We spotted a lone Mallard drake and began to call. Two of us poured our hearts out calling that duck for over twenty minutes. Several times I thought that the duck was close enough to shoot, but Bart, the Captain of the "Turkey" did not fire a shot. After hyperventilating both of us, the drake decided that there was something he didn't like about our decoys or blind and left. We asked Bart why he didn't shoot and he replied.

"I was afraid to shoot. I didn't know how Bobby would react if I missed." He later admitted that after all the hard work that Bobby and I had done calling that drake, the last thing he wanted to do was to shoot at him and miss.

We all had a good laugh and could not wait to get home to tell of our adventure.

I also am reminded a trip to the Altamaha River where Bobby taught us that calling Ducks was not limited to the coastal areas and the large lakes. He proved, without a doubt, that you could call ducks on the upper river too!

We had gone downriver and set up at the beginning of a long reach on the river. Our decoy spread, while not as impressive as the coastal decoy spreads, looked good enough to attract ducks. We positioned the two boats to get the maximum effect from the decoys. We had only been there a short while when another boat pulled up just downriver from us. These guys didn't have any decoys and had pulled into the willows in hopes of getting a pass-shot at some ducks.

We were sitting in my boat eating some smoked Mallard from the coast when Bobby laid his piece down.

"Hush! I hear a Mallard drake!" He said, lifting his call to his mouth and giving out a hail call to the duck.

In a few moments, he pointed to the drake flying down river about two hundred yards high. He called again and the duck turned and came back toward us. The drake passed over our decoys, still way out of range. Bobby wailed a comeback call on his trusty call and the greenhead turned once again and passed over the decoys, still too high. Bobby again pleaded with the traveler, and the duck turned and began to lose altitude. He was coming straight toward the decoys, dropping fast. He came in right over the new arrivals, and they cut loose on him at about sixty yards. The fifth or sixth shot connected and the heavy bird hit the water with a splash. I looked around at Bobby and did all that I could to calm him down. He again was muttering something about duck hunting etiquette or the lack of it. I managed to calm him enough to keep him from making a rude introduction to the two hunters.

Everything would have been alright if they had not come over to our boat to show off their prize. It was dark enough that they could not see Bobby's eyes or they would have certainly been startled. To this day, I am sure that they did not know that what they had done was anything more that the collecting a trophy duck in the Altamaha.

Weyman and I would take the "Squaggin" into the upper arm of the Altamaha to hunt. All things considered, we made a perfect team. We both could call well, and we both could shoot well. We could take the "Squaggin" and hide by a clump of willows, even though the camo was marsh grass. (If we had hunted the upper river exclusively, we would've used Spanish Moss instead of Marsh Grass.) We were successful on many occasions.

We had spotted mallards on the Altamaha and moved around until we pinpointed their flight pattern. The river is high and it flooded the 3-mile floodplain near Ten Mile Creek. Weyman and I were driving the boat on the two path roads on the Tattnall County side of the river, due to all of the water. We drove until we found a "clear-cut" of at least 200 acres. We set our decoys up and prepared to "Shot De Duck" as Justin Wilson would say. Just on schedule the Mallards came, and Weyman and I collected our limit. The only hitch was a duck came suddenly from our rear and surprised us. We both opened up and then realized it was a goose. There was no goose season in Georgia then. One friend, who was not familiar with the waterfowl regulations, caught a group of of snow geese on a sandbar and killed seven of them. He placed them in his pickup and rode all over town showing them off. If it had been me, the game warden would've captured me and put me "Under the Jail".

We used to hunt passing ducks all along the Altamaha. We would position ourselves in strategic places where ducks were known to fly and try to get a few that way. One afternoon when the weather conditions were cloudy and rainy, we decided to go to the river and pass shoot some ducks at one of our favorite "Honey Holes", Sandy Slough. I positioned myself in a clearing on one side of the river and Bart was on the other. We waited for over half an hour without seeing any ducks. Suddenly, I heard the whistling of duck wings overhead and looked up. There were three woodies. I swung my Remington into action and took my lead on the second duck. Blam! I fired at the duck and watched in amazement as the first two ducks folded. In a few seconds, both ducks hit the water. Plop! Plop!

From across the river came Bart's booming voice. "It's a D--- Lie!!"

I had a reputation of, at least once a winter, managing to fall in or at least get wet while hunting or fishing. It had gotten to the point that if I could have just jumped into the water at the first of the season to get it over with, I would have done just that. I have slipped off icy foot logs more times than I care to remember. I have seen the bow of my bass boat disappear from under my feet while trying to free a lure that was tangled in an overhanging branch. I have broken through ice in a ford that I thought to be only inches deep to discover that it was much deeper. You name it and I have most likely gotten wet that way. One event that I will never forget occurred as follows.

The "SS Squaggin," my fourteen-foot aluminum bass boat, was not designed to be used in the sounds. It is a narrow and shallow sided with two high pedestals with swivel seats attached. It is excellent for river and pond fishing but affords very little protection in the rough coastal waters. I once beached it in Crescent Lake in Florida because those whitecaps were too much. But we used it, because it was all that I had at the time.

Weyman and I were on the edge of the sound setting out the decoy spread, with the intention of using a camo net and luring some ducks in. One of the decoys had a neck wrap, which occurs when the decoy line accidentally flips over the neck of the decoy during placement. It is unthinkable for a true duck hunter to leave a decoy like that because it does not look natural. Instead of reaching with the boat paddle that had a hook on the end, I just reached forward to flip the line off with my hand. My seat had been loose for months, and I had procrastinated in repairing it. It took this occasion to demonstrate to me that preventative maintenance is important and broke loose. I plunged headlong into the freezing water, clawing and grabbing at anything to save me from ending up stuck headfirst in the mud on the bottom. Weyman's fast thinking was all that saved me. Seeing me diving forward, he lunged in the opposite direction, which kept the small boat from capsizing. His quick action helped me to regain my balance before completely going overboard. I only got wet from the waist up! As I rolled back into the boat with water streaming off my face, I looked over at him. He was rolling in the rear of the boat laughing. He caught his breath long enough to ask if I was alright.

I sputtered "Yeah, but I just saw Jacques Cousteau, and he said that we might as well go home, the ducks are on the other side of the sound."

My friend Bruce and I were hunting ducks around Hell's Shoals Lake one morning early. I thought that if I went across the narrow opening near the mouth of the lake, I would do better. There was a giant foot log across the water and I determined that it was safe to traverse. It was in the twenty's that morning, and the wind was blowing to make the chill factor much lower. I started across the log feeling secure in my crossing, until I hit a patch of ice on the top of the log. I did a Fandango dance on the log before plunging into the cold water. The water was so deep that my hat literally floated. When I came to the surface, I raised my 1100 Remington out of the water and threw it like a javelin sticking it up barrel first in the mud on the far bank. I floundered to the far side dragging my hat with me. I do not know how deep the water there was because my feet never hit the bottom, although my head went way under. I looked back at Bruce and he could hardly contain himself. He was trying not to laugh but not doing a very good job of it. I guess it looked pretty funny from his vantage point, but not from mine. I regained my composure and carefully made my way back across the log. I was so cold that I was "shaking like a dog trying to pass a peach seed". We got to the vehicle and made a fire to dry me off. I cut a stick and pushed six or so inches of mud from my barrel. After that, I purchased an old pump shotgun that was disposable, so I could let it sink and save my own skin.

Once, I took off my vacation from work and hunted the complete second waterfowl season, fifteen days straight. During that time, I had several partners and thoroughly enjoyed acting the part as a guide in the Altamaha Delta. One of those afternoons my partner was an old skeet shooting buddy, Calvin, who was an excellent wing shot. We pulled up into the best spot in the mudflat that we called the "High Corner" and set up our decoys. As we were settling down to wait for the ducks' appearance, I noticed that he was wearing a pair of Bausch and Lomb shooting glassed with a shiny, gold frame. Thinking that he was using shooting glasses to be cool and fearing that the ducks would see the bright frames and flare, I told him that he needed to put the glasses in his pocket so the birds wouldn't see him. He complied without a question.

The first ducks to make their way into the "slot" were a pair of mallards. I hailed them and they turned and came straight to our spread. I told him to keep down, until I said to take them. When they were at the point of no return, I gave the signal and stood up in the blind. I dispatched my duck with a single shot and swung around to see him take his bird. When I realized that he was not going to shoot, I took the second bird. I was puzzled as to why he didn't shoot but I didn't inquire.

A little later, I called two Black Ducks into the decoys and took mine but he still did not even fire a shot. Curiosity got the best of me and I asked Calvin why he did not shoot at either bird.

"I can't see them without my glasses" He answered.

Boy, was I embarrassed! I didn't know that they were prescription glasses. Needless to say, he was a much better wing shot after I allowed him to see!

By the way, we limited the boat for all fifteen days.

There was one hunt that is easy to remember, because it was about the coldest time that I have ever spent hunting. To set the stage; It was twenty degrees with a thirty -five mile an hour west wind ripping down the Altamaha River. It had snowed on St. Simons Island the night before, which is a rare occurrence in South Georgia. As we launched the "Turkey" and my boat the "S. S.

146

Pond Squaggin", when I was only using a comp net to hide the boat from incoming ducks. It was obvious that there would not be much competition in the sound. We were the only boats in the water.

The arrangements at Two-Way Fish Camp were that we could launch the boats early in the morning and settle our accounts when we returned, and it was certain that Clint and Frank, the operators of the fish camp, would take their time in getting out of their warm beds on this chilly morning. The dock was slippery with the ice that covered it and every exposed object at the landing.

Bart and Weyman would operate out of the roomy "Turkey" and I would set up the net blind on my boat alone. We ran the nine miles downriver in tandem navigating with a handheld spotlight. I was still learning to get around in the delta and was more than happy to follow in the wake of the "Turkey". Finally, we rounded a bend in the never-ending marsh grass and spotted the range marker that marked the entrance into Buttermilk Sound. Bart pulled up in a spot that we called the "high corner" and I began to set up about two hundred yards to the north.

We quickly set up the decoys and I rammed the bow of my boat into a large clump of marsh grass on the mudflat. Using tobacco sticks I set up a blind, that consisted of a mosquito net that had black streaks painted vertically on it. I was prepared for the cold and had brought a small propane heater along, which I lit with freezing hands. The only way to feel any heat at all was to stick my hands almost in the little heater. I tried to pour a cup of coffee from my thermos and managed to spill it onto the floor of the boat. When the steamy liquid hit the aluminum bottom it instantly froze.

Without me knowing it, Weyman had located an old, galvanized minnow bucket and some charcoal and had brought it along. He filled the bucket half full of sand and had placed some charcoal in it. In an attempt to start the charcoal, he had wadded the bag up and saturated the bag and charcoal with a can of lighter fluid. I looked over toward the "Turkey" and saw flames leaping above the marsh grass that was part of their blind and thought that they were on fire. I called over to them and they reassured me that they were in no danger. We used that old heater many a time after that and you would be surprised just how much heat that rig would produce and also just how well the boat blind would contain the heat for the hunters' consumption.

As the day began to break, I was in awe of the beauty of a winter sunrise over the marsh, a sight that I would enjoy many times and always appreciate no matter how many times I watched it. The ducks would be stirring soon so I readied myself. As the first duck came near, I blasted away and forgot how cold my hands were. The drake splashed about thirty yards away near the grass. Since I had no retriever dog, I stuck my paddle out to slide the boat from the clump of grass and discovered that "ice" had formed around my boat and the grass and that I would have to break the ice to remove the boat. I retrieved the duck and flipped him in the bottom of the boat, paddling the boat back into the clump of grass. I reached down to relocate the duck and found him stuck to the aluminum floor. I plucked half the duck just pulling him loose from the floor of the boat. One duck that I shot down later even bounced on the ice as the water around the marsh grass was frozen. The ice extended several feet out into the sound beyond the grass line.

We had an excellent hunt with all three of us filling our limit of ducks including some "prized" Canvasbacks. When we started to return to the landing, we swapped around because of having to head into the fierce wind. My boat only had a small 20 horsepower motor on the stern and it was hard to plane the boat with such a load so we swapped some weight including myself and let Weyman, who was considerably lighter than me, drive my boat. I positioned myself in the bow of the "Turkey" and zipped my float coat up tight. As we plowed into the west wind, spray from the bow would explode up and freeze in midair. Then it would crash into me at full force. It was almost like an "ice shower". I had a full beard at the time and was wearing the "float Coat". The ice covered my front and gave me an eerie appearance.

We tied the boats up to the dock and scampered into the little store at the landing. Clint greeted us at the door and informed us that we were the only duck hunters that went out that morning. Since there were only two other landings in the tidal water and the fact that we heard no other shots, we were most likely the only duck hunters on the sound that morning.

"You all are tough as a gators "tit" to be out there this morning", he exclaimed.

"Or crazy as a Loon," I thought as I splashed down his hot coffee and huddled with the other two around his cherry red potbellied stove heater.

A Boat Limit of Quality Ducks

During a series of duck hunting days, Daddy and I went to the Altamaha Sound to bag some ducks. The tide was not all the way in but thanks to the excellent camouflage of the "Squaggin" we were able to set up decoys and flop the sides of the blind up and do our impression of an isolated marsh island. As day began to break, the ducks began moving around. I began to call and it became hot and heavy for a little while. Daddy shot five times and had five ducks lying on the water. I had shot four times and had three lying there.

Daddy smugly reached for the thermos and poured himself a cup of hot coffee, leaned back in the swivel seat and said, "I have my ducks and am ready as soon as you are." This marked the first time since I was young that he had outshot me with a shotgun, and he was extremely proud of his accomplishment.

150

The first time I hunted with that duck-calling fool Bobby was in Buttermilk Sound. We had taken the "Squaggin" out and had set up the 65 Coastal Magnum decoys in a pattern that I called the flat diamond. It was cat-eye shaped with two landing holes in about twenty-five or thirty yards from the boat. The purpose of the holes was to let the "Candy Bird" almost put his feet in the water there and shoot another duck. After shooting the first duck the "Candy Bird" would usually spring up from there and afford an easy second shot. Bobby learned to call hunting on Reelfoot Reservoir and his calling was like music to my ears. He was the best I have ever heard. I was glad he had married into the family. When he called, the ducks would turn and come to our spread. Now I must admit that I was a decent shot on decoying ducks and when the smoke cleared, we had two canvasbacks, two black ducks, two mallards and the rest were teal for our boat limit. I listened closely to his cadence and the sounds that he would make and went home and took my cheap little call and started feverishly practicing. I had been converted and fully intended to be as good as him one day.

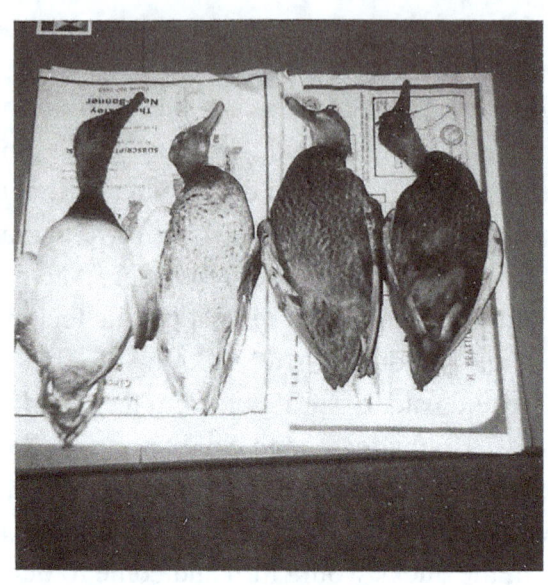

Canvasback, Redhead, Mallard and Black duck

As I said before the first time that I tried to call, all I could do was a feeding chuckle (before I heard Bobby call). Bart would laugh at me for trying to call with the chuckle but that was better than he could call. A few times I actually turned ducks with the chuckle if they were close enough to hear. Bart and I relied mostly on our decoy spreads, which were most likely the best that anyone down on the Georgia coast was using at the time. Most hunters would take a dozen standard decoys but we liked the magnum decoys and lots of them. I have seen ducks that were flying parallel to us see our spread and turn to us, from a pretty good distance. After a while, both Weyman and I could produce a decent call and bring in ducks. We hunted sometimes up the Altamaha River and had pretty good success. We hunted together often, and I really enjoyed the time with my "Old Friend".

On one occasion I arrived to the duck hunting area a little late, due to a slow take off from my home some 85 miles away. After I had landed the boat in at Two Way Fish Camp and made by way the 9 miles down the South Altamaha channel to my favorite spot, I found someone already occupying the number one spot. So, I went to an alternate spot "The High Corner" which was one of the best, second to the "Honey Hole" and set up my decoy spread. As it began to crack day and the ducks started moving in, they of course headed toward the "Honey Hole". As they broke the marsh line in the direction of those other folks' decoys, I cut loose with my double reed call and pleaded with those ducks to come my way. My hail call would turn them and bring them toward my decoys. I would then coax them in with "lonesome hen" calls and feeding chuckle. When they cupped their wings and dropped the landing gear, my partner and I quickly dispatched them. This went on until we had the boat limit. We picked up our decoys and left without ever knowing who was down there sitting in the "Honey Hole". It didn't bother me much then, because I had turned every duck from them and brought them to us. They had had no shooting at all.

A few days later, upon talking to Bart, I found it was one of his dentist buddies, whom he had shown where our honey hole was. He said that he had talked to him and although his buddy didn't say too much about the incident, he knew that it was me in the low corner and told Bart that I called way too much. I guess I may have since I called all the ducks off his decoy spread to mine. Hopefully, he got some ducks after my partner and I left.

On another hunting excursion, I was in the "Honey Hole" and saw someone pull-up across the expanse of the little body of water to an old blind that we had used before we built our boat blinds. I did not know it the time, who was in the other location, but the next week in the newspaper from an adjoining county where I worked, I read an article where the writer had complained about going duck hunting in the Altamaha Sound and someone across the way from him calling in and taking all the ducks that flew over. He made some suggestion to us that the unknown duck hunter across the body of water was unethical because he called in all the ducks that day. The writer and I had both written articles for the original Georgia Sportsman magazine and it was obvious he had a clue as to the identity of the "mystery duck hunter". I saw him later in the week and informed him that my attorney would be getting in touch with him about the libel suit that I had after he wrote so badly about me in the newspaper.

On another occasion, Bart and I were hunting the "Honey Hole" and saw our friend David Earl pull-up across the little sound from us. In short order he had his decoy spread out and was concealed in the marsh grass. A little later I saw a duck come toward him and he shot. It took the duck a long time to finally go down and his Labrador did not range nearly far enough to find him. An hour later a canvasback Drake floated into our decoy spread. Since we neither had a retriever, periodically we would have to venture out into the decoy spread retrieve downed ducks. As we went out to gather in some of our quarry we picked his duck up too. Later when we arrived back at Two Way, he greeted us. As he discussed a morning hunt with us, he mentioned that he thought he had downed the canvasback Drake but was unable to recover it. I reached into the bottom of the boat and flipped the canvasback to him asking, "Did he look anything like this?"

Bart and I got a good laugh out of telling him that was his duck that he drifted all the distance across the sound to our decoy

154

spread. Fortunately for him, that didn't put him over the limit for the federal game wardens were swarming at Two Way Fish Camp that day.

It was David Earl, who shared with me his formula for loading duck shell with P B powder. This was a loading formula that I used until we were required to shoot steel shot at waterfowl. It was a 3 ½ dram 1 ¼ ounce load of number five's that would smoke any duck in range. I used the last of them on a pheasant shoot and dish ragged every bird I shot with them.

A friend that I worked with, Elton, invited me to hunt with him in the Brunswick River on the opening day of the second season one year. Back then duck and dove season was split and every time it opened or reopened the legal shooting hours began at noon on that day. We met up near the Shrimp Boat docks and parked our vehicles. We were to hunt on Andrews Island, which was a dredge island. We had to walk over half a mile in waders and loaded down with decoy bag, shotgun and "Possibles" bag with calls and treats in it, along with a canteen of water. We arrived at the spot early and stood knee-deep on the water contained there. We set out the decoys near a good hiding spot in thick grass, waiting for noon to arrive. There were many ducks flying all around, but we held our fire until noon. Elton was shooting a Model 12 Winchester pump and I had my 1100 Remington. We still could use lead shot although parts of the country with hard bottoms were restricted to steel. My pockets were filled with my favorite reload of 3 ½ dram 1 ¼ ounce load of #5's. Just after we were sure it was noon, I called four teal to us. I told Elton to hold off until I gave the signal. When they were almost right where I wanted them, I said "Now!" I raised up. Since the birds were spread out left to right and Elton was on my right I picked the middle-left bird for my first shot. When the gun went off both middle birds folded. I moved to the left bird and dropped it. I still had not heard Elton fire so, thinking he had a gun problem I drew a bead on the last bird. Just as I was pulling the trigger, he folded the bird in front of my shot. Elton told me he didn't think that I was going to let him shoot, to which I replied that I thought his gun was broken when he didn't shoot at first.

In just a few minutes I dropped two Gadwalls with two shots. I had worked so hard and walked so far and in five minutes I had my limit and should stop shooting which I didn't. This was one of the few times that I did not follow the duck regulations (I hope the Statute of Limitations has expired). I had way more than the limit of ducks stuffed in my decoy bag as we left worrying that the game wardens would catch us before we could get in the vehicles.

We had no goose season for a long time and would see some Canadians and some Blue Geese and Snow Geese, but never were allowed to hunt them legally. One day on the way out to visit another friend, who was also named Billy, I spotted some Canadians in a pond near his house. I knew that he had a Mossberg 500 in 3-inch magnum and I knew he had some 3-inch, number 2's so I hurried to his house and borrowed the gun and shells. When I made it back to the pond half expected them to be gone but they were still there feeding on the grass at the pond dam. Sneaking within range, I raised up and fired at one of them which had seen me and was taking off. I hit him but he kept going, so I placed two more into him and he stopped. When I reached him, the tough old bird was still alive and I had to dispatch him with a lightered knot. He was a beautiful bird weighing over twenty pounds. I put him in the floor of my Ford LTD and quickly drove back to town to show him to Bobby, who had shown me a beautiful Mallard drake that he had killed the day before. I lied and told Bobby that I had killed some kind of duck and I wanted him to identify it. When he looked in the floor he said, "Bill! You sorry so and so! Are you trying to outdo me?" I was!!!

Once I had my friend Bruce with me in the sound. It was a beautiful day for hunting. We were backed up into the marsh grass and were waiting on the ducks. Bruce began to ask me what we might see. I told him that we might see gators, wild hogs, porpoises and lots of waterfowl. "Do you ever see any geese?" he asked. I said that we did sometimes but we could not shoot them. I had not gotten the words out of my mouth, when I looked over St. Simons Island and saw a flock of geese. I watched as the geese drew nearer and realized that they were coming to our decoys. They passed over at about one hundred and fifty yards high and I cut loose with the call. Quack! Quack! Quack! They turned and came back this time passing over at about one hundred yards high. I pleaded to them with the duck call, and they turned once more and came over at about seventy-five or eighty yards. One more time I begged them with a Come Back call. They turned one more time and were about forty yards as they approached us. "Shoot 'em! Shoot 'em! Shoot 'em!" I cried and Bruce and I emptied our guns bringing only feathers.

We watched as they flew away and Bruce asked, "Why did we shoot them if we weren't supposed to"

"I just couldn't stand it anymore," I replied hanging my head in shame.

Louisiana Goose Hunters

There was one second season, that came around Thanksgiving when I took off from work and went to the sound every day whether the tide was right or not. Daddy had to work some so he could not go every day. I sought out my other hunting buddies to accompany me. On one such hunting trip, my cousin Lewis was with me. We had hunted for ducks in the creeks and ponds together but he had never tried the coast. We launched the "SS Pond Squaggin" and made our way down the Altamaha to the sound. We set out decoys and raised up the sides of the "Squaggin's" built-on blind. We were sitting there looking over the sound and the beautiful marsh (The same ones that Sidney Lanier wrote about in the Marshes of Glynn). Suddenly, from my left, I saw ducks. I did not have time to alert Lewis, I just quickly raised my shotgun and fired. Blam! Blam! Blam! Splash! Splash! Splash! They hit the water just to the right of the boat.

Lewis was surprised and looked startled. "Where did they come from?" he asked.

158

`"They just popped up on my right and I shot." I replied. Then I noticed they were Hooded Mergansers, Fish Ducks. Crap!

Lewis asked if we were going to retrieve them and I said that they weren't going anywhere, we'd get them later (hoping something would eat them or they would drift out in the Atlantic Ocean). Then he asked what the limit on them and I said one per day. I had just put three days limit on the water, without knowing what they were before shooting. It takes very good duck hunter to be able to identify the ducks unless they are out front in the decoys and you have watched them for a while. Most hunters have to "brown check" them for identification purposes. I've always been too good a "Reaction Shooter" for my own good.

———————————

Roy and I liked to hunt Butler Island which is run by the Georgia DNR. They have Saturday morning shoots, which you must place an application for and get picked for that date. All the people never come so you could sign up as standby, and if they weren't full, you could draw a blind. We always had a backup to hunt on Champney Island, another DNR island in the Altamaha Delta that did not require a permit so we had our boat. All you needed for Butler was gun, decoys, "Possibles Bag" and waders. You could take 25 shells in and that was all. They had some decoys at the blinds but they were ugly and the ducks were used to them, so we took our own. They had a trailer pulled by a truck that looked like the old plantation hunts. They would drop you off at your area before daylight and would return at noon to get you. If you got tired of waiting you could walk back to the check station. I never did. You can always take a needed nap on the dike while you waited, since you would leave Baxley at 3:00 am so as to get there in time. Sometimes there would be six of us from home there on standby. When you were dropped off there was a boat that you

159

could use to cross the deep canal that rimmed the rice fields of the old rice plantation, that the Butler family owned before the War for Southern Independence. Once across the canal you could either use the blind built by the DNR folks or find a place more to your liking. I learned that the ducks knew where the blinds were so the best thing to do was find another location. You could not stray out of your area because deep canals bordered each area tying into the rim canal. You would then set the decoys up and wait for first light. There was the initial flight in the morning, which would last about an hour. Then stragglers would fly around until the "9 o'clock flight" of returning birds arrived after their feeding. On good, stormy days stragglers would fly around all morning, but on sunny days a hunter was relegated to the two flights.

Roy and I were hunting on a little tusset in our area with about twelve trees on it. We had killed our limit and were fooling around waiting for the morning to be over when we spotted a Wood Duck in the distance. I began to call and it turned coming our way. As it flew past, we did not shoot. I called again and turned the duck one more time. This time he passed closer to us but would not land in the decoys. When he passed, I began a feeding chuckle and it sharply turned coming right back to us a third time. Suddenly Roy and I could stand it no longer. We both raised up and shot dropping the bird. Then we looked at each other knowing we had to take our ducks through the check station to be counted, identified and checked. We searched through our bag and found a less desirable duck and gave him a proper burial, replacing him with the prized and tasty Wood Duck.

We hoped that the DNR folks weren't on the dike as they sometimes were with binoculars and were not counting. We would have been in trouble.

Once I was having my ducks checked out by a cute new DNR Wildlife Biologist girl. She must have been fresh out of college. As she went through my ducks she miss-identified one which was a Redhead hen. She called it a Ringneck hen. I asked her to look at the duck closer. The only noticeable difference is a tan streak around the base of the bill. She was adamant that she had correctly identified the duck when Gene (Who was over all the DNR activities there in the Altamaha delta) stepped up to say hello to me. Gene and I go way back to my beginnings of Coastal Hunting. I asked him to identify the duck. He looked at the bill and said it was a Redhead hen. The girl looked embarrassed that her boss had corrected her but hopefully learned. The limit on Ringneck was 5 a day. The limit on Redhead was 1 a day. Although I sometimes cannot tell what they are when flying over, once I ground checked I knew what they were. One man captured at Two Way had five Redhead hens thinking they were Ringnecks. He was in "Mucho Trouble".

I have taken every species that flies on the Atlantic Flyway except for one. Let me tell you that story. Bart had Weyman with him in the "Turkey" and I had Jackie with me in the "Squaggin". We were well hidden and our decoys were looking good when I heard the loudest whistling of duck wings I had ever heard. I looked past Jackie on the right and saw two ducks headed our way. They were a long way off but had to be Goldeneyes which are also called "Whistlers." I waited patiently as they approached my decoys for them to come in range. All of a sudden when they were about 60 yards away Jackie raised up his Remington 1100 magnum and began firing. Even though I knew they were out of range I joined him. The birds gained altitude and made their escape.

161

Bart's voice boomed across the marsh. "Why did you shoot them? They were out of range!!"

Jackie responded "They were in the range of my Mag-A-Num"

Bart's voice boomed back across the water "Why didn't they fall then?"

That was the only shot I ever had at a Goldeneye. Goldeneye was the only duck that flies the Atlantic Flyway I haven't taken.

I have made three trips to Louisiana to "Shot de Duck" as Justin Wilson would say. The first was with my friend Jack. We had purchased a three-day hunt at a Ducks Unlimited banquet. We packed our stuff and decided to take Jack's dog, Jake, with us and leave my Buck at home. We figured that the two dogs together might present a problem. We took Jack's pickup which was almost identical to mine with his being dark green and mine was black. They were both Ford F 150's with four-wheel drive. We loaded all of our gear and Jake in the back of the pickup which was equipped with a canopy. The other two friends that were with us had made a pile of venison jerky and they gave us several bags. We decided that since we were going to Jones in North Louisiana, we would do best by going to Atlanta via I 16 and I 75 and take I 20 to the West through Montgomery. Jack started by driving the first leg, and I caught a nap to prepare myself to drive the second leg. I slept a while and then began eating jerky. It was salty but good. When we stopped for fuel in Montgomery, I told Jack that I was ready to drive. He then informed me that he did not like riding, with someone else driving, so if I didn't mind, he would continue to drive. I did not object so he drove until somewhere in Mississippi where we got a motel room for the night.

The next morning, he again drove. When we made it to Jones and located the duck camp, we found them cooking a "Cochon De Lait" (a big hog hanging head down on a slow-moving rotisserie). They had the big hog cooking with an oak fire and a big metal reflector. We ate that hog for three days along with rice and beans Louisiana style.

They showed us to our sleeping quarters, which was a metal prefab building with no insulation. We had been told to bring electric heaters with us, which was a good idea since it was 13 degrees when we got there and stayed 13 degrees for the whole three days. The only time that I was warm for the three days was when I was in my goose down sleeping bag. Jack put Jake in the bed with him to keep warm. It was cold cloudy and stormy, perfect weather for the Altamaha Sound. I was excited the next morning as we awakened and prepared for the day. We were up at three o'clock getting dressed and eating breakfast. We loaded our thermoses with hot, dark and strong coffee and headed out. It had been raining and the guide had us stop the pickups over a mile from the hunting area. He informed us that if we tried to drive in the "Gumbo" mud, that it would build-up on our tires and tear our fender struts off the pickup. The guide loaded all four of us on his Honda four-wheeler along with our gear and drove us to the blind with Jake trailing along. When we got to the blind, which was like a dumpster buried in the dike of the rice field, we disembarked and began to climb down into the "dumpster' which was ankle deep in "Ice Water". The decoys were in place but were frozen in the water in the rice field. While we got ready the guide drove the four-wheeler around in the decoys breaking the ice around them so they would look more natural. The guide hid the Honda and came back to the blind.   The blind was deep enough to cause me at 5 foot 8 inches some difficulty in shooting, but we managed to take some ducks. The first one that we shot down behind us Jack sent Jake to retrieve. Jake was not familiar with "Ice Skating" but he soon learned about it. He was no Peggy Fleming but he got the hang of it after sliding all over when turning and stopping.   I wished that I had a movie camera that morning, to film Jake.

We hunted the three days with some success but were informed the "Bluebird" weather produced more ducks and that when it was messy the ducks would fly to the Mississippi.   It would rain a while and the freezing rain would freeze immediately upon hitting the metal of the gun. Then it would snow awhile and then sleet a while. The shotguns would freeze up and would not eject the first shell because of the ice on the action.   After they were warmed by the first shot, they would work better. I was shooting my Remington 11-87 in 3-inch magnum with steel shot and after that trip I acquired and 870 Remington Express for a back-up gun because a pump would cycle better than an autoloader in severe cold and wet conditions.

I brought back ducks and a terrific case of heartburn from the jerky and the hot beans and rice Louisiana Style. The cold messy weather followed us home and turned into a six-inch snowstorm. That was a "White Christmas" in Baxley, Georgia. I worked almost all Christmas trying to keep the highways clear. It stopped late Christmas Eve.

A Limit Of Big Ducks

Best Hunt In Louisiana

Another trip to Louisiana was with my son Billy and a friend Jeff. This trip was to South Louisiana at Lake Charles. We had been in contact with our guide Mark and his wife Cippi. We were guaranteed plenty of Cajun food. I asked Cippi if I needed to bring all my indigestion medicine, remembering the first trip to Louisiana. Cippi told me, "It ain't got to be hot to be Spicy". She was right. I ate her cooking for the whole time without any indigestion or heartburn. When we arrived at the lodge, we unloaded our gear and were called to supper (it might be Dinner in other places but to us Southerners it is Supper). We sat down and she placed a large plate of Et Tu Fay in our front with (I counted them) seventy-five hulled crayfish and a dozen large Gulf shrimp around the outside of the plate. Knowing immediately that I could not eat all of it, I concentrated on the Shrimp and Crayfish. Billy and Jeff did not use this approach and when she sat down a chunk of milk chocolate layer cake, they had to push their plate aside to eat the cake. We later learned that Cippi baked cakes for several restaurants every day.

The next morning, we were to the blind early, and we settled in for the morning. I offered to help Mark call but he declined the help. The weather was cloudy, raining and perfect for the Altamaha Sound but not for North Louisiana, so I wondered how well we would do. The first three ducks Mark called in were three Pintail drakes and at the signal, we dropped them all. Next came a flock of Mallards and we took three of them (I made sure I shot a drake). For the next hour or so Mark called the ducks and we dispatched them. We let lesser ducks like Shovelers (Poor Man's Mallards) go unharmed. I concentrated on Mallard Drakes and when Mark called in two Blue Winged Teal, I stayed in my seat in the "dumpster' (yes, we were in another dumpster buried in a dike.) Billy and Jeff stood up and took them. Earlier Jeff and I had some shots on the right of the blind, where Billy could not shoot, and I told him to let Billy shoot the next bird alone if it was in front. In no time Mark had a Mallard drake bearing in directly in front of the blind. When he said to shoot, we let Billy have him.

Billy later said that when he saw we had stayed down on our seats, that he thought "'Oh! My gosh! What if I miss?" He didn't. He smoked the bird right in front. At first, Mark would bring his gun up, if we needed help. When he decided we did not need help, he began asking if we shot skeet and other questions about our shooting. Then he got out his cell phone and began calling all his guide buddies, telling them that we had Pintails, Mallards, and Teal. When we had the limit, "3 Pintail drakes, 2 Blue Winged Teal drakes, and 13 Mallards, mostly drakes" was what he was telling all of them.

He took pictures, which the last time I looked on his website, they were still on it.

Upon returning to the lodge Cippi had jambalaya waiting for us. As she served the lunch she remarked. "You all shot good today!" to which I replied that I had shot better. "No, you must have really shot good!" she said, "Mark usually comes home fussing that his clients cannot hit anything and he told me that you three did not miss a duck!"

It was one of my top five days of duck hunting ever. My six ducks were a Pintail drake and five Mallard drakes.

Billy and I hunted Geese that afternoon with Mark's partner Frank. Frank actually let me call ducks. We had a great time on that trip and brought a load of ducks home and I killed my first Speckled Belly Goose. The next day I shot a Mallard drake that fell like he was a dishrag when I folded him. He fell on top of a decoy with a thud! I turned and shot a second drake down and when I turned back, I saw my first drake flying low over the water in an attempt to escape. Mark sent his Labrador but when the dog reached the cross dike with bushes growing up, she stopped. It looked to me that the duck dropped just past the cross dike. My old lab Buck would not have come back without that duck. Quit was not in him.

We went back with another group which included three more boys Billy's age. Mark was to guide us again and we had three blinds full. Mark, since I had told him that I was having difficulty walking, drove me to the blinds on a four-wheeler, with the most aggressive tires I have ever seen. I believe that sometimes we were driving on water and those tires were supporting us like a raft. Again, we had a good hunt with two or three incidents standing out in my memory.

The first was a goose that everyone shot and although loaded down with shot he flew at least half a mile low to the water, which is a good indication that it was hit hard. If we could have used lead shot, the goose would have probably dropped right there. When we came out at lunch, we looked all over for that rascal with no luck.

The second was when I was in the blind with two of my friends, Frank was our guide and I was beside him with the two others to the left.   We had taken several ducks that morning, and Frank had another one coming from our left. The duck was coming almost directly over us a little to the front. As he came into range the others emptied their guns and the bird did not even shed a feather nor even wiggle a little bit. As soon as it cleared them where I could, I shot once directly behind the last of their shots and the duck folded. The two of them were both trying to claim they killed it and were arguing with each other about it, when I looked around at Frank, and he smiled and pointed his finger at me indicating that he too knew who killed that duck.

The third is when the four boys went with one of the guides to a dike with cover where we had seen several geese fly over unmolested. The guide and the boys were lying on their bellies on the dike when a small flight of geese headed toward their position. Their guide began to call and the geese began to lose altitude heading toward them. The geese kept dropping as we watched. When they were in the right position, the boys emptied their guns and all of the geese fell almost on top of them. Suddenly the four boys were on their feet jumping up and down and hollering to the top of their lungs. I saw one of them the other day and he began to reminisce about the hunt and that incident.

The best duck load I ever used was a reload. 3 ½ dram 1 ¼ ounce of number five lead shot. That load would dispatch a duck with one shot and dishrag him, if within range. Most of the ducks we took over the decoys were at about 20 to 30 yards. We set out decoys and what I called a flat diamond cat eye shape with two landing holes at around 25 yards. If they intended to land in the two openings and hit the flaps and drop the landing gear, they would be dishragged. (the term dishrag indicates he will stop dead still in the air and drop like a rock). The decoys were set with range decoys left, right and center where the deranged was approximately 45 yards. Any duck within the decoy set was in serious trouble.

A few years ago, when I turned 70, I retired from duck hunting. Then I had two 12 gauge Beretta 390 camo duck guns. I have only been able to hunt doves with mine but I wonder how great it would have been in the duck blind. I gave the other one to my son Billy and maybe he'll get a chance to put it to good use. I might have one more trip to Louisiana left in this old body.

Billy's First Squirrel

CHAPTER EIGHT

SQUIRREL HUNTING

I began my long life of hunting by chasing the little bushytailed gray things we call cat squirrels around here. My first recollection is going with my father and hunting in the branches and drains in this area. I remember he hunted with a 16 gauge double-barrel shotgun which was all he owned at the time. I can remember the crunch of the leaves under our feet, as we walked along together. I remember he had a sewn shell bag/game bag. His mother and Aunt were professional seamstresses, and as a young boy, he learned how to sew so I am sure he made this bag back then.   I can still see it was a blue color and the material seemed to be that of a work shirt. In a little pouch in it he had a nail on a string with a cloth tied on the end that was used to clean the bore of the shotgun after using it. By the way, he used that ability to sew to make hunting gear for both of us, including camo vests, camo shirts and camo clothes, some of which I still use. As we walked through those drains and branches, when he would spot a squirrel, we would begin to use stealth, in order to get close enough for a shot. I learned to lag behind the him and be careful as I could and not make noise that would frighten the squirrel away. He was a pretty good shot and most of the time we brought quite a bit of meat home to be prepared for the next meal. We quite often dined on a repast of fried squirrel served with grits and light brown gravy that my grandmother specialized in. I remember one morning we were making our way through the woods and I started to step across the log.

My father said, "Hold it right there." I froze and then saw the coiled cottonmouth moccasin just on the other side of the log. My father got into position and shortly, the moccasin was no more. We shared many good times in the woods as we hunted for the squirrels.

On one occasion, since I have been asking to shoot the double barrel, he said that I could. I was about five years old. I aimed at a pine and pulled both triggers at the same time. I thought the recall had driven me into the dirt and had broken my shoulder.

It was a long time before I wanted to shoot a large bore shotgun again. I was satisfied with a .410 single shot.

Uncle Jesse and Grady operated a quail preserve near Dunn's Lake. Dignitaries associated with Filtered Rosin Company would come and they would hunt quail on the preserve. The preserve was laid with squirrels. Uncle Jesse would give me a box of 22's and the pump 22 rifle he owned and turn me loose on the preserve. I could easily bag a limit with that little pump. Those ridges were loaded with squirrels.

As I got older, I would go to my cousin Ronnie's house in the country. We would use his .22 semi-automatic Winchester rifle and attempted to bag the squirrels that were raiding pecans from "Uncle Red's" orchard. And that would please "Uncle Red" because those gray squirrels could tote quite a few pecans off in the fall. Although my mother was not fond of the idea of me owning a gun, and even went as far as to nix the Christmas present that my father's company gave to all the boys my age (a BB gun), because of her objection. Nevertheless, when I turned 16, I got a Remington Nylon 66 for Christmas. Mother must have finally relented. I know that I shot at least 100,000 rounds through it because of two reasons. Number one, when I mowed grass, I would go to Ace Hardware and buy a 500 pack of bullets every week. The second reason was that "The Rifleman" was on TV and I practiced shooting that old Nylon 66 from the hip. Most of the time, I would empty the complete 15 round magazine almost as fast as I could pull the trigger. I got to the point where I was extremely accurate from the hip and could place a plastic Clorox jug out into Cainey (Icebox as we called it) creek in front of me and put all 15 rounds in it as fast as I could pull the trigger making it dance down the creek. I also saved up my money and purchased a Weaver D4 scope and mounted it on the dovetails on the rifle. I sighted it in and became a pretty good shot using a scope. I would pride myself in being able to judge distance and adjust my hold. All the shooting with the Nylon 66 made me an excellent rifleman.

I would pride myself in being able to judge distance and adjust my hold to cause my impact point to be on target. This was called "Kentucky Windage". The only trouble was that I brought some squirrels home where my bullet had damaged some of the meat because I had shot in the shoulder. My grandma, Minnie, scolded me severely about messing up the meat. It seemed my grandmother raised the family during the depression and I know for a fact had Scottish ancestors (McKenzie) on her side, because she was very frugal about food. I've often made the statement that if a dog planned on living on what she threw out the backdoor, he might as well learn how to eat leaves, sticks, and grass because she didn't throw anything out. You would get a couple or three opportunities to eat what she cooked in its original form and then if you didn't, it would come to you disguised in what we used to call "Minnie's Goulash". You would not recognize it but you would, in fact, eat it so it wouldn't be thrown away. She stayed on my case enough about not messing up any meat until I got really proficient with that rifle.

We used to hunt with Ronnie's dog, Missey. She was one half July Hound and one-half Collie. She looked like a Collie. She was the second-best squirrel hunting dog that I ever encountered. She was efficient and I was tickled when I got the only puppy that she ever had that looked like her, Sam. Although Sam was a beautiful dog, he wasn't worth a flip for squirrel hunting. I believe it's because he took after his daddy who was one half Chow and one half German Shepherd but looked and acted like a wolf. Sam was one of my favorite dogs to own. He would not eat dog food

174

but traveled around town, getting fed scraps from restaurants and butchers around town. He loved to visit the school close to the house for feeding by the school children at the school. He would come home missing his collar after a trip to the school. When the city voted in a collar ordinance I went to the Chief of Police, Mr. Johnny, to avoid him being captured and put down.

Mister Johnny said, "Beau, we all know Sam and would never do that to him."

I guess he was the town dog.

When he was a puppy, the neighbor's dog Chubby (Chow and Cocker Spaniel) took him in tow like his son. Chubby was the fightingest dog I ever saw. He fathered all the puppies on our side of town and killed several bad dogs that tried to horn in on his territory. My neighbor had him fixed to stop that. The only trouble was he loved fighting and would still whip all the males competing for the female. He would then turn her over to Sam to breed. When Chubby died I was afraid for Sam, who I had never seen fight. When the competition occurred, he fought just like Chubby who would seem to cower away and suddenly turn back and grab the other dog by the throat. Sam learned from the Master.

The best squirrel hunting dog by far that I ever encountered was "old Snooper". Snooper was a Feist dog and hung around the place owned by Mister Seeb. We could pull up in the front yard and park by the gigantic oak tree there in the corner. Before we could get our guns out, Snooper would have a squirrel treed. He would watch the squirrel and would not leave the tree until you shot him out. If the squirrel moved to another tree, Snooper would follow. He would run and bite the squirrel on the head to dispatch him and bring him to you.

I hunted with my cousin, Ronnie, every chance I got. We had several "honey holes" where we could be assured that there would be an abundance of squirrels. There were some places where as soon as we would pull-up, the squirrels would take off. We would have to intercept them before they got to the woods. We had a great time together but when he went off to college is when his little brother Billy started to go hunting with me.

We would go to the river and hunt in the swamp just downriver from Iron Mine Bluff. There was a superabundance of squirrels there and we would get the limit almost every time we went. The only downside to hunting there was that Mr. Woods, who owned the property, did not allow rifles so we had to take shotguns. It was probably a good thing though, because those were the wildest squirrels I ever encountered. We never got a shot at one sitting still because they were always on the move through the treetops and I guess a scattergun was the only way to take them. We would camp there on the bluff and then at the crack of day, we would be lying in wait for the squirrels to wake up. Lots of times we would stay there more than one day so we would cook and dine upon those squirrels by roasting them over coals. They were delicious.

On one occasion we were sitting by the fire when we heard a bobcat squalling. As the sound got closer, we piled more wood on the fire. They got close enough that we set back-to-back with our shotguns on our laps for protection.

I am sure that there is no better training for a young person than to begin hunting for squirrels. There does not seem to be enough of that going on now because the squirrels carry off all my pecans. I need to find some young folks who would like to learn how to hunt and let them practice here around my pecan trees.

My mother loved to eat squirrels as good as anyone I have ever known. She and her neighbor, Mrs. Carter, on one occasion had a squirrel the neighbor had killed out of her yard. Instead of waiting for my son Billy to get out of school or waiting for me to get off work, they made the decision that they could clean that squirrel. They told the story of how they pulled one another all around the yard trying to get the skin off that critter. I am positive if we had a video of that incident, we could've won America's Funniest Videos, hands down. They would get together and talk about that incident and just have the most fun reminiscing how it happened. Those two independent ladies could've just waited three hours and it would've been done for them by either Billy or me. But, they wanted to have that fried squirrel for a lunch and did want to wait to have it that night for supper, ergo the tug of war in mother's yard.

One of my old friends who had 95 pecan trees around his house would entice my son Billy to go visit and to be a "Control Hunter" for him. Billy loved to go out there to accommodate Lamar, because squirrels were everywhere. Billy had a little .410 single-shot youth gun and he became quite deadly with it. His reputation spread far and wide amongst the squirrel community so they tried to avoid him at all costs. I am sure that those early squirrel hunting experiences are the reason he became such a good deer hunter to this day.

There was a time when we would not take a fox squirrel. I'm not sure whether we had heard it was against the law, or whether it was because they were so beautiful and in such various forms of color. I have seen them that were jet black. I've seen red ones, tan ones, brown ones, and even gray ones. I have seen quite a few that had bandit masks on them like unto a raccoon. Nevertheless, we avoided taking them on most occasions. We also found that they were a little tough to chew so that also added to our avoidance of them. We had quite a bit of original longleaf pine trees growing in our area which makes a perfect habitat for the fox squirrels. They eat quite a bit of pine mast which is the seeds of a pine tree. You can be standing under a tree when they were having lunch and it will rain down pieces of pinecone on your head. They can work on a pinecone and in short order reducing it to nothing but the skeleton.

Another great way to prepare squirrel, especially if you have an older tougher squirrel, is squirrel and rice. This is a delicacy in the South and the other day when these stars of "Swamp People" were at the gun show in Savannah, as a draw, they asked a friend of mine if he knew of any restaurant where they could get some squirrel and rice. He scratched his head and told of them he did not know of any restaurant that served it, but he had lots of friends that prepared it but they were about 100 miles away from Savannah, Georgia. I don't know what they had that night, but I'm sure it most likely was not squirrel and rice and I'm not sure whether they were serious or they were pulling his leg.

High Bluff River Buck

CHAPTER NINE

DOGS AND DOG TRAINING

My grandfather on my mother's side was an excellent wing shot. His reputation as a quail hunter was well known in our section of the state. He trained bird dogs and often entertained hunters from Atlanta and other parts. My grandmother used to tell me stories of the marsh hens, ducks, doves, and quail that he brought in for her to prepare. My mother and uncle said that they had so many quail in the "icebox" that they would sometimes spoil, because they could not eat them up fast enough. They also related stories of them only eating the drumsticks and thighs of the quail dipping them into cane syrup.

179

By the time that I was old enough to enjoy hunting, he was too old to share his talent with me. He raised his nephew and passed on the desire and ability to train dogs and hunt quail. Uncle Jesse, as I call him was one of the best dog trainers and field trial handlers in the south and produced some of the best pointing dogs in South Georgia.

I tried my hand at training Brittany Spaniels, one of which was from the fine pair of Brittanys that Uncle Jesse owned and trained. They were as good a pair of quail dogs as could be found anywhere. For a period of time, they probably had more liberated birds shot over them than any other pair of dogs in the state of Georgia. My first pup was a little female named Annie. She was smart and quick to learn. When she died at ten months old, she was well on her way to becoming a fine bird dog. I had started her in training to be a pointing dog and she caught on so fast. Then I changed over and tried to train her to retrieve, which she quickly learned. I had just a couple of weeks earlier turned down a handsome price for her only to have her die of distemper.

My next Brittany was Baron. He was also a quick learner but was not adapted to retrieving. One day when I had finished working with Baron, I flipped my fishing pole, which had the bag of quail feathers attached to it, into the bush where I kept it. It slipped out and fell to the ground at the base of the bush. Baron started toward the bush and I commanded him.

"Whoa! Whoa!" He froze in a point, locked up as pretty as a picture.

Suddenly something moved at the base of the bush. In a flash, Baron snapped and caught a small mouse. I heard it squeak and then he gulped it down. My Gosh! I had trained a "MOUSE DOG".

Later I began to train retrieving dogs to "fetch" the birds for me. Buck was my Chocolate Labrador Retriever male, High Bluff River Buck to be exact. He was a large-framed dog descended from a long line of field trial champions. When he was a puppy, I had doubts about his future as a retriever, because he had no interest in "fetching" anything. Although he was a very obedient pup, he would not even attempt to fetch anything. By the time he was six months old I was almost resolved that I would need to get another dog for retrieving birds because of his lack of interest in retrieving. Suddenly after he turned six months old it was like a switch went off inside him and he turned into an insatiable fetching machine. From that time on, he never got enough of fetching objects. For the most part, when I hunted him in a dove field and had to leave for any reason, I would have to snap a lead on him, because he did not want to leave if birds were still flying and shotguns were going off. He would run over and adopt another hunter so that he could keep on hunting.

I began to train Buck and when he was about a year old, I started going to isolated fields to attempt to shoot a few birds for him to fetch. Usually, it would be just Buck and I in the field. Later, I went with my cousin Henry, so that I could work Buck. Finally, one day the two of us went along with two dogs to a small field to shoot some birds and work the dogs. The hardest thing to control in Buck early was his desire to jump when the gun went off and go after the bird immediately. To correct that action, I bought a belt-lead that was six feet long and attaches to your belt on a web loop. I am a big man and I was sure that I could hold an anxious dog back. This would facilitate my releasing him on the command to fetch and would reinforce the command to stay. I was shooting a lightweight pump, because it had a sling and could be carried on my shoulder if necessary. The only problem was that it did not shoot like the autoloaders that I usually hunted with and could not shoot it as well.

Buck Sit

When the bird flew over, I fired and missed. While I was shucking the pump for the second shot, Buck lunged forward with such force that my feet left the ground as I was firing the second shot. It goes without saying that I missed the second shot also.

I was training Buck and my son, Billy at the same time. I would have Buck heeled up on my left and Billy on a dove stool with his BB gun on my right. I remember the first full-blown dove shoot that I took both of them to. Daylight was just cracking and a hawk flew straight down the field toward us. Both Buck and Billy watched him as he approached and then disappeared over our heads into the branch. Then after following his flight to conclusion, they both looked back at me as if to ask. "Why didn't you shoot it?" I am embarrassed that although I was able to teach Billy the difference between Doves, Ducks and Dippers (as my friend Bobby would call them) I never could teach Buck the difference. Buck was 50 percent eyes and 50 percent nose and he watched the sky constantly for birds in flight. I always intended to teach him to face behind us because when he saw a bird his ears would perk up and I knew some kind of bird was flying. I taught him the command "Mark" which would also cause him to react with perked ears. If I pushed the safety off on my shotgun the ears would perk and he would look to see the bird that he missed seeing.

Bill Casting Buck

Buck was the dog of a lifetime. He was my constant hunting companion for 13 years and during that time I never lost a dove. Buck was not perfect but I most likely will never have another near to what he was. He had some faults. He would get too excited sometimes, but he had the fire to be a Field Trial Champion had I been able to afford it.

I had taught him 59 commands, voice, whistle, and hand signals. The reason we stopped at 59 was that I could not think of any more to teach him. I used him to perform many demonstrations at outdoor shows, schools, and events around. Buck would retrieve up to 10 dummies tossed out in the order I asked him to. I could stop him three steps from a dummy and bring him partially back, then send him left or right, stopping him on the line of another dummy and then send him to retrieve that dummy. His ability to perform like this helped to market the puppies he fathered. Once we had two prospective buyers for a litter that my female Ash had with Buck being the sire. They came into the back yard to the kennel to see the pups. They asked if Buck was the sire and I proceeded to demonstrate Buck's ability. I threw five dummies all over the back yard and began to send him and cast him for retrieves. Ash, who did not like to leave fecal droppings in her kennel, had a certain place, in the fenced-in area, that she frequented and had been there earlier. I did not notice that I had thrown one of the dummies right square into the fresh droppings. When Buck got to the dummy, he noticed what it was in. He reached with his paw and rolled it out of the droppings and then caught hold of the throw rope which had not been soiled and brought the dummy to me. The prospective customers upon seeing this exclaimed that they both wanted a puppy from Buck because he was smart enough to do what he had just done.

On one occasion I let the local game warden, which I had grown up with and was a good friend, ride with me to a dove shoot. I positioned myself about 35 yards from a pecan tree and a friend of mine's son was directly opposite the tree. Early in the morning, someone shot a bird and it flew too low for anyone to shoot. It landed on a deadfall limb under the pecan tree. I noticed that Buck had "Locked In" on the bird. Thinking that he would cause the bird to get up high enough for one of us to get a shot, I told him to fetch. Buck covered those 35 yards in a flash and leaving his feet took the bird off the limb and brought it back to me. My friend's son squealed with delight. Later that morning Buck's brother, Moose, came across the field chasing a low flying bird that was crippled. Moose was not nearly as fast as his brother and Buck was watching the approaching dog and bird competition. I commanded Buck to fetch as they neared. Buck overtook Moose quickly passing him like a relay runner. After passing Moose, Buck closed in on the low flying bird and leaped into the air catching the bird (Buck did this 20 times or more in his life leaping to catch a cripple). Buck brought the bird to me which I had to dispatch like the first one. When the birds quit flying, we all gathered to leave. I had killed 10 and had the two that Buck had caught. I told the warden, James, that I had 10 and Buck had 2 toward his limit so I was going to kill 2 more. He doubted my story and told me so but my friend's son, Art, told James that it was the truth that I never shot at either bird that Buck caught. It did not matter to James and he did not relent.

Another bad habit that Buck had was stealing other people's birds out of their stool or vest. He almost got into trouble with some friends who thought that I had taught him to do that too. He also did not want to leave if the birds were still flying and hunters were shooting. If I did not snap a lead on him, he would adopt one of my friends. He would heel by them and would not go until they sent him but would only bring the birds to me.

Ash did not like the feathers coming off the dove into her mouth. Unlike ducks and quail, dove feathers come off easily in the dog's mouth. The first dove I sent Ash to retrieve she quickly expelled from her mouth and began to make this spitting motion to rid her mouth of feathers. I went to her and talked bad to her putting the bird in her mouth, closing my hand around her mouth and saying "fetch." She looked at me with disdain but never spit another bird out although she would still spit the feathers until I cleaned her mouth out. Buck, on the other hand, was never bothered by the feathers and would have a wad, like chewing tobacco, in his jowls until I could no longer stand it and would clean them out.

On two occasions Buck swallowed birds but quickly expelled them. Once he was retrieving the bird to me and his nose ran square into an electric fence wire which caused him to gulp and swallow the bird. He coughed it up when he got to me. Another time my cousin, Jeffery, went to grab a bird from him as he came through a hole in the fence. Not wanting to give the bird to anyone but me, he swallowed the bird then came to me and coughed it up for me. He looked proud of what he had done. These were a little revolting but caused no harm.

Buck did not like to be left in the kennel or the box and would pitch a fit to come with me. If he saw me come out of the house and go toward the truck with a long gun, he would bark incessantly, even at 4:00 in the morning to the neighbor's dismay.

Buck on Water Retrieve

I have tried in recent years to train two labs that I have. The first, Beau, is as smart of a dog as I've ever seen. Along with that trait came the fact he was the hard-headiest dog I have ever seen. My attempts to train him had become a dismal failure, although he came from fantastic bloodlines, he had just become Deloris' pet. The second, Daisy, came from super bloodlines too and was pretty well trained other than I was not physically able to get out and work her as I should. She also was a little gun shy when she was young. She had gotten over that and if I had been able to get out and work her, I'm sure she would have made an excellent retriever. After that time, both became just consumers of dog food.

Brittany Spaniel - Windy Ridge Baron

CHAPTER TEN

QUAIL HUNTING

Quail hunting in South Georgia is not what it used to be. Several factors will come into play:

1. People are not burning their woods like they used to.

2. Farmers taking down fences and clearing up fence rows.

3. Herbicides for soybeans (I believe).

4. Predators like feral house cats and the re-introduction of coyotes.

Although we have some quail on our farm there are not enough quail to hunt. I have hunted wild Bobwhites and they were great fun. Now if you hunt quail, you most likely have to go to a plantation and hunt released birds.

Back in my grandfather's day, it was different. I remember stories that my grandmother told of granddaddy picking her and the dog up in the family car after work and driving out into the country. Grandmother said that she would sit and tatt (Tatting is a technique for handcrafting a particularly durable lace constructed by a series of knots and loops) which she was an expert at, while granddaddy would hunt quail. She said that he would never get out of sight and would kill 35 to 45 quail an afternoon AFTER WORK. It is almost unbelievable at that kind of proficiency.

Uncle Jesse said that "Uncle Leslie", my grandfather, would kill five on a covey rise consistently. He shot a Remington Model 11 20 gauge (without a plug) and sometimes shot a pump (a Winchester model 12). He related a story where he was home on leave from the U. S. Navy, they went to the Graham farm to hunt. He said that a large covey got up and he fired five times knocking down five birds.

"Uncle Leslie! Uncle Leslie!", he exclaimed." I got five out of that covey."

"Where are your five?" granddaddy asked.

"They are to the right of the fence." Uncle Jesse stated proudly.

"Good," Granddaddy answered, "My five are to the left of the fence."

Granddaddy always told me that there was a cross in every covey rise if you could spot it and you could get two with the first shot. I am doing well to get on birds when the covey lifts off much less look for two to shoot with one shot. Now I have killed three on the rise with three shots and have killed two with one shot (accidentally) before.

It is hard to find any wild game that tastes as good as, South Georgia, fried quail. They are delicious and especially if you can get hold of original South Georgia Bobwhite Quail. The Bobwhite Quail used to be all over these parts and is what most of our grandfather's generation hunted. Later as the Bobwhites seem to get scarce people introduced a small subspecies of Mexican quail. The only problem with the Mexican quail is that instead of flying a short distance and going back down to the ground like the Bobwhites, they fly forever. The first covey I ever got up flew all the way across the 200-acre field before landing. That literally blew my mind because Bobwhites would only fly a short distance and then they were back on the ground so you could hunt them as singles. By the time you get to where that covey of Mexican quail they had landed they had long run off somewhere and the dog that I was using just was completely and totally lost.

I remember on one occasion when using an excellent dog, Dandy, I got up an extremely large covey. Took two on the rise and then finished my limit out with single birds from that covey of over 50 birds. You can only do this with Bobwhite Quail because of the short distance that they would fly.

I took my son, Billy, to a plantation a few years ago, so that he could get some idea of the kind of hunting that his great grandfather did. He started out slowly but quickly caught on and was doing quite well. So, well that I literally had to choke him off, with the birds costing six dollars apiece, he would have broken my bank before he had had enough. We were shooting liberated birds and they didn't get up real well to start with that morning but as the day got warmer, they provided us with some pretty good action. Billy and I were both shooting over-under shotguns so we only had two shots as the birds would get up. We both got to where we could take two quail with two shots with some consistency when suddenly the quail got up in our front and the ones on my side began flying down a 12-foot row between pine trees. As I pulled the shotgun up swinging it to take a lead on the first bird, I quickly dispatched him and moved onto the second. Just as I pulled the trigger two birds were right there together and they both dropped on the second shot. The boy that was working the dogs for us was beside himself.

"Did you just kill two with one shot?" He queried. To that, I replied that I had. He responded to me that he had not seen that before which may be drawn only one of two conclusions. The first being that he had not been doing this very long. The second which was that most of the people that he had been handling dogs for couldn't shoot. It was just blind luck that the second bird flew into the path of my shot column but I acted as though it was commonplace, so he must've thought I was a really good shot.

I had spotted a covey of quail near where I parked to go deer hunting. When deer season was over, I asked Uncle Jesse if I could take Dandy, the best Brittany, to see if I could get a mess of quail there. I loaded him up in our 1964 Fairlane station wagon and headed to the fallow field. I pulled up in the front portion of the field and went around to let Dandy out of the wagon. I opened the back door to get my shotgun and fest. I turned around, and then he was standing there in a perfect point. I scolded Dandy for fooling with me and slammed the car door shut. Suddenly a gigantic covey of quail got up all around the car. I didn't even have a shell of the shotgun and was embarrassed. I noticed that Dandy was watching all the birds go down. I lowered the shotgun and told him to go get him. He started out on the far right and started working the singles. About halfway through the art, I had a limit of birds and took them back to the car. I was lots better off at singles because I only had one bird to look at and one bird to get onto. Dandy most likely had more liberated birds taken over him then you know in Georgia for several years when he was in his prime. He was doing what he did best, hunting singles.

Bill Skeet Shooting

CHAPTER ELEVEN

FIREARMS AND SHOOTING

Rifles for Deer

My first rifle was a Remington Nylon 66 in .22 long rifle. I loved to shoot this rifle at targets and squirrels. I am sure I fired more than 100,000 shots through it and it is the reason I became a proficient rifleman. I became most proficient shooting it from the hip.

Throughout my time hunting deer, I have used many calibers to take deer. I started with military versions of the 7.7 Japanese Arisaka and a British .303 Enfield. I then purchased a sporterized 7X57 mm Mauser and then a sporterized 8X57 mm Mauser. (Sporterized back then was taking off part of the wood stock and cutting the barrel back). This was a fairly primitive era in my deer hunting where, after missing a 12 point with a shotgun, I put shotguns down in favor of centerfire rifles.

My first centerfire rifle was a Winchester Model 70 in .22-250 Remington which I purchased to shoot hawks (then legal) and moved to crows. I had purchased this rifle for its long-range capabilities. It did not take me long to upgrade from a Weaver 2 ½ X to 7 X scope to a Bushnell Banner 4 X to 12 X for the longer-range shooting. I was also reloading and developed a load that would shoot ten shots at 100 yards that a dime would cover. The longest shot I have made to date, on a deer, was with this rifle at a range of 267 yards.

When I decided that I needed to hunt deer with a modern style rifle I settled on a Remington Model 600 in .308 Winchester. I first mounted a Weaver 1 ½ X to 4 ½ power variable scope. I took several deer, since I was shooting at 100 yards or less, with that combination. When I started hunting fields, clear cuts and powerlines, with up to 400-yard shots, I upgraded to 3 X to 9 X power Bushnell Banner scope. This is the rifle that I have taken more deer with than any other rifle or caliber. The longest shot I have taken on a deer with the 600 was just over 200 yards.

All my scopes were equipped with Multi-X or Dual-X scopes with the cross hair being thick and narrowing to a fine hair near the center. This allowed me to get on a moving target fast with the thick hair or fine sight with the thinner hair.

Several years ago, I decided to take a deer with all my deer rifles. I have managed to take them with .22-250 Remington, .223 Remington, .243 Winchester, 6mm Remington, .257 Roberts, 6.5 Creedmore, 270 Winchester, 284 Remington, .7 X 57 Mauser, 7mm Winchester Short Magnum, 7 mm Remington Magnum, .308 Winchester, .30-06 Springfield, 300 Winchester Short Magnum, 300 Winchester Magnum, 8 X 57 Mauser and .35 Remington. All of these calibers work fine for Whitetail-sized game.

I have shot several additional calibers up to a .358 Enterkin Magnum which shoots a 250-grain bullet at over 3000 feet per second.

My latest deer rifle, a Savage, stainless steel barreled, Weather Warrior that takes me back to the .308 Winchester. I have only taken a couple of deer with it, since I got it for Christmas and have only hunted a few times with it.

I plan a trip out west to hunt large Whitetail deer and will take two rifles. They will most likely be the new .308 Winchester and the 300 Winchester Short Magnum. I may take my 6.5 Creedmore due to its long-range capabilities.

Shotguns for Winged Shooting

As I mentioned earlier, my first experience with a shotgun was when I was five years old. I kept begging my father, on squirrel hunts, to let me shoot his double barreled 36 gauge. He finally relented. I accidentally pulled both triggers at the same time. I was aiming up a tall pine tree and it early drove me into the ground. That stopped me from begging to shoot his shotgun. As a side note my grandmother and her sister were professional seamstresses and my dad learned to sew at a young age, He sewed himself a shell/game bag, made from an old work uniform, that wrapped over the neck and was worn on the side. I still have that bag as a reminder of the old times. As a side note he sewed he and I many camouflage hunting vests and outfits through the years,

When I started hunting doves with him at the age of 6, I shot a borrowed .410 single shot. I did not hurt many birds but had great times. Some of the hunters he hunted with have been my hunting partners all my life. It would surprise you how many shots I could take at one dove with that single shot.

Daddy ended up with a Remington Model 11 in 12 gauge, with a Cutts Compensator installed, that he used dove and quail hunting. I would borrow Uncle Jesse's 16-gauge Model 11 Remington for squirrels, rabbits, and dove. I had no idea of what proper gun fit was and never hit birds well with the hump-back Browning types.

When I graduated to the 12-gauge Model 11 I was not very proficient with it either. The sear became worn and the gun would double and really put a hurt on the shoulder. I borrowed my cousin's Remington Model 1100 in twelve gauge and on that first shoot I hit better than I ever had before. The next day I went to the bank and borrowed enough money to buy an 1100. The company my father worked for owned the Ace hardware on the property and the family got a discount there. I paid $135.00 for a brand new Remington Model 1100 with a 30-inch full choke barrel. I shot this for a while and determined that I needed different chokes for different conditions. I had a friend that was a machinist and I purchased a Cutts Compensator which he cut the barrel and installed the Cutts. I not only acquired improved cylinder, modified and full chokes but also later acquired a super-full choke, for turkey shoots, and a skeet choke for quail. I also found an adjustable choke for the Cutts compensator which worked really well and you didn't have to carry a sack of choke tubes. I loved the 1100 and how well I shot with it, still not being aware of fit.

My friend, Bobby, was a skeet shooter. He invited me to go with him to Claxton, Georgia to shoot skeet. This was when my Remington 100 was equipped with the 30-inch full choke. I was informed by him that my 1100 would not work well for 31 yard shots. I had traded for a Savage Fox model BSE in 12 gauge that had improved Cylinder and Modified choke barrels. I decided that the double would be better for skeet. My first experience at skeet was dismal. It was like looking over an aircraft carrier deck. I broke only 6 of 25 targets with it. I immediately went home and ordered a skeet barrel for the Model 1100. I would not let that little game whip me.

I began tournament skeet shooting after much practice in Claxton. My first tournament was in Savannah, Georgia. I started working my way up the classes. Being a shot shell reloader and with Scottish blood, I was having trouble with the rule "All Hulls Hitting the Ground Are Property of the Gun Club". I was entertaining shooting all four gauges in competition and was not desirous of purchasing a twenty gauge 1100 and a matched pair of 1100's little gages at their high price. I was looking at some over under shotguns with Purbaugh tubes to change the gauge of the gun. Daddy had retired the Winchester 1400 semi-automatic 12 gauge that I had traded for and purchased a Winchester 101 over under 12 gauge.

I found two Winchester 101 shotguns fitted with tubes. I shot both and one of them felt better. Again, a trip to the bank to borrow the $700.00 price of the Tube Gun and made the purchase of the new prize. I shot that gun very well for several years winning several times over the years. In Macon, Georgia I shot my four gun best ever, breaking 396 out of 400 shots. I have run 100 straights with the 12 gauge, 20 gauge and 28 gauge. My long run was 235 straight with the 20 gauge. I have competed in the World Championship and the Zone 4 (all southern states). I have also competed in several Georgia State Championships. A friend from Hazlehurst and I became National Skeet Shooting Association referees so as to better afford shooting in Georgia, Florida and South Carolina. Skeet shooting made me a far better bird hunter and shooter. My average on doves went from one for every four or five shots to one per two shots. In Uruguay I once killed 908 with 1000 shots. This was my best day ever.

For the trips to South America for High Volume doves I purchased two Beretta Model 390's in 20 gauge. I shot them on two trips but when I took my son, Billy, with me on the last trip we rented brand new Beretta Model 392's in 20 gauge from the guide so as not to wear out my own guns and to not be hassled in customs with the guns. As a side note, I am well aware of gun fit so three of us used the shims and recoil pads to fit our guns to us. I set my gun at a youth length 13 ½ inch pull. Billy set his at 14 ¼ inch pull and my friend, Bobby, set his for 14 ¼ in pull and left-handed. In the first two trips I shot 2700 and 2500 shells without a malfunction. With the 392, I shot nearly 2000 shells. It performed flawlessly. A "Reactor" shooting pad in my vest reduced recoil by 40% which made the shooting more comfortable.

I recently won a second 12-gauge Beretta 390 Outlander in full camouflage but have not yet put it to the test. After South America I only shoot a 20-gauge shotgun for doves.

When it became illegal to shoot lead shot at waterfowl, I traded my 1100's with my number 5 lead shot to a Remington 1187 with screw in chokes to shoot Number 3 steel shot. I also acquired a pair of Mossberg 835 pumps in 3 ½ 12-gauge magnum for our trips to Louisiana to "Shot de Duck' as Justin Wilson would say. We fixed the stock's recoil pads one to fit me and one for my son Billy.

More recently I won another camo Beretta 390 Outlander which I gave to Billy. We now have a matching pair of 390 in 12 and 20. I suspect my grandson will inherit mine.

I have a camo Mossberg Model 836 Turkey Gun and recently won my fifth Benelli Nova Pump (which does not fit me at all). I traded the first three but the fifth was camouflaged and Billy commandeered it from me for his Turkey Gun. I traded the last one.

I have shot Running Boar at Fort Benning and I also shot International Skeet and International Clay Pigeon, which are the games shot in the Olympics. We used to shoot Five Stand in Odum at the Gun Club which is a combination of skeet and trap on a superimposed field. This utilizes a trap that osculates and gyrates in throwing the targets. And SCRAP which combines skeet and trap.

I once made the statement, "If it goes bang, recoils and smells of gun powder smoke, I love it".

Sighting in Rifles

There was a time when I would sight other people's deer rifles. I would sight in as many as 50 or 60 before deer season. Later as I got older, I reduced it down to 30 or 40. Now my son Billy even sights mine in for me.

I am a big boy, and now have learned how to hold a gun that might kick you tight to avoid that instance. A friend of mine bought a 300 Winchester Magnum. We went to the range for him to sight it in. He did not hold the gun very steady and had it on one of those factory rest instead of the sandbags. When he pulled the trigger, the gun booked up in the scope almost creased his forehead. He turned to me and asked if I would finish sighting it in for him. I think it may have hurt his shoulder and his head. I finished that chore for him but I don't know if he ever shot the gun again.

The same thing happened to my son, Billy. I had traded for a Winchester 300 Magnum model 70 rifle, and we had gone to the range to check it out and sight it in. I had made up my mind that I would give that rifle to Billy, since he shot a model 70 in .270.

That way if he got an opportunity to go out West hunting large game, he would be set up with a rifle that would handle long-range task. He lay down over the sandbags, squeezing the first round off. I watched as a muzzle booked up causing him to look around at me with a funny look on his face. I told him that he would have to hold that rifle a little bit tighter than he did his .270. The second time he fired the rifle he held it steady and made a good shot. He later told me he had no idea that there was that much difference in a 300 Magnum versus a .270. I told him of the first time his grandfather was at the gun club with a friend of ours who had just purchased a 300 Winchester Magnum's, similar to the one that Billy had shot. His grandfather fired expert on everything when he was in United States Marine Corps and that rifles were familiar to him. The BAR that he carried during World War II kicked some, but nothing like that 300 Magnum. He was crouched behind a bench from a picnic table when he touched the round off. The extra recoil from the Magnum overbalanced him, knocking him on his behind. He had a sheepish look on his face as he sat on the ground and looked back at that rifle. The next time he shot the recall did not move him a bit for he was prepared.

Remington Mohawk 600

Jackie, good friend and hunting buddy, was in Atlanta one day and stopped at the gun shop. He noticed a .460 Weatherby

Mark IV, (This was the most powerful production rifle in the world) he inquired about it, and the man told him it was used but had only one shot that had ever been fired in it. The owner of the shop told him that if he would pay for the ammunition, he would let them take it out back to the rifle range and fire it. He went outside, fired the rifle and came back with the rifle handing it to the owner. He told him he was absolutely certain why the previous owner had only fired it one time. He told me it would kick your teeth out. I don't know if that rifle ever got sold, but I am sure there was someone around who was man enough to stand up to it. I bet he had to be the size of Sasquatch. That particular rifle kicked 3 ½ times what a 12-gauge, 3-inch Magnum shotgun will. It had 8100 foot-pounds of energy. Now that's enough to knock an 8100 pound car 1 foot or to knock a 1 pound object 8110 feet. That's some formidable cartridge.

My friend, Gene, the retired Colonel from United States Army who was past National Pistol Champion, developed a cartridge one time that was bodacious. He did this by making up a 300 Weatherby Magnum to .35 caliber. His load for that rifle drove a 250-grain projectile in excess of 3000 ft./s. I witnessed this up close and personal. I shot the prototype rifle that he had, which had been made from a Mauser Model 98. He had taken off the scope in order to address the throat so that the long bullet would feed in the chamber a little better and had placed the scope back in the mounts without resighting it. I started to sit down on the bench but he told me I would probably be better off standing due to the recoil. When I squeezed the trigger, I quickly found out that the scope was not cited in and was shooting to the right because I hit the angle iron target frame, which is made of 1 1/2" x 1 1/2" x 1/8" steel, cutting it off like a chop saw. I noticed that at 100 yards the dust kicked up from the impact of the projectile simultaneously with the blast. He later told me that when a bullet is going 3000 ft./s it will do that.

Pup Tent

CHAPTER TWELVE

CAMPING

I was a Boy Scout and began camping at a young age. I remember so well my first camping trip to the Altamaha River at Buckhorn Bluff and Half Moon Lake. My friends Bart and Bobby were the old scouts in the troop, and my Dad and Mr. Claude were the Scoutmasters. My first night was spent in a World War II pup tent with dirt as my floor. I had no sleeping bag at that time and slept on and under itchy wool Marine Corps blankets that were my dad's. I still can see the fire that was glowing in the middle of our campsite and if I concentrate, I can still remember the buzzing of the mosquitoes and the other night sounds. We sat by the campfire while the older scouts told ghost and booger stories. I was almost terrified but had calmed down after retiring to the tent. As the glow of the fire died down, I began to hear strange noises behind my tent. I tried to identify the source of the noise, but the more I tried the more scared I got. My only implement of defense was the small knife and a flat hatchet set that I had won from the Junior Sales Club of America, so I unsheathed them in preparation to defend my life and limb.

I became aware of a light on the side of my tent moving toward the front opening and I readied myself for action. Suddenly there was a horrible sight in the front opening of my tent. It was an illuminated looking face and I knew for sure that a "HAINT" was about to overtake and devour me. I threw the hatchet in the direction and Guyton, one of the older boys, screamed. I had just missed Guyton, causing him to drop the flashlight that he was holding under his chin and run away. We had avoided an accident but it was certain that was the last time they tried to scare me. I didn't retrieve the hatchet until morning. I, just the other day, tried to replace the broken handle on that old flat hatchet and remembered again that night of terror.

I used the pup tent for a good while and sold greeting cards to earn a sleeping bag to replace that itchy wool blanket. I was sorting through my camping equipment and ran across that old sleeping bag. It brought back many memories.

My friend, Bobby had a hollowed-out section of cypress with a skin stretched over it. it had a string with a button on it under the stretched skin. When rosin was applied to the string it gave resistance as you pulled your fingers along the string and gave out an eerie sound (very similar to the sound that they portray for Bigfoot on the television programs).

It was called a Wang-Doodle and could be made from either a hollow cypress block or an old snare drum. The first time I heard one it scared me out of my wits. Later, when I tried using one, I sure hoped that nothing would answer it because using it sent chills up and down my spine. It made the hair stand up on the back of my neck. When the Boy Scout Troop went camping in the Altamaha River swamp the Wang-doodle would surely be heard at night. The old scouts had already heard the sound but the new scouts would get a scare, especially if they sat up by the campfire telling ghost stories.

I can guarantee that when Bobby went off into the Altamaha River Swamp and began to make sounds with it everyone would get quiet and begin to look around. As I got older, I got to play the instrument and even though I knew what it was, I was always afraid that something would answer me. Bobby called this devise a Wang-doodle but there were several other names for it. Lots of folks fell victim to the fear that this device would bring when heard.

On one occasion one of my friends knew of a house situated down a long lane off the main dirt road. Halfway down the lane crossed a thick branch. The folks at the house were having some kind of party that night. My friend was dropped off at the beginning of the lane and eased into the woods. The first squall from the Wang-doodle and all went quiet at the house. He moved closer and cut loose with a second squall. Immediately afterward, all the automobiles were cranked and the partiers quickly made their way down the lane to the dirt road and left the occupant of the house there without an automobile. My friend moved closer and let out a third squall adding a quiver at the end. All of a sudden, the screen door of the little house flew open and slammed against the outside wall. The patter of footsteps running

205

down the lane could be heard. My friend was near the edge of the lane in the thick brush and as the man came running by. He cut loose with the fourth and last squall. The footstep increased drastically in speed as the man-made his escape from the "Monster" that was after him.

After I became a Scoutmaster of the same troop, my son and one of his close friends were camping with the troop in the Okefenokee Swamp Park. The gators had been swimming around the park all day, some up to 10 feet long. Wayne, one of the Scoutmasters from another troop had a similar device made from a commercial food can. Matt, the other scoutmaster of our troop, and I had retired and the boys were under a shelter about fifty yards from where the tents were pitched joking, talking and making quite a bit of noise. Suddenly, Wayne cut loose on the device and all went quiet. I heard Austin, Billy's friend asked quietly, "What was that?" Wayne waited about five minutes and the boys started to talk and carry on again. He cut loose a second time and you could have heard a pin drop. He let out a third blast and you would have thought that a herd of buffalo was coming our way. The boys quickly got into the tents as though the canvas duck could afford some protection. Needless to say, there was no more noise to affect a body's sleep that night.

We went on a survival camp one weekend to Rock Lake on the Altamaha River. We were allowed three chocolate bars (one for each day), a knife or hatchet or a machete, one canteen of water, a few hooks and some line, one pot or pan, and some salt. We were also allowed one blanket and a piece of canvas. This was tough for us city boys. I managed to eat all three of my candy bars the first morning so I had to fend for myself the remainder of the three days. We quickly located a spring which was a good source of water. Ironically the spring came out of rocks on to a little flat area that had a basin scooped or chipped out that would hold about two gallons of water. When we cleaned the leaves out the water would clear up quickly and taste as good as any shallow well in the county. This solved problem number one. We hunted for some foodstuffs. We found gooseberries which were awful. We began to eat palmetto heart (Swamp cabbage) and it somewhat satisfied our hunger. We found some grubs and cut some fishing poles and began to fish. All we could catch was eels and Daddy took them and cleaned them. No one else dared to do that. He boiled them and offered me a bite. I had long since eaten my candy and the berries and palmetto heart were getting old. The eel tasted like catfish so I went down to the lake and caught a big one. After cleaning him I boiled him in the pot and feasted on the white meat. None of the rest of the boys would try the eel although Mr. Claude, Daddy and I were full of the feast. We never caught anything but eels but by the second day, the whole encampment was devouring them at every meal. It is funny what necessity will do to your taste! On the last day, some of the boys discovered someone's cornfield nearby and we roasted ears of corn which were mighty fine, especially as hungry as we were.

On other occasions, we ate the muscles that grow in the Altamaha. They were a little tough but when you are hungry you will eat almost anything. Along with all kinds of wild game that became available.

Mr. Claude was particularly adept at "Striking" (which is walking at the edge of a river lake with a lightered knot afire in one hand and another in the "Striking" hand). As you walk along the edge there are fish (mostly Jack-fish -Eastern Chain

Pickerel) that are lying along the edge. If you are quick, you can strike them with the lightered knot and retrieve them for the pot. Mr. Claude was also very deft with a machete.

Our Boy Scout troop used to camp at Camp Tolochee on Little Blythe Island in Glynn County, on the Georgia Coast. I was looking over photos from the first time that I went there and the memories literally flooded in. That year we were on the ground with sleeping bags that had inflatable air mattresses. During the night a spring tide occurred. A spring tide is an extremely high tide. Some refer to it as a marsh hen tide. The spring tide covers all the marsh and invades the higher ground. Our campsite was not much higher than the marsh and some of us were floating on our air mattresses in a few inches of water. That is a strange way to wake up in the morning. We relocated the tents on higher ground and had to dry everything including our sleeping bags. They now use that campsite for the Archery range. I have many memories of Tolochee both as a scout and as a scout leader. It has a special place in my heart although Kool-Aid made with sulfur water (the artesian well supplied the camp) and the ice-cold showers that we took in the sulfur water stick in my memory.

We used to camp in the Okefenokee Swamp. Only Boy Scouts could camp on Billy's island back then. Billy's Island is located just south of Stephen Foster Park and is only accessible by boat (with an outboard motor of 10 horsepower or less). It was on Billy's Island that they logged the gigantic cypress trees around a century ago. The butts of the trees were so large that they had to import crosscut saws from the Northwest, United States. We loved the trips where we would see alligators longer than our boats swim beside us and catch large Warmouth's and Mudfish (Bowfins) along with Jackfish, Bream and Suwannee Bass.

On one such campout, my cousin Billy had a visitor in his tent. A skunk. It sprayed Billy pretty well and no one would get close to him for the rest of the campout. You always had to be careful in the Okefenokee, because it contained a wide array of wildlife including Gators, Black Bear, Panther, Moccasins and other things that could do you harm. That is the only place in South Georgia where you had to protect your food from the bears. Raccoons were the normal "masked bandit" that wanted your fig newtons and such.

You had to be careful which wood you cooked with. Fat lightered wood starts easily and burns hot but it will smoke up your pots and pans severely. Oak is the wood of choice for outdoor cooking. It will coal up and cook so fine. I once, early in my Scouting Career, used fat lightered and my little scout cook kit was blackened. I had nothing but a bar of soap to clean it with so I went down to the sand bar and used the sand as an abrasive to clean the pan. It took forever!! I sat down in the sand and wet the pan and scrubbed until it was bright aluminum in color. I learned two things that campout. Don't use lightered to cook with and bring along a Brillo pad.

Once, when my cousin Billy and I were camping out and deer hunting, he received a package in the mail. It stunk to high heaven. He had ordered some Genuine Indian Buck Lure from Cabela's and the glass bottle had been broken in shipping spilling the contents in the package. Relentless as he was, Billy still planned to hang the package near his stand while hunting and try to attract a buck. That night as we started to go into the tent, I noticed he had that stinking package in his hand.

"Where are you going with that?" I questioned.

"I'm bringing it in with me so nothing gets it." He answered.

"Don't you dare bring that stinking thing in here!" I stated emphatically, "Besides if it works, I do not want some turned on buck in the tent with me!"

Thankfully he left that stinking thing outside the tent and I never knew of it attracting anything but gnats and flies.

On our camping trips during hunting season, we often killed and cooked some wild game. Cousin Billy had the phrase "Wild Game Mixed Bag" which meant if it walked, wiggled, crawled, swam or flew; it was in danger of him collecting it for the pot. Hunting etiquette notwithstanding, Billy would gather something. A squirrel or rabbit roasted over the fire was mighty tasty and sometimes we would have quail, dove, and duck on the spit also. We would wrap potatoes (Irish or Georgia Red Sweet) in tin foil and cook them in the coals. We learned early in scouts to cook a coffee can casserole (when coffee cans were all metal including the lid where they would act as a Dutch oven) and later to wrap the meat, potatoes, onions, and carrots in tin foil and make a "Hobo Hamburger". Political correctness caused them to be changed to "Silver Turtle." We had grates that we rested on stones or green hardwood logs over the coals and could cook as good a beefsteak as you could ask for. And we sometimes used forked sticks to make a rack for a shish-k- bob. We roasted corn (in the shuck) which was pretty good too.

I remember that once when we were on a hunting campout, we went to town to a Turkey Shoot. In case you are not familiar with a Turkey Shoot, it is a shooting competition with the prize that goes to the winner being a turkey, ham or side of bacon. That night we won a side of smoked bacon which we took back to camp and feasted on the bacon for the rest of the week.

My hunting buddies Bobby and Bart became assistant Scoutmasters when they became too old for scouts, and they loved camping well enough that they did not miss a campout. I remember well how Bart made coffee for the campouts. he would buy a pound of ground coffee and pour it into the coffee boiler and make the first pot which was as strong as any coffee that you could imagine (unless you have hunted in South America, their coffee does not have to be brought to the table, it walks out there on its own). Bart would continue to add water to the boiler all weekend long. About Saturday night it was decent coffee and at lunch Sunday it was like dishwater. Nothing tastes better or feels better on a cool night than a hot cup of coffee to sip as you sit around the fire. Hot chocolate cannot compare but will suffice if necessary.

Breakfast is the best meal on a campout. Nothing smells better than breakfast cooking in the cool morning air of a camp. As a scoutmaster, we used a big coffee boiler for the boys to make their coco, oatmeal or instant grits. The boys had a tendency to make their pancakes using the mix in the yellow plastic bottles where you just add water and shake it until well mixed. Then all they had to do was pour the correct amount into the pan. One of the scouts in my son Billy's patrol, Josh, passed me shaking the bottle which was making a Thump, Thump, Thump sound.

"Josh. What are you making?" I asked.

211

"Pancakes" he exclaimed.

I again inquired, "Why do they sound like that? What did you put in there?"

"Water from that pot," he retorted, pointing to the coffee boiler.

"Josh, my friend I believe that you have a big biscuit in there now!" I replied.

The patrol did not have their pancakes that morning and this was the same patrol that forgot the syrup the first time that they made pancakes. From that day on they always had plenty of syrup even this time when there were no biscuits. This was the same patrol that one morning Austin was cooking sausage patties for the patrol. Jesse, Billy's cousin, was tasked with holding the plate for Austin to place the finished sausage in. Suddenly the boys noticed that Jesse was eating the sausage as fast as Austin could cook them. Jesse never got the plate holding assignment anymore; they gave him cleanup duty instead.

When the Webelos den, that Billy was in bridged into the Boy Scout Troop from the Cub Scout Pack we were at Camp Hatch on the Altamaha River. This campsite is provided by Southern Company for the Scouts to use and is located on a large bluff overlooking the river. The boys were excited and after the bridging ceremony, they were to sleep in two-man tents that night. Five of the eight boys in the den slept (I use that phrase loosely) in one two-man tent. I know that they had an idea of how a sardine feels after that night because some of them were pretty good size boys.

I was in charge of a camporee at Camp Hatch once when a monsoon type rain came. Although my tent was pitched on what appeared to be a slight rise there was an old yard drain that drained the whole area but it was clogged up. Billy was a Cub Scout but could camp with me. We were sleeping well despite the rain and about four hours into the storm noticed some water trickling in at the seam where the ground cloth (bottom) of the tent and the rest of the tent were attached. I unzipped the door to find that my tent was in six inches of water (just the amount that the floor went up the side of the tent.) I got Billy out and we retreated to the truck to spend the rest of the night. Mine was the only tent that was in the area affected by the clogged up yard drain. All the rest of the tents were in an area that drained well. It demonstrates that a person (no matter how experienced) should check and ensure that there is drainage. Once when I was on a campout as a scout the scoutmasters had us trench around our tents. When the rain came that night the water did not run through the tents and we stayed dry. I wish I had remembered that lesson.

My family camped, on one fourth of July, at the Altamaha. I had a popup camper at the time that I eventually wore completely out. It would sleep six if everyone liked each other and would sleep three that did not care about one another. The problem we encountered was the heat. Because of the canvas sides of the camper, although there were screened windows, it still was hot in the 100-degree weather. I had a 12-foot square screened in dining fly that had flaps and a sod cloth for a floor and in the middle of the night, we moved the bedding out to the dining fly and slept there where there was a little breeze. We survived the heat and the drunks that kept frequenting the landing that was near where we were set up all night long. Nothing will disturb your sleep like headlights shining into your tent and loud country music playing at the maximum that the pickup speakers would allow. I always kept some "protection" with me and thought I might need it to ward off the drunks.

My son Billy's first camping trip was when he was just a toddler. We had gone to spend the 4th of July week at Adams Fish Camp on the Altamaha River in Long County. The camp was located on an oxbow lake adjacent to the river. Deloris, my wife, and I set up my Hillary tent and it was next to her uncle's camper. It was quite hot and we had brought an oscillating fan to ward off some of the July heat. We ran an extension cord from the hook up for the camper to run it. I can still see Bill laying there in his diaper sleeping in front of the fan. I can also see him wading in the slough in his diaper with it soaking up half of the Altamaha River. My in-laws came to fish with us during the day but my father-in-law had an aversion to camping out. He liked to sleep in his own bed if at all possible. We caught loads of fish and had a great time that week.   This was the beginning of many nights camping for Billy.

When Billy was a Cub Scout, we went on a Cub Scout Family Campout in Waycross at the fairgrounds. One of the requirements for Billy's next advancement was for him to prepare a meal. I had given him a recipe for a one-pot meal of beef stew. Instead of getting stew meat he and his mother brought hamburger meat. The old saying is that "you do the best you can with what you've got" applied. He mixed all the ingredients in the pot including the can of cream of mushroom soup and simmered the "stew down". It made a different stew but was quite tasty especially the gravy which was "sopped up" using light bread. We dubbed it "Billy Stew" and he has cooked it many times on Scout campouts and at home. When one of his friends, Austin, was with him he would have to make a double recipe for Austin loved "Billy Stew" and would eat it using almost a whole loaf of bread.

On one occasion two friends and I planned to take a 16-foot runabout, that belonged to Winkie, upriver and camp on the sandbar. When we got to the sandbar we started to prepare our campsite. Now it must be understood that I was the only one there with any camping experience. I began to gather driftwood to ensure we had sufficient fuel for the night's fire. In the meantime, the owner of the boat, Wink, began taking the seats out of the boat and lining them up to make a bed. I began to spread a military poncho for a ground cloth to sleep on. The other friend, Billy (I guess by now you have discovered that there are several Billy's in my life) told me that he hoped that I had two ponchos or room enough on the one for him.   I dug a second one out of my pack and handed it to him.   As night began to fall, I had not noticed that Wink had removed the gas tank from the boat and had poured some gasoline on the stockpile of wood. I said something about getting a fire started and he threw a lit match into the stockpile of wood and "Whoosh" blue flame engulfed our feet as the fumes had spread. Needless to say, we retreated and watched the flames engulf the stockpile. After recovering from the surprise, he announced that we would have to gather more driftwood as our whole night's supply would be exhausted soon in our massive fire.

After the fire had burned down enough, we prepared supper and got ready for bed. Off in the distance, we heard a wild cat scream several times. I got into my bedroll and looked at wink on his "boat seat" bed and Billy laying to my left with his .38 super automatic pistol in the shoulder holster in case the cat came closer. The beauty of sleeping on a sandbar on the Altamaha is that you can form the sand to fit the contours of the body and sleep very comfortably. When I awoke the next morning there was Billy in the same position, I last saw him with his hand on the handle of the pistol. He told me that the cat had squalled all night. I do not think he slept very well.

The essentials of camping include shelter, warmth, hydration and having something to eat. As a Boy Scout, you learn these things and learned that they are vital. It is a given that you must keep dry and keep warm but it is also a given that you must eat. In order to prepare food on a campout, you must have a fire. There are several ways to start a fire but I've always been told that friction is the best method. That is to drag the head of a match across the striking portion on the box. Dry wood is essential to starting a fire although wet wood will in fact burn. That is once you get it hot enough to get the moisture out of it. When I was young, I was anemic and my doctor said to eat beef as rare as I could go and up to, including raw. Since I got used to eating meat on the rare side it was only natural for me on a camping trip to take out a piece of cube steak, salt it and begin to eat it without the benefit of heat or fire. This seemed to bother some of my fellow campers but to this day when I order steak, I tell the waitress that I want to have a conversation with it.

I do cook things on campouts. We had two special ways of preparing fast and easy meals. The first was called a coffee can casserole. Bear in mind that coffee cans at that time were all metal including the lid. What you would do was put your meat and vegetables, onions, potatoes and carrots if you desire into the coffee can. Then the coffee can was placed in the coals with coals placed on top of it. After a while, you would pull the coffee can out of the fire blowing the ashes off the top. After removing the lid, the meal could be eaten directly from the can. The second method was what we called the hobo hamburger, later called a silver turle. The camper would place a hamburger patty along with onions and potatoes and salt and pepper in a tin foil sheet. The sheet of foil would be then closed and sealed. It would also be placed on the coals with coals around it in order for it to cook. One of my Cub Scouts that I taught to make a silver turtle, just told media of the day that as a grown man he still makes silver turtles and puts them in the oven. I once prepared catfish using the silver turtle method. We placed the catfish in the aluminum foil, put butter and lemon juice on it along with salt-and-pepper. When it was removed from the coals the meat would flake off the bones and taste delicious. We have also cooked pork chops, venison, wild hog and almost anything else we could scavenge. I have cooked many a potato wrapped in an aluminum foil upon the coals of a fire, both sweet and white potatoes.

I have several Dutch ovens and a cast-iron "spider that will cook an excellent outdoor meal utilizing the coals of a good oak fire. I bought a propane, two burner stove and a tent four men could get into in 1972, that I still use when camping. I used to take it on their hunts, especially at Fort Stewart, where there was nowhere close to get something to eat. I would just warm some canned Stewart chili for lunch. Sometimes we would eat old military C rations and K rations, when we had them. We have now been introduced to "Meals Ready to Eat" a.k.a. MRE's. A can of sardines, Vienna sausage, potted meat or beanie weenies will do in a pinch.,

My father, who was a Scoutmaster was an excellent cook. He had been a short-order cook after the war and swore to me that mother could not boil water without scorching it when they first got married. He baked all the birthday cakes around the house and made my sister a doll cake for her birthday, every year. Mine was not so complicated. I just required a yellow cake with milk chocolate icing and pecan halves on top of it. He was renowned for his ability to bake a cake on the campfire using a reflector oven. All his old scouts, to this day, when they get around me, talk about those cakes that he used to bake. He and the other scoutmasters never had to wash dishes. They could always find a scout willing to wash dishes for a piece of those cakes.

There is nothing that smells better on a crisp morning than bacon cooking in a frying pan over an open fire. That along with the smell of the coffee perking would make anyone hungry. There is something about cooking and eating in the out of doors that makes everything smell and taste better. I think that is why I love grilling meat to this day. Daddy used to grill the best steak around. I added a special way of seasoning and made them better. My son, Billy, does an even better job of grilling than I do. I wonder if my grandson will be a grill master too.

There are some of us who would rather have all of the amenities we could carry along. I made a Chuckwagon type box for storage and food preparation. It made it much easier while camping to prepare meals and beverages. One of the scoutmasters, Harry, used to carry so much with him because he feared that some of the boys might get hungry. They all knew to come to him if they ran short of or didn't have something. I guess I replaced Harry in being over-prepared for the campouts. I have been replaced by one of the new assistant scoutmasters who has outdone both Harry and I in being over-prepared. Every scoutmaster has his forte in food preparation. We have learned to cook an egg in a paper cup or an orange peel, beside the fire. We have cooked many a shish kebab or another piece of meat only green stick suspended over the fire. Palmetto stems are especially good for this. Another scoutmaster, Matt is the best I've ever seen utilizing Dutch ovens. He can cook anything in a Dutch oven and has taught all his scouts the use of them. I knew quite a bit of Dutch oven cooking but am not in the league with Matt. I cook a mean Brunswick stew in the Dutch oven along with many other one-pot meals. When it comes to cooking breakfast casseroles, biscuits, cinnamon rolls and all those other things I defer to Matt. The meals that I cook in the Dutch oven did not require perfect timing. As a matter of fact, most of them adhere to the rule that the longer they cook the better they get.

At Camp Tolochee, water was furnished by an artesian well and was strong sulfur water. When you would first arrive at camp the water had to be really cold before you could stand to drink it. After a few days there, you would hardly notice the taste except when they made Tang or Kool-Aid from it. Those drinks would be awful all week long. The good side effect to drinking the sulfur water was that the sulfur excreted from the pores of your skin. The biting insects would leave you alone. That was a pretty good side effect since mosquitos and sand gnats abounded at that place.

I have cooked many squirrels, birds and other assorted sundry meats over an open fire. When seasoned correctly they are absolutely wonderful to eat. As they are rotated over the coals, they become a beautiful golden brown and when cooked properly the meat will almost fall off the bone. I have helped cook whole hogs over coals many a time. Some of these were domestic hogs while others were wild. I have cooked chickens over the coals and have helped on large bar-b-q's with 300 chickens and a 40-gallon washpot of chicken and rice or Brunswick stew.

Our ancestors cooked everything over an open fire. Even in their homes, they would rake the coals out of the fireplace in order to cook. They utilized cast-iron pots hanging from hooks over the fire and also things like spiders and Dutch ovens which had legs so that coals could be placed under them easily. I have an antique cast iron spyder and several sizes of Dutch ovens. The best thing to remember about cooking over coals is that if you're utilizing aluminum cookware like Boy Scout cook kits, is to soap them so they will not soot up which makes the cleanup much easier.

My wife does not mind me cooking as long as I do it outside. She claims that I made too much of a mess in her kitchen to allow me access to it. I would rather cook outside anyway because I don't have been nearly as careful as I would have to be in the kitchen. I translate the skills that I learned cooking over open fires to my barbecue grill on the patio. I love to cook on it and partially because it reminds me of all of those times in the out of doors.

───────────────

There is a vast variety of edible things found in the woods of the Altamaha River swamp. The waterfowl that fly along in winter on the river are mostly very tasty. Some, like the merganser, is like eating sardines and coots which taste a lot like mud. The geese that fly along the river are mostly native Canada's and sometimes snows and blues. A guide once told me in Louisiana that those geese graze like a cow so you must treat them like beef. Out there they blunt dissect the breast and cut them in less than half-inch strips. They then batter and fry them like country fried steak. They also use them in the production of sausage. We don't have many speckled belly geese that fly in our flyway but they eat grain and can be cooked like a duck. I have eaten them prepared many ways but smoked duck is at the top of my list.

In the case of furry critters, the deer and the squirrel rank highest with me with the wild hog coming in a close third. I have partaken of most of the rest of the furry things, all of which have some merit but my preference is for those three. Bear and raccoons are a little on the greasy side but are tolerable. From there it quickly diminishes although all are edible the rest do not rank very high on my menu.

Not only are the feathered and fur covered animals good for eating and also those that live in the water which includes channel catfish, largemouth bass, bream, shell cracker and crappie (we call them white perch). There are many other species of fish found in the river some of which are tasty but bony. They include shad and chain pickerel (we call them jackfish). The old-timers claim that if these fish are prepared correctly, they are the tastiest in the river. I was never fond of a bone sandwich so I shy away from them.

All of these taste much better cooked over an open fire than they taste cooked in the confines of the kitchen. There is just something about the clean open air with the smell of oak smoke and the smell of whatever it is you are cooking that will really make you hungry by the time it is done.

Billy the Canoeist

CHAPTER THIRTEEN

CANOEING

From the very first time I laid eyes on a canoe, I fell in love with canoes and canoeing. My first experience was at camp Tolochee my first year. I learned all the strokes and maneuvers involved with canoeing and earned my canoeing merit badge. I looked forward to going down to camp and would canoe at every opportunity. My cousin, Tommy, was about the same strength as me and we soon learned we could canoe together and could paddle with full power strokes and not have to correct course. Subsequently, we became unbeatable in canoe races. Later our troop acquired several canoes and canoeing became a big part of the troop's activities. Our troop has made many trips down the Altamaha River up to 50 miles at the time and almost all of our boys do, in fact, canoe. The troop also went to the Okefenokee Swamp on several canoe camping trips.

On one occasion we were in canoes, on a trip from Deen's Landing to Davis's landing on the Altamaha River. One of our other Scoutmasters, Kelly, who is an avid canoeist, had been sick and unable to make the trip. I decided to put one of the scouts, Casey, in the canoe with me because I thought that he might be the most inexperienced in a canoe. After I had boarded the canoe, I pulled it to the riverbank and was about to use my paddle to steady the canoe for his loading up in it. Before I could brace the canoe with the paddle, I saw Casey stepping into the bow of the canoe-like walking through a door. I opened my mouth to warn him not to but it was too late. When his weight hit on the port side of the canoe it flipped me and the canoe like a pancake in the frying pan. I plunged headfirst into the Altamaha and jumped up trying to get my wallet out and into the air before everything got wet. As I sputtered like Shamu the whale I couldn't help but notice that Kelly was bursting at the seams laughing at me. I asked Casey if he had canoeing merit badge to which he replied that he did not. I told him that was good because if he did, I would have taken it away from him.

"Who taught you how to enter a canoe, Casey?" I asked.

"Mr. Bird", he responded.

I just shook my head

That was the longest trip that I ever took down the river. Every time that Casey saw a slick place in the water, he would jam his paddle into the water to stop us before reaching whatever was under the water ahead. It was twice as hard to paddle the canoe like that as it would have been to do it by myself. Casey went on to get his Eagle Scout Award of which I was extremely proud.

On one occasion we were having canoe races and we had one canoe paired with the nose guard of the high school football team in the stern and a skinny kid who was in the bow. When Pow Wow, the Stern-man would stroke his paddle the bow would lift out of the water like it had a 20-horsepower outboard motor on the stern and the kid in the bow could not even reach the water with his paddle. That was a "Fast" mismatch.

Billy and his friend Austin were good canoeing partners and won in the events that they competed with. They were good friends from the time when they were little and did quite a bit together, especially in Boy Scouts and canoeing. They were on camp staff at Camp Tolochee one summer.

Back in my Boy Scout days my cousin Tommy and I who were close to the same strength were the best Camp Tolochee. Being of equal strength we could just use power strokes and did not have to worry about steering the canoe.

On the occasion that I was partnered up with Casey. They were so fast that they would go almost out of sight down the river then turn around and come back upstream to rejoin us. Now you must understand that the Altamaha River, which is the second-largest watershed east of the Mississippi, moves at a pretty good clip. They were able to buck the current with no noticeable problem. They most likely canoed twice as far as anyone else that day.

Canoes are good for shallow streams and hard to get places but sometimes the canoeist will have to portage to get around really tight places. One such happening occurred when my cousin

Billy offered to take Bobby down Ten Mile Creek to the Altamaha River and shoot ducks all the way down. Bobby, with his foot injury, could not get into the water with that foot and would place a plastic bag on his foot to keep it dry. The invitation was enticing and Bobby accepted. They put the Canoe in at Ten Mile Road and started toward the Altamaha. Neither of them knew that the pulpwood crews had been logging along the creek and had filled the creek with tops and branches in numerous locations all down the creek. Bobby later told me that Billy would pull him and the canoe around the piles on dry land in the canoe. They did not get to shoot any ducks that day but they learned a valuable lesson. That was to reconnoiter before jumping into the creek. Billy never issued that invitation again.

I still have a Chanoe, that my father won at a Ducks Unlimited Banquet in 1980. It is great to paddle and will handle the 7.5 Mercury he won with it. It will go almost anywhere and is stable enough to stand up in it and pole through the shallow marsh. I have fished in many a pond with it since it weighs only 60 pounds. A J-stroke will send it on its way pretty fast. With a small person, the 7.5 Mercury will make it sit up like a feather in the water at over 20 miles per hour just touching at the bottom of the transom.

Although I am getting too old and stiff to canoe, I can't help but look at the canoes at the marine stores and dream of old times when I was able to enjoy the art of canoeing. I also know that if I had a Kayak, back in the day, I would have used it on Butler Island, to duck hunt.

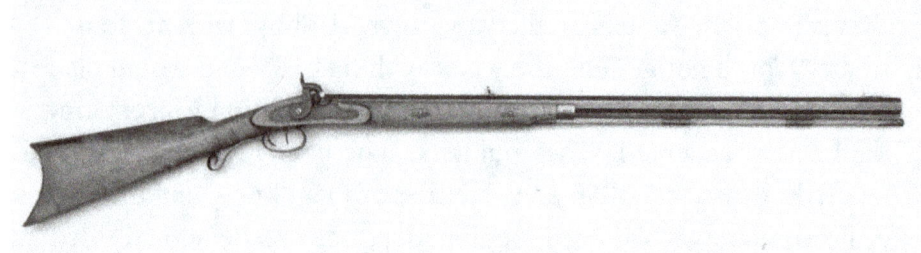

50 Cal Hawkin Rifle

CHAPTER FOURTEEN

Black Powder Shooting and Hunting

Black Powder shooting and hunting can be loads of fun. I originally got into it because it would extend my deer season on the Wildlife Management Areas beyond archery and conventional firearms hunts. It actually would give me one more week at Bullard Creek Wildlife Management Area near my home. At first, I did not own a black powder rifle but Gene, a friend of mine, who I hunted with, had a spare. He loaned me a Navy arms "Buffalo Rifle" which is reproduction of the 1863 Remington Zouave. This was a 58-caliber muzzleloader which shot a War Between the States era mini ball. I hunted with this until I made a trip to Alabama and purchased an in-line H&R 45 caliber muzzleloader. I hunted successfully with this for several years. About a year after I got mine my father decided he needed one just like it, so he acquired it.

I have since acquired a CVA Hawkin Rifle in .50 caliber to hunt with. After getting involved in War Between the States reenacting and living histories, I have obtained several period pieces on .58 to .69 calibers.

For several years four friends who were retired from the military would come and meet my father, my friend Jackie and I for a week of muzzleloader hunting. These guys were all ex-military shooters with one of them retiring from command of the Army marksmanship training unit at Fort Benning, Georgia. We would camp out on Bullard Creek Wildlife Management Area, take our smoke poles out, and pursue the game as they did 200 years ago. Since the rules at the WMA were that when you killed the deer, you could no longer hunt but if you killed a wild hog, you could continue hunting. We would hunt hogs until about Thursday. We knew if we killed the deer early, we would become the camp cook and no one wanted that duty. We would go down into the bays and the river swamp in search of those elusive wild hogs. On one occasion Lloyd, who by the way was a National Rifle shooting champion in the military, and I were headed to where I had located some fresh hog sign. When hunting the river swamp one of the first things you learn is that daylight comes later in the swamp than it does on the hill. As we made our way down the trail trying to keep on the right bearing and locate all of the turn points burned in my mind, we came upon a place that I recognize we were going to have to turn right at. As I stepped over the log, I noticed that the little knoll in front of me look different than it did the day before. It was almost like there was a bump on it. As I continued to stare at it trying to ascertain what was different, the bump begins to change shapes. I quickly recognized it was a pile of wild hogs. Since my .45 muzzleloader was already fitted with a percussion cap, I raised the gun, took steady aim and fired. I heard the telltale squeal of a pig being hit. I dropped to the ground in order to reload and give

Lloyd a clear shot, because the hogs were just waking up. It is a little difficult to lay flat on your side on the ground and load a muzzleloader, but I was hard at work at it. I kept wondering why Lloyd wasn't shooting. Finally, I got my smoke pole reloaded and turned to see that Lloyd was trying to get a percussion cap on the nipple. Before he could get the gun capped the hogs were on the move. There must have been 20 of them and they scattered to the four winds. We went over to recover my prize which I had pinned in its place. We took that hog back to camp and dressed it. That hog only weighed about 50 pounds so we butterflied it and roasted it over coals. After about four hours of roasting the pig, we all sat down to a dinner of succulent hog meat, baked sweet potatoes and baked apples (Joe, one of the other hunters from Virginia had an apple orchard and had brought several grocery bags of apples with him) and other trimmings. The next morning Jackie got one that looked like its twin with a bow and arrow. I heard the squeal when the broadhead hit its mark.

On another occasion, Gene, who was the best all-round shot I have ever seen, snapped three caps on the deer that I had seen a couple of weeks earlier on the last day of bow season. Gene was hunting in a little clearing on the ridge where my favorite loblolly pine tree grew. This was before we had climbing stands so we had to find trees that we could climb and perch on a limb like a Hoot Owl. Not finding a tree that he could climb in that clearing he located the small pile of dirt and took up a stand there. It drizzled rain all morning but rain does not stop a true deer hunter. But what rain does is affect the ability of a black powder gun to shoot. Most people ever heard the phrase "keep your powder dry boys" and it is altogether true. The deer came out into the clearing. Gene, who has taken many deer all over the world, later told me that that was the only deer that he had already mounted and hung on the wall in his den before pulling the trigger. He lined up his sights on the monster buck and squeezed the trigger. Pop! The percussion was all that went off. He flicked the old cap off and replaced it with a new one. Pop! (Another misfire). Once again, he replaced a percussion cap only to have it fail a third time. That afternoon as we met up at my Bronco, he related the story to us. He had placed a fourth percussion cap on the nipple but had decided not to attempt a fourth time as the buck eased on off.

As a side note, during rifle season, Lewis had climbed and that same big buck, again, had managed to stay alive. It was raining that morning and when Lewis put the scope on the deer not knowing that it had fogged up. When the deer went straight under his tree. It was amazing because Lewis missed him too.

Later as we talked about the buck and how large his antlers were, we agreed that we had all three seen the same buck that year.

A friend of mine who owned property adjoining the WMA called me to measure antlers on the deer he had taken on his property there. When I first laid eyes on his buck, I knew without a doubt that the 14-point monster that I was beginning to measure was the same deer that all three of us had lost an opportunity for. The deer was killed less than 700 yards from where we were hunting and was an absolute prize.

Once, due to the fact it had been misting rain, Gene and I decided we would not take a chance of moisture getting to our powder. We made the decision that we would unload the muzzleloaders, clean them well and reload them with a fresh charge of powder. The only way to unload a muzzleloader is to shoot it out unless you want to go through an exhaustive means of pulling the bullet with a bullet puller and then trying to clean it out. Shooting it out is much easier. We went to the check station where one of the game wardens was and asked where we can clean the guns out. He pointed to an area just the other side of the check station and told us we could do it there. As we walked out the door there was a 55-gallon drum of trash. Sitting atop the trash were two of the small orange juice cans. Gene told me to pick those cans up as we went by. When we got into position, he cocked his .45 caliber Kentucky rifle and told me to throw one of the cans up into the air. I threw that can as hard as I could. Blam! Gene fired. Twang! And the can whizzed off out into the woods. He took my .58 caliber buffalo gun and told me to throw the other can which I did. Blam! He repeated with the .58 caliber and the can disappeared off into the woods. As we turned to go back to our vehicle, we noticed the Game Warden looking out the window. His eyes were as big as Buick hubcaps. Later on, he asked me if that guy I was with ever missed. To which I replied that I had never seen him miss.

He told me, "That's some of the gosh awfulest shooting I have ever seen"!

On another hunt, daddy took a button buck on Friday and was the last deer brought into the check station that afternoon. He had been in an accident at work where an electric hoist had broken loose from its moorings falling in peening his hand on the top of a steel drum. All of the bones in his hand had been broken. The doctor, who was a close friend of his had run stainless steel pins through from the knuckle lining all the bones where they could heal properly. He had this funky looking splint on that had all of his fingers separated on one part and his foam on the other. He couldn't climb the ladder stands we were using so he took a folding dove stool and found a good location to hide. The little buck came out about 90 yards from him. He propped his elbow on his knee and lined up his shot placing the gun in the V of the splint. When I came to pick him up that evening in the Bronco, he handed me his gun and stool he asked could I help him with something else. I went across the ditch and discovered he had the little 75-pound buck lying there waiting for me. We loaded him up to get to the check station. Daddy decided instead of staying that last night with us that go on home and prepare to go to Atlanta the next day and see his new grandson.

The next morning, I climbed my ladder with my trusty .45. Right at the crack of day, I saw a movement off to my right. It was a doe moving through the planted pines. My ladder stand (hokesits – I hope I spelled it right) was up against a spindly Oaktree. The leaves had dried and rattled almost every time I breathed. This would prevent me from shifting around to my right to take the shot right-handed. Years ago, as a young Boy Scout at summer camp, I could only close my right eye. I had not practiced winking at the girls enough to be ambidextrous with this eye closing business. So, I had to shoot left-handed at summer camp. I did pretty well because I scored Sharpshooter. But later I was able to close my left eye so I shot right-handed which was more natural to me. I didn't know it at the time if you know what your dominant eye is and shoot from that side you don't have close either eye. I shifted my rifle to take a left-handed shot. The pine trees must've been spaced at about 10 feet apart so I lined up on an opening in front of the deer and when the deer stepped into the clear and squeezed the shot off for the vital area. The deer took off but I knew it was hit. I reloaded my smoke pole and set out to track the deer which I found the deer after about 90 yards. When I got to the check station mine was the first deer turned in that morning. Daddy had gotten the last one turned in the day before and I got the first one turned in that morning. I guess you could consider ours to be back-to-back. As we hung my deer up preparing to "Jeep Skin" the deer (in order to Jeep-skin a deer you split the skin up the underside and each leg run the end of the cut on the legs. You peeled down the skin on the neck just enough to tie a rock or golf ball inside it. The other end of the rope to the front of the Jeep, or Bronco, as my case was and backup peeling the deer like a squirrel.) Daddy and mother pulled up on the way to Atlanta to see how things had gone that morning. He was pleased to see that I already had one and even more pleased to know mine was the first one turned in the next morning. He only had to go 3 miles out of his way to come by where we were camped.

Since that time, I acquired a .50 caliber Hawkin rifle with double set triggers, for very accurate shooting. I had heard that you could shoot a maxi ball with 120 grains of black powder and have an excellent load for deer. When I attempted at my friend Lamar's house to try the load, I sat down at the beach pull the set triggers first then test off the second trigger and thought I had lost my shoulder. The curved brass butt plate of rifles made in that day in time were a weapon to use after you had shot your one shot. The sharp points of that butt dug into my thick shoulder and was extremely painful. I just decided to try a slightly lighter load. So, I loaded 90 grains of black powder and shot that maxi ball again. This was a much more comfortable load and was plenty powerful enough to do what it needed to do since in my .45 caliber I only shot 80 grains of black powder. I had read that you could load it with two .50 caliber balls on top of each other pushed by the 120-grain load and they would impact side by side. It might be deadly but severely uncomfortable to shoot.

232

I have gathered several muzzleloaders including one that I have absolutely no need for, a 36-caliber squirrel gun. I also performed living histories and fire salutes at memorial services with my War Between the States era replicas of Springfields and Enfields. These .58 caliber and .69 caliber behemoths would take a deer but are much too cumbersome to attempt to get into a tree stand with. Of course, you could put the bayonet on it and toss it toward the deer to impale it until you got there.

They are fun to shoot as is a rifled cannon one of my friends has. We had several reenacting cannon crews in neighboring towns and my cousin had a coehorn mortar who all my kinfolks were part of the reenactment crew, including my son who was their "powder monkey." My son and his wife have uniforms and performed salutes fired at grave marking ceremonies. At the 150th anniversary of the battle at Sharpsburg, Maryland (Antietam), I bought my daughter in law an Enfield carbine to use.

———————————

It is also loads of fun to shoot cap and ball revolvers and single-shot muzzle loading pistols. They are the devil to clean, as all black powder guns are, but they are worth the trouble you have to go to. Samuel Colt did well in developing his revolver and it is said that Colonel John Singleton Mosby, of the Confederacy, made it famous. He would not allow his troops to carry a saber because they made too much noise and he said they were only fitting for roasting a piece of meat over the fire. He insisted at the least that they carry at least two Colts on their belt with fixed or loaded cylinders handy but really preferred them to have two pistols on their belt and two on pommel holsters on the saddle. This would give them 24 shots as they entered into battle. This was a definite advantage. You have to be careful when you load the doggone things because you have to put some kind of grease in over the ball in order to keep the fire from one cylinder opening from leaping into another and thus causing a chain fire. I saw one chain fire at a reenactment one time and the fellow looked like he had a handful of firecrackers. I bet that would be uncomfortable with lead balls in all the chambers.

With the advent of substitutes for black powder and also with new projectiles, called such as sabots, it is possible to develop more accuracy and more stopping power and the cleanup is much easier.

The way I learned the cleanup was to pump hot soapy water back-and-forth through the gun after taking the barrel and the breach out of the stock. Place the breach end into the bucket of hot soapy water and using a cleaning rod with a tight patch pump the water for a good time then place the barrel in hot clean water pumping to see if you have done a good enough job of removing the residue. Once you are pumping clear water out of the nipple it is clean. If the water is hot enough the barrel will completely dry if you turn it upside down to drain after being heated up. All you would need to do then would be to lightly oil it. Window cleaner with vinegar will also break the black powder residue up pretty well. When my water heater in my shop went out, I cleaned the muskets just using the window cleaner and vinegar. I am such a purist that I prefer to use black powder and I also prefer to mold my projectiles. "To each his own", as they used to say, "Whatever floats your boat".

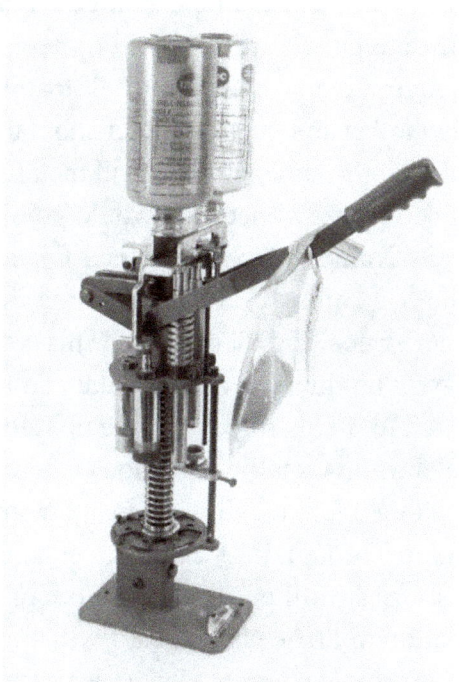

MEC 650 Progressive Loader

CHAPTER FIFTEEN

RELOADING AMMUNITION

I have been a reloader of ammunition for a good many years. My first exposure to metallic cartridge reloading was a neighbor, down the street, who used an old Lyman 310 tool to load his .22 Hornet. My first exposure to shotshell loading was a childhood friend who became an avid skeet shooter and had begun loading his shotshells. I first began to reload metallic ammunition with a Lee Loader for my .38 special. I would go out into the country to a friend of mine's place and reload five at the time, stepping out to the edge of the shed and shooting them at a target, stepping back in and reloading them again. This was in the mid to late 1960's and I was not making a large salary so in order to shoot as much as I wanted to, I was forced to take up reloading. I have progressed to the point in metallic cartridges where I load everything that I shoot and have dies for many cartridges that I no longer own or shoot. Through the years I have gathered and amassed the accessories from people getting out of loading. I am so persnickety that on my rifle cartridges, I will cut a powder granule in two to make the charge balance perfectly on my scale. This is unnecessary but is the way I choose to load. A person asked me the other day how much I would charge to load them some rifle ammunition to which I remarked you probably can't afford it.

I have developed rifle loads through the years that were tuned to the rifle that I use them in, in an effort produced some tight groups when shooting them. My first attempt in loading for rifles came for my trusty .22-250. It was not illegal to hunt members of the raptor family so we would take my accurate model 70 Winchester and ride the roads looking to collect our specimens. When legislation was passed protecting the raptors we began hunting crows. My friend acquired a bull barreled Mossberg 800 on which we placed a 36x Unertl scope. By that time, I had replaced the 2 ½x to 7x scope that I had with a 4x to 12x to facilitate longer shots. The funny thing about crows is that they are pretty smart animals. They got to the point where, I believe, they were able to recognize our vehicles and would not sit on a tree limb long enough for us to get out and line up a shot. But if we used someone else's vehicle, they would sit there which was a bad move on their part. There have been reports in some areas where people do a lot of crow hunting and believe that the crows were able to tell whether they have a scoped rifle or a shotgun. I don't know about that but I believe they knew our vehicles. I developed a load with the 50 grain super explosive projectile that I believe if it hit them on the toe would blow them up like opening their mouth and dropping a cherry bomb down their throat. That reload also worked well on coots. My buddy shot a coot one day, swimming in his brother's pond and blew him up. All of the coot exploded, with the exception of the gizzard which was still floating out in the pond. Of course, anyone who's ever tried to eat a coot gizzard knows that that dang thing is darn nigh indestructible.

We were riding on the other side of the county one evening looking for crows. We knew there were several pecan orchards in that area and knew that the pecan orchard owners hated the crows with a passion. They are reputed to be able to carry away seven pounds of pecans a day each. Anyway, we rode for a while looking for crows and got thirsty so we stopped at a small country store. We went in to get us a drink and a pack of crackers and one of my distant cousins was standing outside. He glanced in the backseat of the car and saw my rifle lying there. He asked me what kind of rifle it was and instead of trying to explain I just said a .22. He wanted to know why I had such a big scope on it and of course, I replied so I can see how to shoot a long way. He started making fun of my rifle and scope saying that no .22 needed a scope that big. I reached into the back seat and withdrew the rifle looking for a target to demonstrate that I did need that larger scope. Way across the highway in the bottom of a round head was a dead tree standing in the middle. Perched in that treetop was a bird. I didn't know what kind of bird it was and I knew it was a long way away.

So, I told my cousin, "You see that Mockingbird in the top of that tree."

He said that he did and I told him to watch. I propped on the pillar holding the roof of the porch of the store up, ran my scope up to 12 power and lined up my shot. My rifle was sighted in for 250 yards and I knew that this range for something beyond that so I tried to estimate the distance and held up over the bird's head, hoping to get close enough to at least make it fly off. I squeezed my shot off. The bird tumbled out of the tree to the ground which literally blew my cousin's mind. He ran across the highway with disregard for traffic and it was a good thing nothing was coming because he didn't look either direction. He ran all the way over to that tree. Picking the bird up he began to pace back to where we were. When he arrived, he had the "Mockingbird" in his hand and announced it was 347 paces.

Upon making the shot, I had quickly slid my rifle into the gun case and zipped it up for fear someone would want me to duplicate that shot. It was by far the very best shot I've ever made with a rifle and although I really did not believe that I was going to hit the bird. I tried to do everything right and must have. I guess I was a legend from then on in that neck of the woods.

I later began skeet shooting and for purely economic reasons had to get geared up to reload my shotgun shells. Dad and I started with a single-stage MEC loader. My dad would've been great on an assembly-line because he could get geared up for any repetitious act and perform it flawlessly time after time after time. I have witnessed him on many an occasion reloading over 250 shotshells and hour on that machine. He would load shells on Saturday night. Then he, my cousin Ralph and I would go on Sunday afternoon to Claxton and shoot them all up. He would take the same hulls and repeat the process for the next weekend. We were using Winchester AA hulls which would load 20 times before failure. Remington and Federal later came out with a unibody hull like it but they were not as good.

When my friend Bobby started me shooting skeet in competition. I was not making enough money to buy new shells so it was a necessity to shoot reloads even in competition. I got loaders for all four gauges and begin to load up shells to shoot in the tournaments. I practiced some to improve my skill and loaded for that also. I became so conscious of my hulls that I switched over from a Remington 1100 autoloader to a Winchester 101 over-under. Most gun clubs had rules that any hull hitting the ground became the property of the club and they would sell hulls to reloaders after the tournaments. Once I acquired the 101 which was fitted with Purbaugh tubes for the other three gauges, hulls were no longer a worry. If you were to look in my shop now, I have boxes on shelves that are over 12 feet long and four shelves high that are filled with the empty hulls awaiting an appointment with the reloader.

Later when I began to referee shooting events my shells were included in the compensation package.

Although I no longer shoot tournaments and do not hunt birds nearly as much as I would like, I am geared up for and can produce many reloaded shells when needed. I have 30 or 40 pounds of powder and at least a ton of shot waiting to be used.

Although it costs, at one time, half the cost of a loaded factory shell and less than that if one shopped judiciously for components the price of lead on the world market has driven the cost of reloading up along with the cost of new factory loaded ammunition. Now my reloading is more therapeutic than it is of necessity and remains very satisfying as a pastime.

I still love to shoot rifles and pistols and on occasion will go to the range and spend two or three hours sighting in rifles for just recreational shooting. There was a time when I would sight in at least 75 to 100 rifles for people in advance of deer season. That was later trimmed down to 35 or 40 and although I'm not as steady as I was at one time, I would state matter-of-factly that I can sight one as good as anyone around. My son now does all the sighting in around here. By the way, he still loves the smell of gunpowder like his dad.

I'll never forget one of my friends had purchased a Weatherby 300 Magnum. That is quite a lot of gun for this area of the country but nevertheless, he had acquired it. We went to the range where he could sight it in. I had my trusty 5-gallon bucket with my shot bags filled with sand and sewn up to utilize a rest. I ask him if he wanted to use them and he informed me that he had something better. He pulled out one of those adjustable varmint rifle rest. I advised him against using it but he insisted. When he touched off the first shot the old Weatherby jumped so high that the scope almost creased his head. He turned around me and had the funniest look on his face and then asked, "Bill, you think you could finish this up for me?" I knew that the old Weatherby had whipped him. I hauled out my sandbags and promptly sighted the rifle in for him. I don't know for sure if he has ever shot that rifle again.

The same thing happened to my son Billy. I had traded for a Winchester .300 Magnum model 70 rifle and we had gone to the rifle range to check it out. I had made up my mind that I would give that to Billy since he shot a model 70 in .270. That way if we ever got an opportunity to go out West and hunt large game, he would be set up. He lay down over the sandbags squeezing the first round off. I watched as the muzzle bucked up and he looked around at me with a funny look on his face. I told him he would have to hold that one a little bit tighter than his .270. On the second shot he attempted, he held the rifle steady and later told me he had no idea there was that much difference in the .300 Magnum versus his .270. I told him of the time when his grandfather was at the gun club and a friend of ours had a 300 Winchester Magnum similar to his. You need to understand that daddy fired expert in everything when he joined the Marines and that rifles were not unfamiliar to him. The BAR that he carried in World War II probably kicked some but nothing like that .300 Magnum. He was crouched behind the bench of a picnic table when he touched the round off. The extra recoil of the Magnum overbalanced him and knocked him on his behind. He had a sheepish look on his face as he sat on the ground and looked back at that rifle.

Jackie, a good friend and good hunting buddy, was near Atlanta one day and stopped in a gun shop. He noticed on the rack a Weatherby Mark V chambered for 460 Weatherby Magnum (the most powerful production rifle in the world). He inquired about it and the man told him it was used but had only had one shot fired through it. The price was pretty good on it and Jackie inquired further. The owner of the gun shop told him that if he would like he could take it out back to the range and fire it as long as he would pay for the cartridge, which was pretty expensive. He liked that idea so he took him up on it. He went outside, fired the rifle. He came back with the rifle and handed it to the owner. He told him he was absolutely certain why it had had only one shot fired through it because it would kick your teeth out. I don't know if that rifle ever got sold but I'm sure there was someone around who was man enough to stand up to it, but I bet he had to be the size of a Sasquatch. That rifle kicked 3 ½ times what a 12-gauge 3-inch Magnum shotgun will and had 8110 foot-pounds of energy. Now that's enough to knock and 8110 pound car a foot or to knock a 1 pound object 8110 feet. That is some awesome cartridge. I have shot a .358 Enterkin Magnum and withstood the recoil.

One friend of mine, Gene, was a retired colonel from the United States Army and was a past national champion pistol shooter, developed the cartridge one time that was bodacious. He did this by necking up a 300 Weatherby Magnum cartridge to .35 caliber. His load drove a 250-grain projectile in excess of 3000 feet per second and I witnessed this up close and personal. I shot the prototype rifle that he had which was made from a Mauser model 98. He had taken the scope off to try to dress the throat where the long bullets would feed a little better and placed the scope back on but he had not resighted it yet. I was in Columbus, Georgia at the AMTU range at Fort Benning with him and he offered to let me shoot it. I started to sit down at the beach and he told me I would probably be better off standing due to the recoil. When I squeezed the trigger, I quickly found out that the scope was shooting to the right because I hit the angle iron target frame which was made of 1 ½" X 1½" X 1/8" steel, cutting it off as a chop saw. I also noticed that at 100 yards the dust kicked up from the impact of the projectile almost simultaneously with the blast. He later told me that when a bullet is going 3000 feet per second it will do that.

Throughout the years I have owned rifles of several calibers. Although I have preferences, I've enjoyed shooting all of them. It's funny how some like the .22 -250 can shoot with such accuracy. I had some friends at one time that had special built .22-250 bench rest rifles. They were something with laminated thumb through stocks, high-powered scopes with dots placed at minute-of-angle increments. This was way before you could buy a scope with Mill Dots in it. They would shoot what they called fly spec targets. Which was a circle that was about .300 in diameter and had a dot in the center. They shot this at 25 yards. The object was to shoot the dot out without breaking the circle. It takes a pretty good shot to put a .224 bullet through a .300 hole without breaking the circle. One of them had a little farm and hunted deer in the cornfield. He had built a blind with a bench rest in it and had measured the field, color coding the fence posts to coincide with the distances. This was a pretty scientific way of deer hunting and was pretty successful for him to be involved in. He reloaded his ammunition and was more persnickety than I was. He would weigh his brass to make sure they were all the same and would cull any that weren't the same weight. He would do the same with his bullets. Any that were not the same weight as the others were set aside and not used.

Ponsness Warren Shotshell Loader

I always wanted a Ponsness Warren shotshell loader. Some of them were capable of loading 1800 shells per hour. I have friends that in fact bought them one and fell in love with it but they were so fast that it had taken all the pleasure out of reloading.

My sister helped me reload one time. It was two times, the first and the last. I don't know what she did to those shells but when you fired the shell it was like it was lobbed out there and then would explode about 30 yards away from you. One of my friends, Billy, saw one of those crazy shells and what it did and begged me to load some more of them but I didn't know how she had done it. I was uneasy with it anyway, what she did was almost like somebody smoking a cigarette while they loaded. All that gunpowder and one spark would be all it would take. Although smokeless powder won't explode unless it is confined, it is still scary.

I must confess that I have not always done the most perfect job of loading ammunition. This has occurred more with shotshell than anything else because of the need for high production and also because of the use of a progressive loader where several steps are occurring at the same time. Sometimes you catch it when the machine messes up sometimes you don't. At times I have been exposed to ridicule by my shooting buddies when one of my shotshells would make a funny sound. Sometimes it would be so little powder inside the hull that the shot in the wad would just barely make it out the barrel. There are other times when the shot load is so light that it will barely break a clay pigeon. On all of those occasions, it was a matter of me not noticing when a powder charge didn't drop or the shot charge hung up. On a progressive loader when it does goof-up it takes a little while to straighten out the mess. The good thing about a single stage loader is about the worst you can do is pinch your thumb. You know when something malfunctions because you're only dealing with that single stage.

No progressive loader is totally failsafe. Some are better than others but they all can produce faulty ammunition for a number of various reasons.

There is no telling how many hundreds of pounds of powder and how many tons of shot I have loaded and shot through my shotguns. I was shooting up to 400 shells per week, in practice and competition. For the most part, there aren't any problems with it but only upon occasion that it does malfunction and most likely is never on the dangerous side, it is just on the goof up side, that can cause you ridicule from your shooting buddies. I have developed my favorite loads through the years for different applications. In my over-under shotgun, I prefer a 2 ¾ dram 1 1/8-ounce load of number 8 ½'s for skeet. In a semiautomatic shotgun for skeet, I prefer to go to the 3-dram load. For trap, international clay pigeon, wobble trap and sometimes sporting clays, I have been known to use even a 3 ¼ dram load and almost always will use 7 ½ shot. All of these loads can be produced in my reloading shop.

The greatest advantage to reloading is when you shoot .410 or 28 gauge shotguns. Those shells are quite expensive bought over the counter, which is not understandable to me since the price of a shotgun shell in 20 gauge, 16 gauge, 12 gauge, and 10 gauge is driven by the weight of lead shot used as projectiles. The .410 in the 2 ½ in shell contains ½ ounce of shot while in the 3' version contains ¾ ounce, which is the same as the 28 gauge load. Most of the time they cost more than 20 gauge, 16 gauge and 12 gauge shells although 7/8-ounce, 1 ounce and 1 ¼ ounce are their normal loadings. The 28 gauge is by far the best to train a young child the art of shot gunning with. But 28 gauge shells are scarce except in the skeet shooting realm and very expensive to purchase. They used to refer to the 28 gauge as the rich man's gun. The only ones who would use it were some prosperous quail hunters.

Someone asked me one time if I reloaded .22 long rifles to which I responded, "If I could figure out how to place the priming back in the rim, I probably would load them also".

Sometimes reloading includes the use of cast bullets used especially for target shooting with a pistol. A lead wadcutter or semi-wadcutter is the best bullet to shoot targets with. It cuts a pretty, round circle in the paper and therefore is very easy to score. I have tried my hand at casting bullets and have surely not perfected this yet. The fumes from the melted lead are not good for you, so I use an electric fan to blow them away from me when I am trying to make my bullets or fishing sinkers. My most success has been molding round balls, mini balls and maxi balls to shoot in black powder rifles. Nevertheless, I will continue until I am quite a bit better at this if the lead fumes don't get me first.

The suggestion I would make to anyone interested in loading rifle, pistol or shotgun ammunition, would be to get some good literature and do a lot of reading before you get up and get started. This may save many mistakes on the part of the novice loader. Maybe even save some fingers and eyes and such. There are lots of great books on the subject. I have a shelf full of them that I still consult them when trying some new load or loading for some new cartridge. I keep loading notes on everything I load and refer to them often. The other suggestion I would make is to keep good records. Mark your ammunition box with the appropriate data including caliber, bullet, powder charge and feet per second. I utilize old factory cardboard boxes for my handloads but prefer some of the plastic boxes with flip-top lids. I also incorporate a sighting in book with the rifle, load, and distance sighted for. I have records going back to 1966.

CHAPTER SIXTEEN

TRAINING YOUNG PEOPLE

It is every parent's responsibility to ensure that their child is trained in at the very least, gun safety. The National Rifle Association had the Eddie Eagle program that went to the schools in order to train children about firearms and how to treat them in a safe manner. I was a National Rifle Association Hunter safety instructor even before it was required by the state of Georgia. I began to teach my son at about the age of three. The first thing I taught him was respect for firearms and a healthy respect for what they could do. I trained him that he was not to touch a firearm unless I was there and told him that it was okay. He learned that well and to this day he practices safe handling of firearms.

I have been a range officer in the Boy Scout program and have the opportunity to work with young boys from the first grade through the twelfth grade. I tell them at the outset that I do not care if they cannot hit the side of the barn. What I care about is that they know gun safety and they know how to act around firearms and they know what to do even if they find a firearm in the woods.

Daisy made a short-stocked BB gun, with a safety, to use in training a young person in shooting proficiency and gun safety. My son had one and I would go to the appliance store, get a box that a washing machine came in and put it in the backyard for him to use as a backstop. The BB would penetrate the front layer but it could not penetrate the back layer so all the BBs would wind up in the bottom of the box and could be recycled. This was a very inexpensive way to train both safety and proficiency at that young age of three. The stock was short enough that it actually fit him. He got pretty good at it and I savored the time that he and I spent while he was out there practicing on his skill set. I would take him on dove hunts and allow him to take his little Daisy BB gun along. He would fire at doves that were flying over. Of course, the chances of him scoring a hit were very slim, but that was the beginning of his dove hunting.

I looked far and wide for a youth model single shot 28 gauge shotgun. Although they were manufactured for years the source had dried up. I finally bought him a youth model single shot .410 to train him in the art of shot gunning. Even with the short stock on a youth model I had to remove the recoil pad and replace it with a one-quarter inch the piece of leather since he was so young. The gun was then short enough to fit a four-year-old. He would take that trusty .410 and use it to fill his grandmother's larder of squirrels. He became quite a proficient squirrel hunter and as we went on those squirrel hunting trips, I would note his observance of the safety rules and if he violated one would call it to his attention. I would also take him on dove hunts where he would practice more and more learning wing shooting. He dropped his first dove at age 7. Although he did not kill them with regularity after that bagging that dove set him on fire for wing shooting.

At the age of 10, Billy and one of his cousins, whose father had spent an equal amount of time drilling safety into his head, were eligible to take the Georgia Hunter Safety Course. They blew the doors off the test because they had been living it for seven years or so. Older boys did not make the grade and had to retake the test because of it. Any person born after a certain date in Georgia has to have the completion of the hunter safety course in order to attain a hunting license.

That year for Christmas he got a Remington 870 youth shotgun in 20 gauge. Come that fall I instructed them that he was only to load one shell until I was sure how competent he was and how safe he acted with a repeating shotgun. He hunted all that year and did what I call the "Barney Fife" where he had only one shell. He demonstrated to me his awareness of safety and his proficiency that year and after begging me all year long to let him load more than one opening day the next year I told him that he could fill the magazine up which he did. The first bird that flew over him his shotgun reported. Blam! Blam! Blam! The bird flew on. I walked over to him and informed him that he was going to have to play "Barney Fife" again. He was very disappointed but learned to live with it. All that day he loaded one shot at the time.

On the next hunt, I again allowed him to again load the magazine and he acted way more responsible at that time.

It is so important that these young people start out right. It is important that they learn the basic rules of gun safety. Number one: always treat a gun as if it's loaded. Number two: always point a gun in a safe direction. Up. Down or downrange. Number three: never point a gun at something you do not intend to shoot. Number four: make sure of your background (know what is beyond your target). There are many other rules of safety but, without a doubt, if these four are followed the child will be safety conscious. The other rule I like teaching my Cub Scouts and I told my son is that you do not handle a firearm without permission. As Eddie Eagle would teach if you're walking around in the woods and find a firearm do these things. Leave it alone. Go and find an adult and show them the firearm.

A parent and child can have many rewarding experiences on shooting outings for target practice and on hunting trips. By doing this a bond can be established between the parent and the child that can last a lifetime. I have so many fond memories of hunting and shooting with my father and also an equal number of memories hunting and shooting with my son.

In this day of "Political Correctness" and "Zero Tolerance" in schools, children are taught to fear and not respect a firearm. I personally believe that they should be taught about firearms and how they are safely handled (or left alone) and how to properly use them.

Some school systems around here have shooting programs and the 4 H has BB competition. One of my cousin's daughter, was just awarded a college shooting scholarship. I told them that I hope to see her in the Olympics one day.

CHAPTER SEVENTEEN

MISCELLANY

THE DEVIL AT THE RIVER

There was a time when stories of the devil of the river were circulating. One such tale was that a man was tied up to the shore and the devil surfaced by the boat scaring the man so badly that he jumped out of the boat and swam to the sandbar then running just as hard as he could back home. Another story was of a man who had said that he would shoot the devil if he came near to him. He lived in a cabin on the river and was cooking breakfast one morning and turned around to find the devil sitting at his table. It was told that he threw his frying pan in the air and ran out of the house screaming and did not stop until he got to his neighbor's house out of breath and scared to death.

There were numerous alleged sightings and there was some suspicion that two young men, from the county, who were scuba divers had a "Creature of the Black Lagoon " outfit and were behind it. Nothing was ever proven but all the folks who lived along the Altamaha sure kept a sharp watch of anything suspicious happening.

RAFTING TIMBER ON THE ALTAMAHA

My family, the Middletons, were some of the first to raft timber to Darien down the Altamaha. Their property bordered the Altamaha River. They would cut the timber and build the rafts and then drift down the Altamaha to the delta and get the timber to the sawmills located there. Afterward, they would make their way to Brunswick and ride in the cars of the Macon to Brunswick Railroad back to Surrency and walk the eleven miles back to their homes and begin again. It is said that one of my grandmother's uncles slept on a coffin on the way back and caught cholera and died. It was a rough life. Sometimes those rafts were not built well enough and broke up. Some of those logs are still in the river and present a navigational hazard to fishermen and boaters when the river is low. I have hit them before and damaged a prop. I know several folks who have broken the foot of their outboard motors on them.

A friend of mine, Weyman, hit one near Carters Bight running wide open in his bass boat. The foot of the 150 Mercury broke off and they almost hit the cut bank on the Tattnall County side when the bow of the boat came down slowing the uncontrollable boat. We went back looking for the foot of the motor. I had a frog gig and was slowly moving downriver from the gash made in the log where the foot hit. Suddenly I found something metallic and held the gig in place while he donned a scuba outfit and went down the shaft of the gig. The gig began to thrash violently and he appeared at the surface with the foot of his motor in one hand.

GERMAN SPY ON THE RIVER

We used to hear tales of a German spy that had come in on the coast and made it up-river to near Buckhorn Bluff and lived there during World War II. During that time the river swamp was so dense and the population was so sparse that anything could have remained hidden there easily. From Buckhorn Bluff to Upper Sisters Bluff is as thick a swamp as there is along the Altamaha. Is it possible that a German Spy could live there undetected for any length of time? It would have been possible to hide in that dense swamp without detection for a good long time.

When we would camp there as Boy Scouts, we would go into the river swamp and explore looking to find his shack of some sign or skeleton or something. We never found anything but had a great time looking for evidence. It is known that German U-boats were operating all along the Georgia and Florida coast and our Navy and coast watchers searched the entire coastline looking for German infiltrators. There were cases of German spies landing on the East Coast and working inland. It is very possible that one was there.

BOATS

It has been said that the two proudest days in the life of a boat owner are the day he buys it and the day he sells it. I have owned several boats since 1970 and have often made the statement if cars and automobiles were as much trouble as a boat and trailer, we would still be riding horses. It seems that every time you go out in your boat there is something that has to be fixed. A good portion of those items is involved with the lights on your trailer. But other things will literally drive you crazy. I have broken shafts, torn up propellers, lost propellers, dead batteries and even once, in a tournament, a screw went up into my stator coil which left me dead in the water with a crippled boat. I learned early in my motor boating life to go upstream from the landing so if anything tore up it would be easier to get back to where your truck and trailer were. I also learned to have a spare prop, spark plugs and other necessities in the boat.

I have paddled many a "dead in the water" boat back to the landing and I can tell you for a fact it is not fun trying to do it upstream. You hope and pray for someone to come by who can pull you there. Ergo always go upstream for you can float back down.

I have found is much easier to have a pond boat. If you put it in the pond at your house all you have to make sure of is that it doesn't leak and you have a paddle. That is a lot less complicated than going to the river or to lakes with your boat.

FERRIES ALONG THE ALTAMAHA

AND

CONFEDERATE GOLD

After the 1813 Creek Cession and the 1818 lottery when the west side of the Altamaha was open to settlers there was a need to be able to cross. Stafford's Ford, close to Carter's Bight, is indicated on early Spanish maps in the 1600s. It later became Stafford's Ferry and eventually became the property of my great-great-grandfather Middleton.

My ancestors also operated Halls Ferry (later Nails Ferry), Town Bluff Ferry, Kemp's Ferry (later Mann's Ferry and Piney Bluff Ferry), Tippins Ferry and Tillman's Ferry. It appears that if you crossed the Altamaha back then you paid some of my family.

Town Bluff Ferry is where my Uncle Seaborn Hall supposedly brought General John C. Breckinridge (Confederate Secretary of War) across the Altamaha when the confederate government was breaking up. General Stoneman of General Sherman's hordes was in pursuit. Uncle Seaborn then destroyed the ferry so Stoneman could not pursue Breckinridge. That was the winter of 1864 and the Altamaha was wiregrass to wiregrass impassable without a ferry. It is said that General Breckenridge had some of the Confederate Gold from the Richmond Treasury and some folks think it is buried near Towns Bluff to this day.

RABBIT HUNTING

When I was a teenager my cousin Billy and I would hunt rabbits at night. I know that "fire Hunting' was not legal but the statute of limitations had long since run out. We usually took my 1951 International pickup truck. We had a green wooden box (that used to be my toy box) in the back. One would drive and the other would stand in the back of the pickup and shoot any rabbit that would freeze in the headlights. We would fill the back and sell the rabbits the next morning for $.50 each. This would help pay for the gasoline (at $.25 per gallon) and shells (at $1.00 a box). We would sometimes hunt with another friend in his father's pasture which was about 200 acres. That pasture was full of rabbits.

One night we drove by the Game Wardens house and Billy decided to shoot a house cat in the Game Wardens yard. The road by his house was a dead end and realizing the Billy had messed up by shooting the cat I quickly got the pickup turned around and as we passed the house again the lights were on and we quickly saw the Game Wardens pickup lights come on. I ran that old International as fast as I could and hollered to Billy to get rid of the rabbits in case we were caught. Just as Billy had thrown the last rabbit out, I managed to elude the Game Warden in the dust storm I had created on the dirt roads. We lost all our profit that night and decided to call it quits while we were ahead.

On another occasion, we were using the family 1864 Ford Fairlane on which I was seated on the hood. Billy was driving the car while I was the designated shooter. Our signal was to tap the windshield once to slow down and twice to stop. Suddenly I spotted a rabbit on the left edge of the headlight beam. I tapped once on the windshield with no response. I slammed my hand on the windshield unaware that Billy had fallen asleep at the wheel. As I clicked the safety to the shotgun off preparing to harvest the little furry prize, Billy jolted awake and slammed on the brakes. I slid off the hood in front of the car. I pulled the shotgun in and extended my elbows and hit the ground hard. As I was rolling it looked as though the tire was going to come across me and I rolled into the road ditch. It scared me half to death. As I scrambled out of the ditch, Billy had jumped out and was laughing wildly. I frapped him up beside the head out of frustration and then calmed down and started to laugh also.

WILD CATS

Two types of wild cats live along the Altamaha River. One is the Bobcat which is abundant in our area. I see them regularly at our farm on the river. The other is the Panther (Felis Concolor) which at one time inhabited the entire continental United States. The Georgia DNR will try to tell folks that they are no longer here in the Altamaha River area. The big cats like to range far and the last two sightings I had were in the Bullard Creek Watershed which is over 18,000 acres and the Ten Mile Creek Watershed which is more than 20,000 acres. Both of those areas are plenty large enough to support some cats.

I can still remember the first Panther that I saw in the wild. I would spend a part of my summers with my Aunt Myra and Uncle Buddy between Bunnell, Florida and Flagler Beach. Uncle Buddy had a military jeep in the 1950's and I loved to ride in it with him. We were riding near where they lived on the Bulow Plantation Road when a panther jumped into the road in front of the jeep. It was a magnificent animal, tan-colored with a very long tail. It stayed momentarily in the road looking toward us in the stopped jeep then bounded into the palmettos and disappearing into the dense woods.

In 1971 when I was returning from Savannah, late in the afternoon, and had just crossed the Altamaha River I saw an animal on the right shoulder of State Route 144. At first glance, I thought it was a deer due to the color but when the cat bolted across the highway in four bounds. I quickly recognized it as a Panther. The pavement was 21 feet wide and I could estimate the length from nose to tail at about six feet. There was a dirt road on the left that led off at an angle and I saw the cat hit the middle of the dirt road. Turning around I went to the place where it had crossed and found the tracks in the dirt. I measured the tracks with a cigarette pack and they were almost as long as the pack of king size cigarettes. Far larger than any house cat or bobcat I have ever seen.

In 1996 while I was working on dirt roads near Bullard Creek in Jeff Davis County, I saw an animal larger than a Labrador retriever on the base of the cut bank of the ditch. The animal was a dark tan color. It looked toward me momentarily then sprang to the top of the cut bank with its long tail flowing behind. The same day my Uncle Jesse was training bird dogs on the edge of the Ten Mile Creek area and saw one. Two other Panthers spotted on the same day. They were 25 miles apart, which eliminates the chance of it being the same cat.

The old folks used to say that a Panther sounded like a woman screaming and I have heard that sound before while camping in the Altamaha River. It will put chill bumps on you when you hear it.

My cousin Billy and I were camping on Iron Mine Bluff one night before a squirrel hunt toward the old landing downriver from the bluff. We had cooked our supper over a small fire and were preparing to turn in for the night when we began hearing cat squalls. It sounded as if they were getting closer. We added more wood to stoke the fire to see farther around our campsite. The sound was even closer until it seemed that the cats were just outside the light that our fire provided. Billy and I loaded our shotguns and sat back-to-back in a defensive position so we could stop the critter if it decided to attack. The sounds stayed close for a while and then sounded as if they were moving away. We did not sleep a wink that night because we were sure that they would quietly return. I know we were not in Africa where Lions and Leopards stalk at night but we might as well have been.

BEARS

Yes! We have bears in South Georgia! We have black bears that some of the old-timers called "Hog Bears." These bears are located all around the state and one was trapped by the Department of Natural Resources just outside of Baxley on the edge of a residential area where it was feasting on the honey that the bees of some beekeepers were housing.

It has been said that if a pine needle falls in the woods, a deer will hear it, a turkey will see it and a bear will smell it. They have an acute sense of smell which is how they locate food they will eat almost anything but they especially love sweets like honey. They will brave the stinging hordes of bees just to get some honey. They can be dangerous also since lately we have heard of many Black Bear attacks around the country.

The Georgia record is 578 pounds which is quite large and capable of doing damage to a human. A 574 pound bear was killed on the western edge of the Okefenokee Swamp and one was taken a few years ago on the eastern edge of the Okefenokee with a .44 magnum pistol. The Okefenokee is around 50 to 60 miles from the Altamaha.   I had two friends that I worked with who lived on the edge of the swamp. They invited me to come and hunt bear with them in the swamp. There were two problems with the invitation. One was I did not own a high-powered rifle at the time and the second and most important was that there was no Bear Season in Georgia at the time. Those two guys were "Swampers' and did not pay any attention to game laws. One later died from a rattlesnake bite.

When I was a teenager two friends, Ray and Lamar were riding around with me one night drinking some cold ones when the call of nature hit us. We pulled down a firebreak on some of Lamar's family's land on the edge of Sweetwater Creek to get relief. We got out of the car, leaving the engine running and the lights on and started to do our business. Suddenly a black bear stepped into the firebreak in the headlights and stood on his hind legs not far from the front of the car. In retrospect, he probably was not a very large bear but he looked like a King Kodiak to me at the time. We suddenly did not need to go anymore and jumped back into the car making a speedy exit from the woods. After our escape, we stopped about five miles away and compared our remembrances. Every time I pass that place, I think about that little bear and look down the fire break expecting him to be standing there. He made a lifetime impression on me.

When my father was a teenager, before joining the Marines, he lived in Bunnell, Florida. He had gone to Flagler Beach for the day and had overstayed his visit, missed his ride and darkness had fallen. He decided to walk the 8 miles back to Bunnell. About 3 miles out near the old coquina rock quarry a black bear wandered out in the road in front of him and stood up on its hind legs. Daddy quickly decided that retreat was the best option and ran the three miles back to the Beach. He slept out on the pier that night.

There has been much discussion about what caliber rifle to use when hunting for black bear. Some will say that any caliber that could be used for Whitetail Deer would work for taking a bear. One thing that a prudent bear hunter might think about when choosing a caliber is that there has never been a reported case where a wounded Whitetail has climbed up the tree and attacked the hunter.

ROCK OVEN

Rock oven is a series of caves located downriver from Iron Mine Bluff on the Appling County side of the river. I have explored it and been there many times. It is speculated that Native Americans once lived there. There are rock formations all along the river but this one is unique. When you stand there and muse about what happened there in times past. The Altamaha River was the red man - white man divide until the 1813 Creek Cession. Surely a place such as this would have been a handy place for an abode. All along the river artifacts have been located including pottery, projectile heads, and tomahawk heads. It is a fact that the Yemassee and then later the Lower Creeks lived in the area. At Rock Lake which is not far upstream from Buckhorn Bluff. We found a basin scooped from the rock under a spring which empties into the lake. We surmised that the Native Americans had scooped this to obtain water to cook with and to drink since the Altamaha River water looks too muddy to want to drink.

HOUSEBOATS

At one time there were quite a few houseboats on the lower river. They were from Barrington Lake to downriver from Altamaha Park. Some were on the main river and some were back in the lakes, especially Swan Lake. I kind of always wanted one for the convenience of being able to fish or hunt and just come back to the houseboat, tie up and rest or eat or whatever you had in mind. With the use of one of them, you could have a weekend getaway with no phones, TV or any other distraction. There was a movement a few years back to clean up the river and get rid of the houseboats. When they are gone there will be some nostalgia and history lost forever.

Weyman and I were bass fishing in the upper end of Swan Lake when a terrific thunderstorm suddenly appeared. We cranked the boat heading for shelter. No! Mind you. I do not have an aversion to fishing or hunting in the rain as long as the zigzag bolts stay away. As a matter of fact, the world record largemouth bass was caught in a rainstorm. The first one of them I see will put me on the hill. I have never been struck but like Lee Trevino holding an antenna in my hand during a lightning storm is not smart. The zigzags were present and the rain had become heavy. The raindrops felt like .22 bullets hitting me as we went as fast as we could in the lake. Up ahead someone under the shelter on a houseboat motioned for us to pull up alongside his houseboat. It did not take much encouragement for us to do so since we were at least five miles from the landing. We quickly tied up the boat, turned the bilge pump on so the boat would not fill up with rainwater and jumped under the shelter. He invited us to come in and have a cup of hot coffee which we thought was a great idea.

The layout of the houseboat was a gas stove on a cabinet, two coolers on the floor beside. Shelves with pots and pans and canned food were above the table with the stove. A dinette set with four chairs was nearby. On the other end were an old, overstuffed couch and a bunk. Cozy little place it was.

As we sat around his dinette table sipping on the warm brew, he offered us some jerky which we readily accepted. While we were drinking and eating the subject of wild game came up. He commenced to tell us how you could make jerky out of not only beef and venison but the raccoon and possum made good jerky also. The jerky that I was chewing grew larger in my mouth as I looked over to Weyman. He had a funny look on his face. Since I had already swallowed some of the jerky, I went on and swallowed what was in my mouth although it continued to seem to get larger. I chased it down with the coffee and announced that I was full and could eat no more. Weyman did the same. We were really happy when the storm ceased and we could get back in the boat. After we pulled away from the houseboat and had moved out of earshot of our host Weyman asked me what kind of jerky did I think that was? I had no answer.

Every time I fished in Swan Lake after hat occasion, I would pass the houseboat and wonder what I had eaten that day.

SASQUATCH

One of the other strange occurrences that are talked about from time to time in this area is sightings of a strange animal in the woods. In Florida, they call in the skunk ape. In the Himalayas, they call in the abominable snowman. And the Pacific Northwest they refer to him as Sasquatch or Bigfoot. Whatever you want to call them people indicate they have seen him roaming in the woods. They are described as big, hairy thing that does not smell good. Last week in our local newspaper there was a picture from a trail cam of some white hairy object holding something that looked like a small deer. Then the second picture of a deer with scratch marks on his side was also on the page. I don't know if I believe something like that does exist in our woods but the only woods in this area that I would believe capable of supporting an animal of this type would be the Altamaha River Swamp. It is surely vast enough for something to hide out and remain undetected by man. It is for sure and certain that you can hear some strange sounds after dark in the river swamp.

I believe it was the "Survivor Man" series that had one episode filmed in the Altamaha River Swamp. The best I could tell by their location description they were located in the upper Altamaha River about 17 miles from where I live. They were in what is called the Three Rivers Area. That is where the Ocmulgee and Occone rivers join to form the Altamaha. Just before they come together the Little Ocmulgee joins the Ocmulgee near

Lumber City Georgia. It was amazing because the main character who seems fearless on some of the episodes seemed to be worried about alligators and moccasins. Much more worried than he normally seemed on the other episodes. I don't know what he would've done if someone had whipped out a Wang-Doodle and pulled on that string. I will wager he would have left his cameras and set off that little emergency beacon thing that I know he has with him and got the heck out of Dodge.

I do believe though if there is some creature like that roaming the woods of the United States that as many trail cameras as people are putting out in the woods (we have six on our property at the river). Could be we will eventually get a photograph of him are it for the whole world to see.

About the Author

William A. Bowers, Jr. was born August 5, 1947 in St. Augustine, Florida to William Alfred Bowers Sr. and Lora Elizabeth Tuten. When he was young, his family returned to Baxley, Appling County, Georgia, where he lived, was raised and educated. He is a 1965 graduate of Appling County High School, an Eagle Scout and is retired from the Georgia Department of Transportation as an Area Engineer in South Georgia. Worked as a Consultant Engineer with EMC Engineering for ten years after retiring from the DOT. He is married to Anna Deloris Willis of Toombs County. He is a member of the First Church in Baxley, Georgia.

William has given speeches and performed living histories at State and National Parks, Historical Societies and other organizations for several years in Georgia, Florida and South Carolina.

He resides still in Appling County and has served as a Boy Scout leader for over 30 years, a charter member and officer in the Appling Grays Camp #918 Sons of Confederate Veterans, the Appling County Board of Education, the First Church Administrative Board and the Appling County Heritage Center Board of Directors.

He has published three Confederate regimental histories with *the History of the 47th Georgia Volunteer Infantry* being published in May 2013 and *the History of the 27th Georgia Volunteer Infantry* being published in February 2014. In 2016 he published *the History of the 54th Georgia Volunteer Infantry*. This completed the trilogy of Confederate Regimental Histories which encompasses the four companies of Confederate Infantry which originated in Appling County, Georgia. In 2017 he published the *Bowers Genealogy, the Descendants of Benjamin Bowers, Sr., of Pitt County, North Carolina*. And his first novel *Two Rebels from the Altamaha.*

This book is a collection of stories, funny events, miscellany and strange things collected a lifetime of hunting fishing, camping and boating all up and down the complete system of the Altamaha River.